In Spite of My Resistance

I've Learned From Children

Thomas C. Lovitt
University of Washington

CHARLES E. MERRILL PUBLISHING COMPANY
A Bell & Howell Company
Columbus   Toronto   London   Sydney

To Polly, the kids, and Fritz

The author wishes to express his gratitude
to Dr. T.C. Owen for his editorial assistance.

Published by
Charles E. Merrill Publishing Company
A Bell & Howell Company
Columbus, Ohio 43216

The book was set in Optima.
The Production Editor was Linda Hillis.
The cover was designed by Will Chenoweth.

International Standard Book Number: 0-675-08528-4

Library of Congress Catalog Card Number: 76-44048

2 3 4 5 6 7—82 81 80 79 78 77

Printed in the United States of America

Foreword

So many books about education are not worth the paper they are printed on that it is a rare delight to find one—like this one—worth far more than its list price. Worthless books have been written by people who confuse social and political reform with education, take the nihilistic stance that you can't teach children anything (only love them and leave them alone so they can learn), arrogate teaching to a practitioner's guild, or turn education into a technological nightmare. It is refreshing to read that children can be taught effectively and that teaching—even teaching *exceptional* children—does not require membership in a guild, complicated methods, or social revolution.

Not everyone will like this book. Some will hate it passionately, for it will strike educational dilettantes to the quick. Others will not recognize its worth because it is not filled with technical jargon or "humanistic" sentimentality, even though it is scientifically rigorous and grounded in humanistic sentiment. But I believe the majority of readers will love it for its easy "home-spun" grace and the way it gets to the heart of the matter of teaching.

Tom Lovitt writes with authority, and it is important to recognize that his authority derives not only from long experience as a teacher but also from a vast amount of relevant data. He has written a book without pretention because he has done precisely what he set out to do (and what many others have suggested or aspired to do but never accomplished)—painstakingly researched teaching and learning over a period of many years and interpreted his research for teachers. His is not a book tossed off in a fit of emotion following a few months of traumatic experience during which he became a critic of contemporary education. His book represents reflection on more than a decade of careful observation and measurement of what works and what doesn't work in teaching.

This little volume will fool some people because it is deceptively simple. People who do not understand that simple things can be important and that there can be a special eloquence in simplicity may be tempted to call it simplistic. Lovitt has not written here about unspeakably complicated things, and he has not complicated simple things, but the things of which he has written so simply and eloquently are essential considerations. Besides the value of Lovitt's research and the importance of scientific data, this book represents, I think, a long overdue recognition of the principle that the simplest way to accomplish a task is the best.

My family and I were reminded of the value of simplicity by one of our experiences this bicentennial summer. We were in New England·for the first time in our lives. Having great expectations for a two-week vacation in an ancient farmhouse, we were more than a little disappointed by our inability to locate the property. Driving for twelve hours had worn us out, and the prospect of wandering vainly through the forests and mountains of New Hampshire in the dark was not a pleasant one. We had driven to the end of a mile-long dirt road only to find a farmhouse that was not "ours." In the dusk we could barely make out a hulking figure standing in the doorway, watching us turn our car around in his driveway. Yes, we decided, we'd better ask (and look like fools in our own eyes, if not his, for being unable to follow a map). Timidly, I approached the door, trying to think through an explanation for my predicament and the small talk I might make as an opener. He didn't wait for me to knock or to stammer something incoherent.

"You're lost," he said with finality.

Would I spend eternity in the bottomless pit with Satan (the message crudely painted in bright red letters on a sign down the road a bit), or did I simply not know where I was? Not sure of his meaning, my only response was a moan.

"You're in New Hampshire," he continued with certainty.

"Oh, God, I hope so."

Small talk now seemed out of the question. Get to the point, I thought.

"We rented the Sirkin's house."

"You sure did."

Suddenly, I got his message. Simplicity. Directness. No hostility, rejection, or threat. Just plain, uncluttered communication.

"Go back down to the end of this road. Take a right. Go to the next right. Down that road on the left. Remember, a right and then another right."

"Thanks."

We laughed as we drove away, and we've laughed about the incident many times since; not only, I think, because the conversation was so different from what we had expected but also because of the delightful simplicity and effectiveness of this stranger's behavior. He took the time to diagnose precisely the exact nature of our problem, and his subsequent instruction could not have been simpler or more helpful.

The chapters of this book, like the New Englander's directions, are elegant in their simplicity and utility. It is not surprising that they are, for in preparing this volume Lovitt has carefully followed his own first bit of advice—he has diagnosed precisely the exact nature of teachers' instructional problems.

JAMES M. KAUFFMAN
The University of Virginia

Preface

Chaos. For many generations, changes brought about by whim, superstition, and a quest for novelty have resulted in chaos in educational practices. As a consequence, teachers, parents, and others concerned with teaching children have worn themselves out keeping abreast of the changes. Or they've decided they weren't "expert" enough to keep up and have simply dropped out of the race altogether.

To keep everyday teachers from seeking basic improvements in their profession is unfortunate enough, but the real irony is that the abundance of solid educational research over the past fifty years has had little impact on common teaching practices. More often than not, researchers have presented their findings to other researchers—not to teachers and others who could use the results to implement changes in the ways they teach children.

Evolution or chaos? It is my firm conviction that research can promote an orderly evolution of our ideas and practices of teaching. And that is why I have tried, in this little book, to digest the research I have conducted for several years—to make it easier for practicing teachers to understand and implement.

In this effort to interpret my research so that it may more easily be incorporated into common practice, I have elected to communicate through a series of adages, much in the manner of Ben Franklin in his *Poor Richard's Almanac*. Each adage in this book is, like those of Ben's, based on a goodly amount of experience; but, unlike most of his precepts, those offered here are supported by hard clinical data. Each is backed by a number of research studies as well as by a significant amount of down-to-earth experience.

Contents

IN SPITE OF MY RESISTANCE,
I'VE LEARNED FROM CHILDREN   *1*

DIAGNOSIS   *21*

When we take time to diagnose precisely the exact nature
of a child's problems, subsequent teaching can be simple.

BEHAVIORAL OBJECTIVES   *31*

If you have some ideas as to the extent you want to teach
something to someone, you might make it; if you don't
have an idea, well . . .

CLARIFYING EXPECTATIONS   *40*

Some children will do what you want them to if you just
tell them what you want.

COMMON TEACHING PROCEDURES   *48*

Some teaching procedures that have been used for a long
time seem to be okay, others aren't too great.

SOME TEACHING PROCEDURES ARE COMPLEX   *57*

Some of our teaching procedures are a conglomerate of
many techniques; for some kids this amounts to instructional overkill.

THE BENEFITS OF PRACTICE   63

Practice, in itself, probably won't make perfect, but it sometimes helps.

TEACHING YOUNGSTERS AND OLDSTERS   70

You can teach a young pup old tricks and an old dog new tricks if you want to.

EVALUATING CURRICULUM AND TEACHERS   81

We don't need to use expensive techniques to evaluate curriculum materials or teach effectiveness; the data from kids will do these jobs for us.

MOTIVATION   95

Children are often good motivation analysts.

REINFORCEMENT CONTINGENCIES   102

Reinforcement contingencies can shape up some kids who are erratic performers.

A HIERARCHY OF REINFORCERS   111

Sometimes it is necessary to arrange reinforcers, but don't give away the store.

CONTINGENT FREE TIME   117

Leisure time is as big a reinforcer for youngsters as it is for adults.

PUPIL MANAGEMENT   126

Kids are turned on when you give them a piece of the action.

RELATIONSHIP BETWEEN ERRORS AND LEARNING   132

Some children, even when they've made the same mistake over and over again, can still learn to do it right.

DIRECT TEACHING   137

If you want to teach kids to crawl, do it; if you want to teach them to read, do that. Just don't expect that when you teach kids to crawl, they'll learn to read.

MORE ON DIRECT TEACHING   144

Focus on the behavior you want to develop, not on the one you don't want.

GENERALIZATION   154

Some pupils, when taught something, actually *do* generalize that skill to different situations (just as they're supposed to).

CHILDREN AS MANAGERS   162

Sometimes youngsters are better managers of behavior than adults.

PARENTS AS TEACHERS   172

Even parents can teach their children if they follow a few simple rules.

EVERYONE MEASURES   183

Measurement: if it's good enough for children, it's good enough for big people.

ENJOY YOUR CHILDREN   198

Teach those kids, but along the way get some laughs.

EPILOGUE   205

REFERENCES   227

Acknowledgments

Figures 2 and 3 from T.C. Lovitt, J.O. Smith, "Effects of Instructions on an Individual's Verbal Behavior," *Exceptional Children* 38 (1972): 689-90. Reprinted by permission of The Council of Exceptional Children.

Figure 4 from T.C. Lovitt, K.A. Curtiss, "Effects of Manipulating An Antecedent Event on Mathematics," *Journal of Applied Behavior Analysis* 4 (1968): 331. Reprinted by permission.

Figure 5 from Eugene Ramp, George Semb, *Behavior Analysis: Research and Application*, p. 291, © 1975, Prentice-Hall. Reprinted by permission.

Figure 6 from T.C. Lovitt, C.L. Hansen, "Round One—Placing the Child is the Right Reader," *Journal of Learning Disabilities* 9(1976): 351. Reprinted by permission.

Figures 7 and 12 from F.S. Keller, E. Ribes, *Behavior Modification: Applications to Education*, pp. 32, 50. © 1974, Academic Press. Reprinted by permission.

Figure 8 from E.A. Ramp, B.L. Hopkins, *A New Direction for Education*, p. 64, © 1971, University of Kansas. Reprinted by permission.

Figure 9 from T.C. Lovitt, K.A. Esveldt, "The Relative Effects on Math Performance of Sing 6—Versus Multiple-Ratio Schedules: 4 Case Studies," *Journal of Applied Behavior Analysis* 3 (1970): 263. Reprinted by permission.

Figure 11 from T.C. Lovitt, K.A. Curtiss, "Academic Response Rate or a Function of Teacher-and Self-imposed Contingencies," *Journal of Applied Behavior Analysis* 2 (1969): 51. Reprinted by permission.

In Spite of My Resistance, I've Learned From Children

Most teachers, parents, and educational writers would agree that educational practice has changed over the past few decades. These changes have made their appearance in every aspect of education: from the basic philosophical underpinnings to the methods for grouping children; from weighty curricular issues to the most minute procedural details.

Most individuals who have studied the process of education would also agree that these modifications have been more cyclical than evolutionary. Many of the current techniques, thoughts, philosophies, and procedures were the vogue twenty or thirty years ago. Some educational practices keep coming back like old familiar songs.

We are constantly reminded of this cyclical process by our elder statesmen in schools of education who point out to their younger brethren, each time the latter present ideas, that they have been there before. The same thing could be said about educational practice that is often heard about the weather in Kansas: "If you're unhappy with the conditions now, just wait awhile; they will change."

Most educators and critics of education would further agree that these changes have not been brought about by educational research. Educational practice has not awaited the new discoveries of science before effecting change. Change has been prompted by whim, boredom, necessity, and frustration.

This constant change has made it difficult to interpret, much less evaluate, the cumulative progress of our educational program. In this regard, Joseph Featherstone (1975) recently complained:

> In one sense, it seems discouraging that our efforts to improve practice have not gone beyond the formulations of the Progressives. The general lack of cumulative development makes a good deal of our educational reform seem terribly faddish. In what I sometimes think of as the United States of Amnesia, we keep rehearsing the dilemmas of the past, and I suppose we will continue to start from scratch each generation until we develop a sixth sense of the past to add to our other five senses. (p. 3)

The agencies of education have done little to stem this incessant change, this perpetual and unfounded quest for novelty. Certainly the schools of education have not succeeded in abating the pell-mell fashion parade of educational practice. Neither have they convinced the general citizenry that change, in order to be developmental, should be based on research. On the contrary, the colleges of education have usually supported every educational movement. Ordinarily, they cautiously observe the current effects of changes, then if they speculate that the modification will endure for a few weeks and that they can profit from it in some way, they will endorse it.

There are a number of reasons why colleges of education have contributed to the unsystematic course of educational practice either by design or through neglect. I will comment on only two of them. One of the reasons they have not been seriously committed to rigorous, systematic programs of research that might well contribute to a steady improvement is that they have, instead, supported departments of psychology, history, sociology, and other areas which have little interest in the study of systematic curricular and technological development. Colleges of education have long ignored, avoided, even escaped from the crucial problem of education by overintellectualizing the many aspects of education. Whenever a new type of child is discovered, for example, the learning disabled, many schools of education establish and require courses on the psychology of the learning disabled. Whenever a new region or area is highlighted, for example, the inner city, sociology courses in education are set up. Whenever an educational thinker or technique has run its string, a new course (or at least a new chapter) in educational history is written.

The publishers of educational materials—another powerful educational agency—have done nothing to stem the tide of confusion. They have profited from the fact that educational practice, particularly in the form of materials, has changed so rapidly. If a given aspect of educational thought and practice persisted for any considerable period of time, for whatever reason, the publishers of curricular materials would dry up. For once they had sold their latest model or kit to everyone, there would be no one left upon whom to unload.

Indeed, the publishers of educational materials deliberately stimulate change. One of their techniques is to borrow the tactics that toy producers use at Christmas time. They offer a "new product" and bombard the public with cries of the novelty of this merchandise and with pleas to buy it and be the first on their block or the first in their school to be so blessed.

In their efforts to continually market new products, the publishers of materials also use the favored technique of the automotive industry, that of insignificantly altering their product each year. Both industries turn out new models by adding a little trim here, a new stripe there, without appreciably changing the basic structure of the product. Potential consumers are, of course, informed that although last year's model was fine (certainly better than the model the year before), the new model is even better. One aspect of the automobile industry the publishers have not yet borrowed is the trade-in policy. Were they to do this I can imagine a showroom full of last year's books, kits, packages, and games.

In order to keep their merchandise flowing, the publishers have also taken a cue from the life insurance people; they try to program guilt. By constantly harping at teachers to buy the best, the latest, publishers are often successful in making them feel guilty. They make the teacher who does not have the new updated books and instructional packages feel like a "klutz." Like the life insurance industry, the publishers promote the idea that if you care you buy; therefore, if you do not buy you do not care.

The third educational agency that has served to inhibit the systematic development of educational practice has been the bureaucracies of education. They have used a tactic different from those of the other two agencies to thwart steady growth, one often employed by many social and welfare agencies: administrate the problem into oblivion.

When an educational problem arises, one agency or another seeks to bury it under a blanket of bureaucracy. Education has mastered the art of identifying a current fad and drowning it with words and meetings. When concerns such as ability grouping, the treatment of dyslexic children, team teaching, accountability, performance contracting, or collective bargaining have been identified, the bureaucracies of education engulf them with task forces, colloquia, symposia, and short courses. Later, if those concerns continue to be topical, courses are developed in their behalf, perhaps even degree programs; often, associations and journals are created for their furtherance.

Although there have been many instances of bureaucratic burial in education, one of the most recent has been the Right to Read program. In 1969, President Nixon authorized this program at the urging of James Allen (long since departed commissioner of education). It was the charge of this commission to attack the problem of illiteracy in the United States. One of the first acts of the commission was to form a national council. Next, a national reading center was organized. This group spent the first year, according to the director, "laying the groundwork." As of September 12, 1971, according to the New York Times, not one illiterate child or adult had been taught to read as a result of the program.

Finally, a director of the entire organization was appointed who, in turn, encouraged many states to organize their own Right to Read programs. In the state of Washington, for example, a Right to Read advisory committee was formed. This committee was made up of twenty-one professional people from the state. Phase I of the Right to Read program was to select twenty local education agencies which agreed to receive the technical assistance offered by the superintendent of public instruction. Next, local reading directors were to be appointed and local Right to Read councils established. Later, during Phases II and III, regional personnel would be named.

Think of that! Our Right to Read program has continued to keep resolutely away from illiterate readers. As of November 1, 1973, I could discover no evidence that a single illiterate reader had yet benefited from the program.

So it appears that three large and powerful agencies of education—schools of education, publishers of educational materials, bureaucratic agencies—have done little to halt the proliferation of numerous changes in educational practice, changes that have not, for the most part, been based on data. In fact, a strong case can be made that these agencies, in their efforts to maintain their own power and prestige, have actually fostered the development of an ever-changing atmosphere in the educational world.

As a result of these unstable conditions, several consequences have ensued. For one, the emergence of a science of education has been severely frustrated. Although the development of sciences such as chemistry, physics, and biology has not always proceeded at a smooth, steady pace, those disciplines have reached levels of sophistication far beyond their points of origin because of a willingness to modify their principles and practices to accommodate each significant discovery. Rarely did they shift from one procedure or point of view to another simply because of obscure testimony or because they grew weary of one set of ideas and turned to another.

It is likely that had the educational founding fathers supported a strong educational research program and encouraged educators to modify their practices only after data had been duly considered, more people would be better educated today. It is quite possible that had such a strategy been adopted and continued there would have been far less need for such special programs as Head Start, Follow Through, and Right to Read, and less need even for special education in general. It is highly probable that millions of dollars would have been saved had the evolving of education been based on science. Throughout the years poor, unsuspecting teachers and parents have spent many precious dollars on materials and procedures of only little or no worth. There has never been a government act, a consumer's union, or a better business bureau to protect them. It has always been a matter of "the buyer be bilked."

A second consequence arising from these rapid, unsubstantiated changes has been that educational practice has been kept out of the hands of the populace at large. Many parents are extremely hesitant to instruct their children; that is, to teach them such school-associated tasks as reading, writing, and arithmetic. They are aware that educational practices change, that their children are not taught as they themselves were. They are constantly informed of the "newness" in education—the new math, the new methods of teaching composition, phonics, or spelling.

Many parents equate the rapid rate of change with development and improvement. They believe that educational practice has changed in the past twenty-five years as much as have the fields of the computer, aircraft, or communication. Assuredly, there has been as much change in education as in these other areas, but the change, to a great extent, has been sporadic or irregular.

Because of their conceptions—or should we say misconceptions—of educational change, many parents avoid any efforts to teach their youngsters. They believe their ideas about teaching are as antiquated as modes of travel and communication of a bygone era and would retard the progress of their youngsters. It is a pity that some parents, particularly those of children in need of additional tutoring, hold this belief for these youngsters will suffer from this withholding of perfectly valid help.

Many teachers are also convinced that educational practice has become highly efficient because of the new "methods." Those particularly in small towns or rural areas always want to know about the new educational techniques and materials. Indeed, many a circuit speaker has made his bundle by telling those receptive, but uninformed, teachers away from the cities all about the most recent educational innovations.

Many teachers actually feel guilty because they do not know about or do not own the most recent kits and packages on the market. They believe (and publishers and others feed on this belief) that they are not doing the best job possible for their youngsters because they could not afford this year's packages for the teaching of the language arts and science.

Some who have been out of the business for a few years are afraid to return to teaching. Recently, I spoke with such a person. She had taught for five or six years, then retired for a time while she had her family (as they say). She had thus been out of teaching for about four years and now was afraid to return, believing that since there had been so many significant advances in education that she was unaware of, she would be an incompetent teacher. I tried to tell her that, to a great extent, not being informed of the new programs and trends in education for four years was about as serious as missing out on four years of TV commercials or, for that matter, missing four years of TV.

Many teachers today are also convinced that since there have been many changes in education, educational practice has in turn developed into a precise, even scientific, craft, one that only the up-to-date and highly trained specialist can deal with. Others believe that only *they* can teach. They do not want non-sanctioned teachers to meddle in their stew. Many kindergarten and first grade teachers, for example, do not want assistance from parents; such teachers send parents notes and do everything they can to discourage parents from working with their own youngsters. I recently read such a note sent to parents. It said, "Try not to instruct your child in reading. To do so is like a surgeon performing an operation on a member of a family: too much emotional involvement."

Think about that. If all parents heeded such advice, they would rarely speak to their children, never differentially reinforce their efforts by praising some behaviors and correcting others. They would never buy books for their children, certainly they would never read to them. Parents who followed this advice would neither take their children on trips nor talk to them about history, geology, or geography. Heaven forbid: too much emotional involvement!

But many parents *have* heeded such advice. They are reluctant to teach their own children. They are convinced that the certified teachers are the licensed educational surgeons, and only they can impart knowledge to children and alter their minds. These parents honestly fear that if they attempt to teach such highly complex skills as reading, composition, or spelling, they might louse up their children forever.

Parents are also warned by many child specialists and the press that they should not attempt to teach their children complex skills. This advice generally comes to them in an effort to counter the strong emotional attachments already apparent, and not because of any anticipated lack of instructional savvy. But pity the parents who receive warnings from the teachers and child development specialists that they should keep hands off their children. Those who actually heeded these admonitions would soon find themselves merely serving their children as simple caretakers, providing food, shelter, clothing, television, and transportation service, but nothing more.

To summarize: educational practice, because of the many changes and perhaps for other reasons, has been kept out of the hands of the common folk. In this respect, the business of education is deserving of the same criticism Ivan Illich leveled at the business of medicine in 1970 when he said that it had done everything possible to hide the simplicity of its basic procedures from the public.

So now what? We can see that changes in educational practice have been rapid, that the innovation of today will be forgotten tomorrow, only to appear again in perhaps a slightly modified state. We know that, generally, these modifications have not been fortified or prompted by research. We realize finally some of the consequences of this unchecked and disorganized state: improvement in educational practice has been thwarted, and education has been kept out of the hands of ordinary people.

So whose responsibility is it to clarify these matters, to develop a system whereby education, like other sciences, progresses systematically, to disseminate the underlying truths of education, and finally to place these truths in the hands of common practitioners? I suppose any one of several groups could assume this charge: a children's crusade or revolution could be formed; a parents' movement could be organized; a teachers' federation could be developed. Frankly, I would support all of the above as efforts to simplify and bring educational practice back home. For the time being, however, I believe that it is the responsibility of educational researchers to set us on course. They should be obligated to promote a system which requires that changes be supported by research, to conduct research which focuses on current problems, to share and report their findings in such ways that they can be effectively implemented.

I am not, however, recommending that educational research of just any type be encouraged, for there has been a superabundance of educational research over the past fifty years. Simply to recommend that more of a given "cure" be provided when a problem persists would be to follow the program orientation of the well-meaning but shallow-thinking liberals of the late 1960s who sought to solve all social problems by forming agencies and allocating funds.

It would be a mistake to support the majority of the existing types of educational research, for it has failed to deliver. There are, I believe, at least five important reasons why educational research has not contributed significantly to the development of systematic and uncluttered educational practice.

One reason which greatly explains this failure is that many educational researchers have chosen to deal with rather insignificant, at times even esoteric, matters. For instance, many of them have for years required children to operate form boards, to solve mazes, and to associate nonsense words with various shapes. Educational and psychological researchers have subjected children to these tasks because of their quest for information about the abilities of children to acquire information, to generalize, to discriminate, and to remember. Certainly, information about those processes is needed. But most teachers are unable to make practical applications of findings from research in laboratories where nonschool tasks are assigned, even though they might be concerned about the general processes being investigated.

Another reason for this failure to contribute is that too many researchers have been concerned only with general effects and statistical significance. Ordinarily, a researcher can publish his findings only if the results of the treatment are beyond the .05 level of significance. One way to increase the probability of obtaining data of this weight is to select a large sample of pupils: the more the better (easier). A researcher, for example, might investigate the effects of a special reading treatment on one group as compared to the effects of a traditional treatment on another group. He could administer a pretest to both groups prior to treatment and a posttest following the treatment period. He could then treat his data statistically and perhaps discover that the gains of the children in the special group were significantly greater than the gains of those with whom the traditional program was used: significant, that is, beyond the .05 level. The researcher might then recommend that teachers use the special rather than the traditional technique in their classes.

Many good teachers, upon learning of such recommendations from researchers who have used many pupils in their studies, are cautious about adopting the findings. They know that although the special technique may be more effective in general than the traditional, they are uncertain about its effects on specific youngsters, especially on the unique children in their classes. These teachers are concerned with finding an effective technique for Billy Joe who has problems with blending, for Melinda who has troubles with digraphs, and for Peter who cannot remember what he has read. They are forced to deal with individuals. After all, haven't they have been told for years that they should individualize their instruction?

Furthermore, teachers are often intimidated or unimpressed by the type of research I have described; hence they do not readily implement the findings from such investigations. Some teachers are baffled by the methodology: the research groups, pretests and posttests, and statistical treatment. They do not understand all the talk about levels of significance, t tests, and homogeneity of variance. They are not certain to just what extent such highly scientific terms and concepts can be related to their little second graders in a rural school.

Other teachers are unimpressed by the concept of statistical significance, for they are well aware of differences between actual and statistical significance. They have perhaps known of instances where a child's ability to read was statistically improved, but neither the teacher nor the youngster's parents could notice the difference.

A third reason for the failure of research to influence practice is that the researchers have too often tried to scale the Everests of educational theorizing. In their efforts to make a deeply significant impact on teaching, they have sought to supply answers to concepts and processes as esoteric and lofty as the true nature of intelligence or motivation. Others have tried to discover the basic truths about language development, locus of control, and anxiety. Without a doubt, all thinking people—the world, certainly teachers—are interested in learning more about these matters. But researchers with such grandiose aspirations all too often fall lamentably short of their aims. The results gained from such research must be so watered down and interpreted with such caution that the immediate implications for teachers are highly nebulous. Although some teachers are willing to accept research of this type and patiently await more relevant findings, others, those with more immediate concerns, grow weary of pie-in-the-sky promises. Many want only the most direct, clearcut answers to today's problems.

Researchers have also failed to influence educational practice in a systematic, meaningful way because they are more responsive to their guilds than to the educational community. Though they allegedly set out to influence educational practice, they are reinforced far more by their associations and societies than by classroom teachers. One way to substantiate such a claim is to examine the journals used by our educational researchers, many of whom report their findings in the *American Journal of Educational Research* or in the *Journal of Applied Behavior Analysis*. Most of these reports are excellent methodological treatises seeking to answer serious educational questions. But sound as they may be, they are rarely read by teachers. I have yet to visit a library of a public school and find copies of those journals. Those I see in classrooms in Washington are the *Reading Teacher, Arithmetic Teacher, Instructor,* and *Learning*. Only on rare occasions do creditable educational researchers write for these journals, particularly the latter two.

Why *should* aspiring or established researchers publish their material in these teacher journals? The aspiring ones are busy trying to survive in university environments. They must conduct elegant research, write it up, and publish it in journals that are recognized by their peers. Often these journals are of the American Psychological Association or American Educational Research Association variety. Many of these educators realize that it would be more harmful to their careers to publish in low-level teacher journals than not to publish at all. Meanwhile, the established professors—those who have attained tenure and have been blessed with full professorships—do not wish to publish in teacher magazines because they are bucking for higher prizes. They aspire to be department heads and deans. They realize that a vita containing articles published in teacher journals would only harm their claims to sophistication.

Occasionally, full professors write for the teacher magazines, but simply because they have run dry. They have, perhaps, been away from teaching and research for many years, and their only source of inspiration is their fading memory. Summoning these recollections of yesteryear, they sit down and knock off position papers. The unfortunate consequence of such writing, particularly upon the readers of magazines, who are inclined to think of themselves as uninformed and who hold people of eminence in great respect, is that they accept these words as gospel and immediately attempt to implement the article's suggestions. They fail to realize that these printed words of wisdom are, at best, hazy recollections, which are rarely substantiated by data, current or otherwise.

That many investigators do not care one whit about the classroom teacher is also indicated by the symposiums and federations they choose as sounding boards for their findings. Many times, educational researchers simply talk to one another.

(They are an incestuous lot!) As a result, they often focus on irrelevant and dated topics. I must confess that I have attended many meetings where so-called educational research was presented, but there were no teachers in the audience. The scientists simply fed on reinforcement from one another. Their actions were not monitored by the reality of today's school problems and needs.

When researchers do communicate with practitioners, they rarely capsulize their information so that teachers can use it. They devote large sections of their manuscripts to the integration of their findings with those of other researchers or to contrasting their results with those of others. To some extent this is justifiable. It is a good practice insofar as science is concerned, for the blending and contrasting of knowledge among researchers is a necessary step in developing a science. But the practitioner is more in need of immediate solutions for today's problems than of discussions as to the background and theory of such issues.

Researchers also tend to elaborate carefully the procedures of their studies. They often go into great detail to explain how the characteristics of their subjects were matched, how they were instructed, how the curricular materials were developed. Again, this is good research practice, for if studies are to be replicated the procedural details must be carefully explained, to the extent that they can be repeated. But the teacher could well be spared some of the fine details, for she needs to have information that can be readily interpreted and implemented.

Furthermore, researchers tend to describe at formidable length the results of their studies. Often, in their attempts to explain their findings, they use many complicated statistical tests. They also tend to use many tables, graphs, and charts. This, too, is good practice—particularly in the scientific community—to explain convincingly one's results. But the teacher who is seeking immediate assistance is often overwhelmed by so many numbers and data displays. Basically, she simply needs to know whether or not to use the researched technique or procedure in her classroom.

Finally, when researchers do halfheartedly attempt to communicate with teachers, they too often fail to supply a final guiding summary, brief but pointed, for the reader to follow. Even though they attempt to blend their research with the investigations of others, they rarely come up with a precept which teachers can hold in mind and follow. No one expects researchers to arrive at rules that carry the authority of Pythagoras each time an investigation is reported, but they should provide some notion, some capsulated conclusion, that the commoners can identify with.

Some teacher journals and magazines attempt to digest the research of educational investigators. Many of them provide a column in which an attempt is made to abstract recent research. They are given such headings as "Research Says" or "What's New in Research." Although the intent of these features is admirable—to digest recent research so that teachers can draw upon the current ideas—the efforts often fall far short of the objective. The research may be so distilled that only the most creative teacher would be able to implement in her classroom even the most general notions of its findings. Furthermore, the person who summarizes the research is only rarely able to extract its primary essence.

There is, of course, another major reason for the failure of educational research to contribute significantly to the smooth development of educational practice. Educational researchers (often misled by governmental funding agencies) have conducted some pretty shoddy investigations, many of which were extremely expensive. Some of the most expensive, yet educationally insignificant, educational masterpieces that come to mind are Head Start, Follow Through, and Right to Read. Such obvious failures have done little to enhance the credibility of educational research as a guiding force in the school world.

My reason for writing this book is to explain my own educational research in such a way that it may be better understood and used by everyone, teachers and parents alike. As I have stated earlier, it is my belief that education should develop as a science, that is, systematically rather than haphazardly. Moreover, it is my belief that educational research should provide the basis for such consistent growth. It is also my contention that if research, not blind chance, is used to guide change, there will be fewer changes made, and those that do prevail will be more straightforward than many of those in the past have been. It should follow, then, that if the changes are fewer and more straightforward, more people will be able to understand and hence cope with educational practice. Therefore, more parents and educators will be able to qualify more speedily as good teachers than is true today.

In an effort to explain my research, I have introduced each of the next twenty-one chapters with an adage. These adages are, in a way, like many of the familiar educational precepts: "You can't teach an old dog new tricks," "You can lead a horse to water, but you can't make him drink," and "If at first you don't succeed, try, try again." I have used adages to introduce each chapter because it seems to me that people remember aphorisms such as these. Almost everyone can repeat numerous bromides, maxims, and bits of proverbial lore, those which pertain to education and learning as well as others: "A rolling stone gathers no moss," "Still water runs deep," and so forth. The point is, they do stick in the mind.

I also have a strong hunch that since people do remember adages, their behaviors are correspondingly influenced. These correspondencies seem to be particularly vivid when it comes to educational sayings.

There are two significant differences between the adages I have used to introduce the chapters and those which permeate the folk thinking about education and psychology. One difference is that mine are not as bold and as sharply defined as those of my forepersons. Many qualifiers, such as *can be, might be, some, probably, often,* and *sometimes,* are sprinkled throughout my pronouncements. A second and more significant difference between my adages and those of yesteryear is that most of mine are based on a fair amount of data. In most of the chapters, two or more research reports which support the theme of the adage are summarized and digested. To my knowledge, no research has ever been submitted to support any of such educational bromides as "Practice makes perfect." Some erstwhile educational philosopher or psychologist simply dreamed up this catchy phrase many generations ago, and we have been stuck with it ever since.

This being the case, since I have gathered a significant amount of data in support of each adage, I should explain the system used to generate the data of each project included here. I am convinced that the data system I have employed is not only a reliable and valid means of discovering the underlying truths of education, but it is also a simple method. Many have learned to use it in a short period of time. It is my hope that the reader will agree, after reading this book, that this is indeed a simple, yet effective, method of obtaining educational data. I believe that if enough workers seeking to clarify the practice of education will use these procedures, they will be more clearly discerned, and, therefore, more readily and widely taught.

HOW THE DATA SYSTEM WORKS

In contrast to the complex measurement systems often used to obtain statistical data, the method used in the research projects presented in this book is quite simple. There are five characteristics of this approach that account for its simplicity and ultimate effectiveness.

First of all, it is *direct*. That is, the exact behavior of concern is measured. If, for example, the focal behavior is a pupil's way of speaking to peers, that behavior would be precisely defined and counted. If the behavior of concern is reading orally from a reader, a pupil's number of correctly and incorrectly read words in a specific reader would be counted. In the first case, a social adjustment test would not be given; in the second example; neither an achievement test nor an intelligence test. Although behaviors are sometimes measured by these instruments, such findings would be only indirect assessments.

The second characteristic, a feature that adds tremendously to the truthfulness of the data, is that of continuity. Once a behavior has been defined and the decision has been made to count it, that behavior would be counted *daily*. If, continuing with an example used earlier, the focal behavior was talking to peers, that behavior would be counted over a period of days. The obvious reason for doing this is that if only one day's data are obtained, any conclusions made from that score might be erroneous; hence, an inappropriate judgment of performance might be made. On one day the pupil might be in a vile mood and speak to no one, and on the next day he might feel more benevolent and speak freely to everyone. Such extreme performances would be tempered by more normal displays, if the behavior were counted for several days. Daily measurement stands in contrast to more traditional assessments, whereby the important behaviors of children are monitored only once at the beginning or the end of a year.

A third feature of this simple measurement system is that *common*, single-element teaching procedures are recommended. A majority of the teaching procedures used in the projects in this book have been used by good teachers for many years and consist of a single feature. To teach reading, the following are some of the straightforward techniques I have used. Most of these are represented in the projects that follow:

1. tell the pupil to read faster

2. have the pupil read silently before he reads orally
3. schedule practice on newly introduced words
4. schedule practice on missed words
5. provide points or chips for correctly read words
6. schedule practice on simple phrases
7. schedule practice on various phonic elements, for example, initial consonants; medial, short vowels

In arithmetic, some of the common procedures used to increase computational accuracy have been these:

1. show the pupil how to perform a certain type of problem
2. tell the pupil which problems were correctly or incorrectly solved
3. give points for correctly computed problems
4. tell the pupil to work faster or to compute more accurately
5. provide the pupil with various aids as he works the problem, for example, abacus, number line, Cuisenaire Rods, flash cards

Other common teaching procedures have been used to assist pupils to become better spellers and to write more legibly.

Such procedures are in marked contrast to the multi-element instructional packages sometimes used. More will be said about this type of teaching package later in the book, but the reader should be alerted at once to the fact that many educators and publishers recommend using procedures that are extremely complex. Some current methods for the teaching of reading, for example, require students to be drilled on the shapes of letters and their sounds, to study word families, to study the derivation and meaning of words, and to engage in many other exercises. As the reader will surely agree, it is much easier for a prospective teacher to learn one simple instructional technique than to develop the many proficiencies recommended by some producers of curriculum materials.

A more important reason for using single-component teaching procedures is that if the data revealed that the measured behavior was changed, that change could be attributed to the single procedure. Obviously, if the procedure comprised several elements, any of which could influence performance, the evaluator would not know which element was influential in causing the change.

A fourth feature, one that also relates to procedures, is *consistency*. Once a teaching procedure is selected, it is generally scheduled for several days. If a teacher has decided on a certain procedure for a pupil who is not computing addition facts satisfactorily, that procedure will be used for at least three days. Most techniques, even common, single-component ones, need a few days before effects can be noted. Obviously, if after a short period the pupil's performance is worse than it was before that procedure was used, it should be withdrawn and replaced by another.

Once a new technique has been adopted, many teachers are reluctant to wait for results. Some schedule a procedure one day, and unless instant success is evidenced, they withdraw the technique and make a substitution. Any technique must be given a fair trial; even some of the miracle drugs require some time to become effective. In this connection, however, I must point out that when a teacher takes time to identify a child's problem and adopts a procedure that is appropriate, instant success is often achieved.

It is obvious that procedural consistency makes for more accurate measurement. If the same situation is maintained over a period of time, the data then obtained reveal performance throughout a common set of circumstances. If, however, teaching circumstances vacillate from one day to the next, the data obtained are extremely difficult to interpret. One day's data will reflect one set of circumstances; the next day's, another, and so forth.

A fifth feature of simple measurement is the ease of analyzing the data. Most teachers and many parents, in their undergraduate days, took classes in educational measurement. But these courses, far from providing them with the simple analytical tools required to make judgments and decisions from the measurement data, often frightened them away from all numbers: mathematics, logic, and science. Because of these traumatic experiences many teachers not only shy away from measuring the progress of their pupils, they shudder even at the thought of calculating their monthly bills. Calculation, quantification, and evaluation have often become their mortal enemies.

The type of analysis used in the projects included in this book is easy, yet effective. This approach recommends the analysis or inspection of data in two ways. One is to determine the average of a set of scores; the other, the direction, or trend, of these scores. The average is calculated by adding a series of scores that pertain to performance and dividing by the number of scores. Anyone can do this. Bowlers and golfers regularly calculate their averages to determine their handicaps. To ascertain the direction or trend of the data, the teacher simply inspects it; no addition or division is required. She needs only to scrutinize the data over a period of time to decide whether the performance is generally the same, improving, or worsening.

The following is a sample measurement project that illustrates the five components of this simple method for obtaining data: direct measurement, daily measurement, common procedures, consistent procedures, and easy analysis.

I have selected a spelling situation to demonstrate this method. The pupil was given ten words to spell each day. After each session, the correctly and incorrectly spelled words were checked, and a correct percentage score was calculated. Each day this score was graphed. Thus, his behavior was directly measured; an outside test that might relate only indirectly to his ability was not used. It should also be pointed out that his performance was measured over several days, not just one or two.

This project consisted of two phases. The baseline, or diagnostic phase, ran for five days, and the teaching phase lasted for seven days. In the first phase, no teaching was scheduled. The teacher pronounced the words every day, and the pupil wrote them. After the ten words were written, the teacher corrected his paper and handed it back. That was that.

During the teaching phase, a simple procedure was used. Throughout that period, the pupil was required to write each word missed on the test five times. This procedure was consistently followed throughout the teaching phase. Although this program was effective, the reader should note that it took four days before much progress was observed.

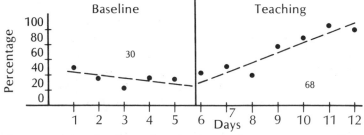

Figure 1. Sample data of a pupil's performance in spelling.

In order to evaluate the results of this little project, average calculations and trend observations were made, according to the easy analysis method described earlier. The average of the baseline data was 30 percent and the average during the teaching phase was 68 percent. These averages were obtained by adding the baseline scores and dividing by five and by summing the scores in the teaching situation and dividing by seven. In respect to the direction of the data, the scores throughout the baseline phase gradually went down; whereas during the teaching period the scores went up.

These data revealed that the average score in the teaching phase was higher than the like score in the baseline condition. As to direction, the data in the instructional phase showed more improvement than did the data throughout the baseline condition. Based on these average and direction comparisons, the teacher concluded that the procedure she had selected to improve her pupil's spelling was successful. Not only did these data inform her about the effects of the intervention, but the chart also provided evidence that she was, in fact, able to teach. These data were subsequently used to interpret progress to the child, his parents, his next year's teacher, and his principal.

But ever onward. I apologize for delaying you from getting to the heart of the book—the ideas about learning I have acquired over the years. I wanted to explain first the rationale for writing such a book and to describe briefly the system used in obtaining the information.

As I mentioned earlier, I have drawn upon my research experience to substantiate the twenty-one adages presented throughout the book. I have personally conducted research and have assisted dozens of other people in carrying out research projects with children since 1965. Throughout that time, my colleagues and I have published over seventy-five research articles in numerous education and psychology journals. In the past few years, I have inspected thousands of graphs that depicted various performances of children. I have spoken with students and teachers for many hours about the development of children, and I have listened to the stories, laughter, and groans of the children themselves even longer.

I must confess, however, that I have been distracted from time to time and have not always attended properly to the input I received. This was particularly true of my relationships with children. There have been many interesting and charming incidents that passed by me daily, and too often I let them pass me by. For one reason or another, I did not always pay attention; the phone rang, someone unexpectedly came into my office, I daydreamed, or I was otherwise occupied with an activity that competed with kid attending. But in spite of my resistance, my inattentiveness, and distractableness, I have managed, over the past few years, to learn a few things from children.

On the basis of these lessons, I have written this book, whose primary purpose is to help bring education back to the people. I am becoming more and more impatient with the spectacle of education drifting away from people who should be teaching. In effect, this book is an educational counterpart to Fred Harris' text, *The New Populism*. As he seeks to return government to the people, so I would like to see education returned to the citizenry. In order to accomplish this, I have attempted throughout this book to identify and explain the essential simplicity of many educational procedures—so simply that they may be used by the many.

Following are my twenty-one adages about learning. They are, to some extent, arranged as they arise in a teaching situation; that is, beginning with diagnosis, then setting goals. There is, however, no particular order in their arrangement; they should be consulted as the exigencies of teaching may direct.

Diagnosis

WHEN we take time to diagnose precisely the exact nature of a child's problems, subsequent teaching can be simple.

Some exceptional children have been frequently diagnosed. They have been to many clinics, hospitals, and remedial centers. They have been asked questions, probed, and thoroughly interrogated by pediatricians, psychiatrists, psychologists, neurologists, opthalmologists, and many others.

Well-meaning parents and teachers have kept some children on the run between one diagnostician and another for weeks, sometimes months. Some children, during these diagnostic periods, spend more time being diagnosed than being taught. Many of these "diagnostic" children, when not being diagnosed, are waiting to be. During those waiting periods their teachers or parents are, of course, afraid to tamper with them for fear that they will invalidate the impending diagnosis. It's rather like not eating or drinking for so many hours before an operation (once again the medical analogies may have screwed up education), except that many of these children must wait months before their first diagnosis.

We might refer to this type of activity—jumping from one expert to the other, hoping and waiting for the expert to tap the magic engram and thus be able to prescribe the magic pill—as "clinicide." The child is the victim of clinical death. She has been deprived of instruction because of the long waits for so many diagnostic interviews.

Education has built a huge subindustry around diagnosis. As a result, many publishers and clinics have profited greatly. Diagnostic tests and kits by the hundreds have been developed and marketed. To verify such a statement one need only consider the advertisements in the many educational journals and magazines. Another way to become informed of the plethora of diagnostic packages being marketed would be to scan the mail received by educators over a period of a few weeks. I receive as many advertisements for diagnostic kits, tests, and packages from publishers as I do flyers from gasoline companies trying to sell me luggage, stereo equipment, and binoculars.

Many professionals—pediatricians, psychiatrists, opthalmologists, educators—have used the diagnostic business to supplement their practices. Some of these people have fantastic moonlighting projects on the side because they diagnose the learning, social, motor, emotional, or you-name-it problems of any and all children.

Large and expensive centers have been built and staffed by professionals who devote the major part of their time to diagnosis. In these centers, there are diagnosticians from many disciplines. This multi- or interdisciplinary form of assessment has carried diagnosis to extreme lengths. The apparent hypothesis upon which such centers are predicated is that the reason some children's learning problems have not been discovered in the past is simply because there has not been *enough* diagnosis. Therefore, many centers attempt to make up for this lack by staffing their facilities with numerous diagnosticians, engaging the services of at least one specialist of every type.

Apparently, it is the rationale of these centers that if enough people evaluate a child from their particular vantage point, then put together all their collective wisdom, a complete picture will emerge, one that explains all the social, educational, and psychological facets of the child's psyche. Following upon this total description, the diagnosticians also apparently believe that either diagnosis itself will cure the child, or, as a result of the complete checkup, a treatment will magically appear that can be prescribed to solve whatever problems have been detected.

I have had the opportunity of witnessing firsthand several multidisciplinary meetings regarding children. These meetings are commonly called staffings. I have been the token educator in two medical centers where these staffings are common practice. I have sat in with pediatricians, psychiatrists, psychologists, social workers, speech therapists, neurosurgeons, psychomotor specialists, and many, many other -ists. I have been with many diagnostic wizards as they "staffed" children. In many instances, what has in fact happened is that the children were shafted rather than staffed. Let me explain.

After my twentieth or thirtieth staffing, where dozens of people described the referred pupils from their professional vantage points, I became convinced that these gatherings did not serve the purpose I had naively thought they were meant to serve. I had believed their purpose was to offer practical recommendations to someone responsible for the treatment of children so that those children would be cured and would subsequently thrive. To my dismay, I discovered that the suggestions offered were rarely based on data and those that were relied on the briefest amount of data. I discovered that the recommendations offered by these highly paid specialists were about as empirically derived as those of Ann Landers or her sister. The few suggestions I heard that *were* derived from fact were not operational because they were obtained in a laboratory environment, one that was invariably different from the client's natural setting. Other treatment suggestions were so steeped in theory and imagery that not even the proponent's erudite colleagues could translate them, much less put them into practice.

Occasionally the teachers of the referred child attended the staffings (the child, of course, never attended). Often, throughout the deliberations, the teachers were even allowed to describe the children from their point of view. Many teachers I observed, however, were so intimidated by the high-powered diagnosticians surrounding them that they were afraid to speak. When they did, they were often apologetic about the fact they did not have Ph.D.'s and could only explain actual happenings during recess and the reading period. The professionals often talked down to the teachers, thinking, I suppose, that the teachers could not actually know anything about the children, even though they were with them several hours each day. After the diagnosticians had advanced their theories and conjectures as to why a particular child was in her current state, the teachers were even more intimidated. They had always been taught to worship and revere the medics, and during these meetings they were in their actual presence! Many left these meetings in a state of shock; they had been made to believe they were instructional illiterates, totally incapable of assisting their charges in developing their skills. The day following the staffings their morale was even worse, for not only did they feel insecure about their own competencies, but they also found themselves quite unable to translate the many recommendations that were offered at the shafting into solutions for their child's problem.

About the only purpose served by these staffings is that they maintain clinics and diagnosticians. The only way these facilities and professionals can survive is to find more and more children to run through their diagnostoriums. For unless the high-powered probers are kept busy staffing children,they will have nothing to do. Many of the practical clinical or research skills the diagnosticians may have had have long since atrophied. Therefore, the shafters must continue to practice clinicide.

I certainly wouldn't want to leave the impression that I am antidiagnosis, for diagnosis is essential; that is, if its purpose is to determine what is wrong so that it can be fixed. It's that I am violently opposed to the strategy of current multidisciplinary diagnoses.

Some garages are in the business of diagnosis in a rather practical way. They have computerized diagnostic centers that supposedly tell the mechanic exactly what is wrong with a car. Some claim that thirty items of diagnostic information can be supplied by such a process—that most of the important features of a car's operation can thus be described. From this information the car owner is told about wheel alignment, the condition of the shocks and brakes, all about the compression, battery, radiator, starter. These automotive diagnosticians explain that when the problems have been pinpointed, the mechanic knows where to start to work. He knows where to adjust, rebuild, or replace. In this example (ideally, of course) diagnosis leads directly to remediation.

If a person goes to a medical clinic for general diagnosis—to have a physical—he will also receive many tests. Urine and blood samples will be drawn, his blood pressure is measured, his heart rate calculated. He will be probed, questioned, and looked at, over, and into. Often, as a result of such a general diagnosis, physical problems are disclosed. The diagnosis may reveal a circulatory, respiratory, digestive, or elimination problem. Moreover, if the diagnosis has been precise enough and the doctor is skilled enough, diagnosis will lead directly to remediation. The doctor will be able to take over where diagnosis left off. He will presumably be able to prescribe some course of treatment that will cure the malady.

This should be the purpose of diagnosis: it should lead directly to remediation. Unfortunately, the type of educational diagnosis I have described earlier, and many other forms of educational diagnosis, do not lead directly to remediation. They simply lead to further diagnosis.

The primary reason for this dismal failure is that the diagnoses are not direct. They do not focus exactly on the behavior of concern. Often, when a child is referred for diagnosis because of her inability to read from the blue Science Research Associates (SRA) book, she is diagnosed in a dozen or so indirect areas before someone listens to her read.

Educational diagnosis—the type conducted in schools rather than in medical centers—often consists of a standardized test. If intelligence is to be diagnosed, the child is given an intelligence test. If social adjustment is the concern, she is given a social rating scale; for motor development, a motor test; for personality, a personality test.

There are thousands of tests from which to select. To measure intelligence, for instance, the diagnostician can choose from an array of at least thirty tests. There are nearly as many for social and personality adjustment and dozens for such skills as reading, spelling, and math. But in spite of the abundance of tests, they still are not specific enough. Almost invariably they do not focus precisely on the behavior of concern.

As I have mentioned, one of the requisites of good diagnosis is that it be direct. If the teacher wants information about a child's ability to read in an SRA reader, he should listen to the child read from an SRA reader. If he wants to know how often the student swears, he should count the cusses on a given day. The teacher, in other words, should monitor directly the behavior of concern; he should not administer an intelligence, personality, or motor development test that might be only indirectly related to the behavior of concern.

During this diagnostic period, the teacher wants to know the extent to which the pupil does something: reads, writes, walks, talks, rides, rows, or whatever. In order to obtain this information he must do more than directly monitor the pupil's behavior; he must monitor the behavior over a period of time.

As Jacqueline Susann has said, "Once is not enough." Since all of us have good days and bad days, the behavior of concern must be measured on several different days in order to obtain a realistic impression of the pupil's performance. The teacher must also watch, listen, and carefully study the way in which the pupil responds during those situations. For example, if the teacher is monitoring the pupil's oral reading, the teacher must write down the mistakes the pupil makes and other details of the situation in order to understand totally her style of responding.

By measuring directly and frequently the behavior of concern, and by carefully studying the response patterns of the child, the teacher is in a position to learn of at least two vital features of the client's behavior. One is in reference to the breadth and consistency of the referred problem. If, for example, in an arithmetic situation in which a pupil's ability to add facts is being measured, it could be discovered that she has difficulty with only one fact, $6 + 2$. Or it could be revealed that she cannot accurately add any of the facts. Consistency refers to the variability of the child's performance. It might be that the pupil occasionally errs on the problem $6 + 2$ or, on the other hand, that she can never solve that particular problem.

The second item of information is that the teacher will learn about the consistent, but misleading, notions of children. Often, they respond logically to various problems, developing logical, although mistaken, strategies for solving them. Some, until told otherwise, use these private strategies consistently for long periods of time. If the teacher can detect them, users are often willing to adapt immediately to an alternate, correct approach. Many examples of such aberrations could be offered, but a common one is when children subtract in reverse; their answer to the problem $43 - 15$ would be 32.

Perhaps another reason why some of the current educational diagnoses are not effective is that once again the medical model has led educators astray. In the medical system, diagnosis seeks the cause of a problem. Medical people attempt to discover why the person's head, back, or toe aches; they want to know why his urine is red or his blood amber. Once they have pinpointed the reason why, they proceed to recommend one of several therapies. They prescribe drugs, exercise, surgery, psychiatry, diet, transcendental meditation, or lotus-posture yoga in the hope of curing the diagnosed malady.

Many of the educational diagnosticians I have criticized are like the medical people: they seek to discover the reason for some abnormal behavior. They want to know what *caused* the reading failure or the deviant personality. Then, they believe, some type of educational therapy can be prescribed, and the client will be cured.

(Perhaps, since the term *diagnose* means to identify a disease, it should not be used in education. Though it may be appropriate for the medical people, who must determine the nature of the disease in order to prescribe for it, educators should not use the word since they deal with educational matters that do not necessarily originate from diseases.)

Be this as it may, in education it is more important *to find out where to begin instruction* than it is to know why the person is not behaving as he should. It is imperative to know where to begin the child's reading instruction. The teacher must know what behaviors in reading the pupil has and what ones she does not have. Once this information is known, the pupil can be started at a point where she can learn new material. We do not need to know about her reading disease (if she even had one); we want to know where to start teaching. The same approach goes for other academic skills, if not for all physical and personality skills. We do, indeed, need to search for a better term than diagnosis, one that means "finding a starting point." Perhaps the word *revelation* would be more accurate. But until a more accurate and acceptable term is found, we will have to use diagnosis.

To illustrate the type of diagnosis (revelation?) I have been talking about, one that focuses precisely on the behavior of concern, I have selected two projects. The first illustrates the way in which precise and direct diagnosis can determine the breadth of a problem. The second serves to point out how pupils' faulty strategies can be detected by teachers who carefully study the response patterns of their children. In both projects, it is demonstrated that when enough time is spent focusing directly on the behavior of concern, subsequent teaching can be relatively simple.

FOCUSING ON d—b REVERSALS

The director of this study, a graduate student in special education, noted that when a youngster wrote during spelling and writing periods, he occasionally reversed some letters. Most often he reversed *d*'s and *b*'s. (D. Smith & Lovitt, 1973).

In order to determine how often and in which position (initial or final) the boy reversed either letter, she organized four lists of words. Two lists featured the *d* in final and initial positions; two *b* lists were also constructed.

For several days the teacher read these words to the boy; his task was to write them. From day to day, the presentation order of the words was mixed. After each session, she checked his answers. He was credited with a correct answer if he wrote the *b* or *d* accurately (he was not required to spell the entire word correctly). Each day's performance was graphed as to the percentage correct. Four graphs, one for each letter in both positions, were maintained.

The data during this baseline, or diagnostic, phase revealed that the boy's most frequent error was the *d* in initial position. It was further revealed that he rarely erred when required to write *b* in initial position, and his performance was inconsistent when he was requested to write *d* or *b* in final position.

Using this information, the teacher designed a remediation strategy that focused on the *d* in initial position. Each day, during the remediation phase, instruction consisted of the following steps. First, a card was shown the pupil on which was printed the word *dam*. He was asked to read the word, name the initial letter, then print the word. Next, the teacher showed him a card on which was printed the word *bam*. The boy was told that he often incorrectly printed *bam* for *dam*. He was asked to read the word, name the initial letter, then print the word. This instruction lasted about thirty seconds and was administered each day during the remediation phase. Following instruction, the word lists were presented just as they had been throughout the diagnostic phase.

After six days of instruction, the pupil's performance was 100 percent for all lists. To make certain that he could discriminate *b* from *d*, at least in the context of the study, the instruction phase ran another two days. These results revealed that not only did the pupil's accuracy for the initial *d* continue to be at 100 percent but also that his scores were perfect on the other three word lists. Thus, the teacher had determined by a precise diagnosis the extent and nature of the boy's problem. Remediation time to correct the error was only about four minutes over an eight-day period.

HORIZONTAL AND VERTICAL MATH PROBLEMS

The boy in this project was assigned addition problems, presented to him via a computer program. The teacher of the study noted that the pupil's scores were much higher on some days than on others. Since he was curious about this inconsistent performance, he studied several days' papers and noted that the assigned addition problems varied as to format; some of the problems were vertically written and others, horizontally (J. Smith & Lovitt, 1973).

By studying the boy's papers, the teacher learned that the pupil always answered the vertical problems correctly, but invariably erred when the problems were horizontally written. Furthermore, his errors for the horizontal problems were consistent. If the problem was 14 + 2 = , his answer was 52. He added the two digits in the left numeral, entered that in the tens column of the answer, then placed the numeral on the right in the units column of the answer.

In order to confirm that the pupil could compute vertically but not horizontally designed problems, the teacher scheduled a baseline, or diagnostic, condition. During this phase, the pupil was given two sheets of twenty-five problems each. On one sheet the addition problems were written horizontally; on the other, the same problems were written vertically. From one day to the next the sheets were reversed; one day the pupil initially worked the vertical problems, the next day he first solved the horizontal items.

During the six-day baseline, the teacher's hypothesis was confirmed. The pupil rarely erred on the vertical problems, and his answers to the horizontal problems were consistently incorrect. The only horizontal problems he answered correctly were those that had a zero in the units column of the left addend (10 + 4 =). This information verified the teacher's suspicion that the pupil consistently used his own private rule—to obtain the answer he added the digits on the left and combined that total with the digit on the right.

During the remediation phase, the teacher demonstrated how to compute one problem. He drew a line from the units digit of the left numeral to the numeral on the right, told the boy to add those numerals, and then to place the tens digit in the tens column of the answer (14 + 2 = 16).

This teaching procedure required less than thirty seconds a day. Following the instruction, the pupil completed the two sheets of problems as he did during the baseline condition. In two days, his accuracy was 100 percent for both sheets of math problems.

In both projects, the instance of the b - d reversals and the example of format confusion, the instructional effects were significant and immediate when the problem was clearly pinpointed, when teaching was direct, and when instruction was simple. It should also be noted that in these projects the diagnosis was conducted by the classroom teacher; the youngsters were not sent to clinics far from school, receiving diagnostic information that would have been imprecise or useless. The subsequent remediation techniques for these pupils, too, were managed by persons in their classes; they were not sent to remediation clinics where they more than likely would have received indirect, hence useless, instruction. Invariably, when diagnosis is direct and undertaken by the person responsible for instruction, the chances of a happy match between diagnosis and instruction are extremely good.

Behavioral
Objectives

IF you have some idea as to the extent you want to teach
something, you might make it; if you don't have an idea,
well. . . .

Goals and objectives have been around for ages. People have always thought about, talked about, or written about behavioral
objectives, either for themselves or others. Some people engage
in this exercise only around the first of the year, but other
people are concerned with goal setting the year around.

Early in their lives, children are exposed to the process of
specifying goals and objectives. Beginning at about age two they
are repeatedly asked what they are going to be when they grow
up. Most youngsters readily reply to these perfunctory queries.
They have learned to indicate some vocational choice—a fire-
fighter or an astronaut—if for no other reason than to get the
adults off their backs. Some children are asked about their career plans so often—and they of course always reply to these
queries—that they probably program themselves into jobs they
never really took the time to consider seriously.

Parents have many goals for their children. They want them to be good students, make good grades, be happy, be successful, develop sparkling personalities, and become skilled conversationalists. Teachers also have several objectives for their pupils. They want them to be quiet, polite, happy, attentive, punctual, cooperative, and to understand and apply what has been taught.

In the past few years, many educators have talked about performance criteria, desired outcomes, terminal objectives, and management by objectives. As a result, significant pressure has been brought to bear on the educational system to declare its objectives. Much of this pressure has come about because educators have traditionally been hazy about specifying the proposed outcome of their product.

In 1962, Robert Mager wrote a clever little booklet entitled *Preparing Instructional Objectives.* Because it was published at a time when people were becoming concerned about educational objectives, the book has been widely acclaimed. As evidence of its popularity, ten different education courses at the University of Washington listed it as one of their texts a few years ago.

Mager's book greatly influenced many people in education and related fields. Even today, many years after its publication, whenever the conversation of educators shifts to behavioral objectives, Mager's name and his little book will be mentioned. He has become synonymous with the specification of objectives.

Perhaps the primary reason for his success in influencing people to think more about objectives was his insistence that when people specify an objective they must consider an aim that is both measurable and quantifiable. He would say, for example, that the objective "to become an avid reader" is, although admirable, unattainable, because the definition does not include a measurable component. He would accept the definition, however, if it were "to read fifty books each year."

Mager's rules for establishing behavioral objectives have greatly influenced the public schools, at least insofar as the writing of objectives is concerned. Many school systems insist that their teachers write out detailed behavioral objectives for the pupils in their classes. A few years ago, for example, when my daughter did her practice teaching in a Seattle first grade, she spent hours each evening writing out detailed behavioral objectives, one for each skill every child was being taught.

The objectives she came up with, however, often had little bearing on her teaching. Although she and the head teacher assisted the children in the areas which generally corresponded to the detailed objectives, for example, reading or arithmetic, their instruction did not necessarily focus on the specific behaviors defined in the objectives. Furthermore, they did not monitor periodically the target behaviors in order to learn whether or not the specified objectives were being reached. In that classroom, the writing of objectives was merely an end in itself. Once written, they were filed on a shelf. When space becomes critical in a few months, they will likely be piled in a basement, along with other educational trivia.

My daughter's experience with writing phantom objectives is like that of many teachers in situations where they have, by fiat, been required to perform this busywork. Many, in such circumstances, treat the specification of objectives as an exercise quite apart from teaching. They write the objectives simply to satisfy their supervisors. Once written, they are forgotten, and the teachers return to what they consider the important business of the classroom.

More's the pity! It would seem that good teachers should not only specify behavioral objectives, but also should use those objectives as targets for their teaching and should occasionally monitor the progress of their pupils toward those targets. We have all heard and recognized the wisdom of such truisms as, "If you don't know where you want to go, you may end up someplace else," or "You should be careful about the objective you set up, for that's where you might end up." Both sayings suggest that the specification of objectives is indeed one of the basic tactics of good education.

Admittedly, there are some problems involved in specifying objectives, particularly when it comes to establishing such aims for others. A philosophical concern of many teachers, when they are asked to specify behaviors for others, is that they do not wish to assume that much responsibility. They are afraid that if they specify, for example, that a child should learn to read or compute, they are to some extent stripping him of his freedom of choice; they would apparently prefer to stand aside and assist him only if and when he asked for help. Most parents and perhaps all teachers of exceptional children would roundly disagree with such a philosophy, arguing that if we waited for some children to clamor to read or compute, we would have a long, long wait. There is the added fact, too, that if objectives are not specified, some people may never develop at all, or they may develop in ways quite contrary to our expectations.

Another problem in establishing objectives is raised by individuals who are willing to take the plunge and specify what behaviors should be taught, but are not certain to just what extent, or what degree of competency the pupil should be expected to develop. Some people, when they are faced with this problem, respond much as did the first-mentioned group of teachers—they back off and refuse to become involved, so fearful of setting an unreasonable requirement that they specify none at all. This group, unlike the first, goes ahead and teaches specific skills (they are not worried about this), but they teach without having a clear end in view. The consequences of such teaching may well be that children are either over- or undertaught.

In either situation, the child's time is wasted. If a pupil is overtaught some behavior, if he is asked to perform a certain skill over and over again after he has demonstrated he can do it well enough, he will become bored and disgusted with the whole process and perhaps with school in general. This has happened many times with children and their math facts. Some have been asked to do their addition or subtraction facts over and over again, long after they have proved their proficiency. Pupils may be required to do page after page of writing drills long after their penmanship abilities have peaked. Often, the teachers who overassign their children work at school are the same ones who complain loudest in their college classes about being required to do busywork!

Another catastrophe that befalls the pupil who has been overtaught is that he has been delayed from advancing to, and hence from learning, a more advanced skill. Perhaps he could have mastered beginning algebra, even trigonometry, during those hours he was required to practice the addition facts.

And what about the child who is undertaught? He is a loser too. Often, children are only partially taught certain skills; they can read, write, and type a little, but they are not really proficient at anything and are, therefore, unable to use these half-skills in applied situations. For all practical purposes the time they spent only approaching competence was wasted.

All of us have these only partially developed and, therefore, nonfunctional skills. Although we began, at one time, to learn a "skill," we did not, for one reason or another, become proficient. Consider, for instance, the multitudes who have wanted to play the guitar. Thousands of enthusiasts have purchased guitars, bought dozens of instruction books, taken private lessons, and bought Segovia or Chet Atkins records. They had dreamed of inviting their friends over, sitting around the fireside, sharing a bottle of Thunderbird, and playing the current hits for them. Or they dreamed of strapping the guitar on their backs, along with some bread, cheese, and another bottle of Thunderbird, getting on their Yamaha, riding off into the hills to rendezvous with their loved one, and serenading their partner with seductive Spanish tunes. Those two fantasies have sold a passel of guitars and related items.

After a few weeks, during which time those romantics practiced a little and experienced a great deal of guilt for not practicing more, most of the guitars ended up in attics or pawnshops, the books and records were given away or forgotten, and the lessons were discontinued.

These zealots did not invest enough time or effort to develop anything, and their feeble efforts yielded, at best, only partial skills, utterly nonfunctional. They got off the blocks but never finished the race. In fact, some of them never got into the race.

Another example of underteaching lies in the thousands of severely handicapped children who have been subjected to thousands of hours of reading instruction, yet never learned to read. Many of those youngsters were initially placed in basal series and failed. They were then drilled, prodded, and coaxed to read. They went from one teacher and school to another, facing a new technique or approach at each change.

The major portion of the school day, for many of these children, was spent "learning to read," but the investment yielded little or nothing. They could not read Chaucer or Rabelais, Hemingway or Proust; they could not read pamphlets, newspapers, church bulletins, advertisements, or governmental forms. Many could not, in spite of the countless hours of instruction, even read the signs in their surroundings that told them where to go and how to do it. Results such as these are the regrettable consequences of underteaching.

Although under- and overteaching are both the result of not specifying what behavior should be taught and to what extent, underteaching is perhaps the greater of the two evils. As I have indicated in the guitar-playing and reading examples, those who are undertaught all too often spend many hours and much too much money, yet come away empty-handed.

Had a clear objective been set prior to attempting to learn the guitar or to read, this time and money might not have been so wasted. A well-specified objective prior to teaching, and some reasonable estimate as to how soon the objective can be reached, will often make all the difference.

For example, if the guitar player had specified as an objective the ability to play five songs containing three chords, and if he had reason to believe (based on his guitar teacher's honest appraisal after the second lesson) that this competency level could be achieved within two months if he practiced thirty minutes each day, he could come to a decision. He could quit, believing the gain would not be worth the effort. Or he could, of course, opt to continue studying, believing that the end was worth the means. The point is that when an objective and its presumed cost are known, the decision as to whether or not to invest time and money in an experience can be intelligently made before training ever begins.

The same strategy applies to reading. The teacher could specify as an objective for the severely retarded pupil with no reading abilities that he be able to read fifty-three signs of safety and convenience. In addition, she might estimate the cost of teaching such a skill to be 30 minutes a day for forty-three days. Knowing what was to be achieved (the ability to read fifty-three signs) and the cost (1,290 minutes distributed over forty-three days) the teacher could then decide, prior to beginning her teaching, whether or not the acquisition of the skill would be worth the anticipated cost.

We see, then, that the steps involved in setting up desired objectives are the following. First, the teacher should determine the pupil's present level of competence in relation to the desired behavior. That is, she must know how well the pupil can perform the expected task prior to initiating the teaching of that behavior. She must also know what portions of the desired behavior are currently in the pupil's repertory. And she must know what other similar skills have been learned.

Second, the teacher must determine how competent the pupil is expected to become in regard to the target behavior. She—or someone—must decide whether he will be trained to be a record holder in that behavior, a highly competent professional, a so-so performer like most students his age, or an incompetent performer. She should not begin this teaching without a competency level clearly in mind, for that is how people end up with nontransferable behaviors.

Third, the teacher must determine, as nearly as possible, the cost of developing the selected behavior to a specified level of competency. This is often extremely difficult to do. Currently, little help is available when it comes to attaching a cost figure to the development of most behaviors. One factor that must be considered is the time per day or week that will be required. Another requisite is to determine how much of that effort is required over a longer period of time. To illustrate: the teacher should determine the optimum amount of time per day, such as twenty minutes, and also specify the total number of days that should be devoted to this task, for example, 100, 250, or 500.

Obviously, about the best assistance teachers have when it comes to making these estimates is to ask people who have either acquired the skills or who have taught them to others. And in evaluating these statements, the inquirer must, of course, take into account the characteristics of the person who learned the skill, the type of instruction he received, and other important conditions that prevailed throughout the learning situation.

For instance, if we wanted to know the length of time required to teach a child to read from a first grade reader, we would naturally go first to teachers of first grade children. From them, we would obtain some idea as to how many minutes each day they generally devoted to reading instruction and how many days throughout the year reading was taught. We would also learn much about the types of children they had worked with, the kind of instruction they had offered, their own classroom style, and the nature of other important environmental factors. With this information, imprecise though it might be, the "cost" of teaching other first grade children to read from first grade books might be fairly accurately assessed.

At the risk of elaborating on the obvious, let me cite one more instance. If an ambitious young man with a horn wanted to know the cost of becoming a symphonic trumpet player, he should interview all the orchestral trumpet players he could possibly buttonhole. Only they could provide information as to the number of hours per day they practiced and how many years it took them to attain their skills. They could also provide information about their instructors and the conditions under which they developed their skills. They could describe the books and exercises they were required to know, the sequences for developing various skills, and the drills they had found particularly effective in mastering specific aspects of their playing.

The fourth requirement for specifying objectives, once the cost of teaching a particular skill has been estimated, is for teachers or pupils to readjust their goals. They may now be willing to spend more time on the behavior than was thought necessary to reach the initially specified competency level and so will want to raise their sights. On the other hand, they may be unwilling to pay such an added price, and it would be to their advantage to be content with a lower level of achievement. Instead of aspiring to play the guitar like Segovia, they may be happier to strum a few folk ditties for their friends. Their friends may be happier, too. And of course a reckoning of the cost may induce the aspirant to drop the whole thing and become neither a Segovia nor a parlor balladeer, but, instead, a proficient disc jockey or a mediocre autoharp player. Such are the rewards for the specification of behaviors.

As important as it is, however, this specification is regrettably not an easy assignment. There are sketchy, if any, data available as to how many hours, over a total period of time, are required to develop many skills. The military has, I have been told, some approximate information as to the average time required to learn to assemble and fire Browning automatic rifles and other weapons. Industry probably has some data on the number of hours required to teach certain skills to varying types of individuals. I recently read, in fact; that a certain firm claims they can teach the essentials of the metric system to their workers in six two-hour sessions. We educators need to study their approaches to this problem.

But as difficult as it is to specify even general cost estimates, we must still make the effort. Unless we establish these projections, many people will develop only bits and pieces of behaviors that are never transferable, and others will continue to be wastefully taught certain behaviors long after they have been learned.

Many times in school situations we are concerned with bringing certain behaviors of children into greater accord with those of other children. Such a practice may be good or bad; many debates have raged over the issue of conformity and norms. Some argue that it is bad practice to try to make all the children behave alike and that it is quite absurd to expect all youngsters to read at the same level of competency, recite with the same readiness, or develop the same insights into history and social studies.

Others maintain that it is impractical not to strive for certain standards. They argue that it is one thing to foster individualization, but the child who cannot read, write, and compute as well as his peers is in these respects, less proficient. Later, if that child must compete for his livelihood with other children who are more competent, he will be at a distinct disadvantage.

Everyone must make her own decision on this matter of similarities and differences. I would only hope that every teacher, assigned as she is the responsibility for developing and nurturing the growth of each of her pupils, will seriously consider the consequences of either approach.

I believe most of us take a moderate stance in this matter. Few teachers are hung up on the idea of making every child look like one another in every respect. In fact, most of us are such sloppy teachers we have little to worry about even if we wanted to "make" all kids look alike. The kids are going to come out of it (education, that is) behaving very differently from one another in any event—and in spite of our best or our worst efforts.

Some teachers use the data of their best students as the target objectives for those who are not doing so well. And many times this little game of catch up is successful in such academic areas as math, writing, and reading, as the less competent children in the class respond to the challenge. Although such an achievement does not guarantee a continued parity of competency or that the striver has attained a securely negotiable skill, it does mean that, at least in regard to these matched behaviors, both youngsters are at the moment alike. The less gifted pupil has been brought up to a competitive level.

Such an equalization, however temporary, can do wonders for some youngsters. Imagine the little fellow who has always been slower than everyone else. Now, after he has been taught a certain skill up to another student's level, he is as competent as the other, at least in respect to that behavior. It might well be that knowing he is this "teachable" is enough to motivate him to become generally a more competent person. It is also devoutly to be hoped that his teacher will be sufficiently motivated to keep up the good work herself.

In sum, although specifying objectives is not as easy as Mager has led us to believe, it is an eminently good idea to make the effort. And it is a still better idea to specify the level of competence desired and the anticipated cost. For if we do not specify objectives in this manner, who can say what our pupils will be taught, or to what level, or at what cost?

Clarifying
Expectations

SOME children will do what you want them to if you just tell them what you want.

Sometimes the attempts of teachers to solve educational problems are very complex. Perhaps the reason they tend to use complicated solutions to potentially simple problems is that they have invested heavily in acquiring sophisticated approaches to educational issues. Most teachers have devoted at least four years to obtain an undergraduate degree and a teaching certificate, during which time they were provided with many complicated and intricate tools for their trade. Many have even returned to college for fifth-year courses and masters' degrees. Others have spent their hard-earned cash to buy books and materials guaranteed to help solve their various instructional problems. Still others have spent time and money taking special in-service and summer-session workshops that were designed to give them expertise in dealing with such specific educational phenomena as "modern math" or "productive thinking."

40

If, for instance, a second grade teacher was concerned about children who had reversal problems, those labeled as dyslexic, he might have built up a small library on the subject, attended workshops or conventions, and enrolled for in-service courses dealing with individuals of that type. As a result of these efforts, he might have amassed a huge arsenal of tactics to use with children displaying dyslexic symptoms. (A later chapter, Some Teaching Procedures Are Complex, deals with the use of multiple and varied techniques.)

Armed with such an array of techniques, he could sit back and eagerly await a victim. Woe be unto the poor unsuspecting pupil in his class who one day behaves as a dyslexic; for the teacher could then unleash upon her his barrage of dyslexic remediation techniques stored up over the year.

Possibly the child would be cured by this vast array of techniques. But, alas, she might also become the victim of remediation overkill. She might have been helped with a less massive onslaught.

Examples come to mind of such overzealous, overcomplicated tactics. I once heard of a teacher, for example, who discovered that one of his pupils misread a number of words. In an effort to help her, this teacher subjected her to a multi-sensory remediation program. She had the girl trace various letters on sandpaper, write words in the air, cut out magazine pictures of objects that began with various consonants, and practice on short and long vowel sounds.

Then there was the instance of the girl who was always tardy. Her teacher, in an effort to solve the problem, established a contingency system whereby the girl earned apples for coming to school on time. First, she was given an apple each day for being no more than ten minutes late, then for being only five minutes late, and, finally, on an intermittent schedule for prompt attendance.

In both examples, the problems actually were solved: eventually the first girl read more accurately and the second girl became more punctual. There is a possibility, however, that the same results would have been noted had the first girl simply been told to make fewer mistakes as she read and the second girl requested to show up on time.

Following are four instances where positive effects were noted when children were simply told what was expected of them.

ORAL READING WAS IMPROVED

In this project, the teacher obtained data in oral reading from an eleven-year-old boy. Each day, during the baseline phase, she required him to read from a basal reader for five minutes. While he read, she followed along in another reader and noted the words that were read correctly and incorrectly. Errors included substitutions, omissions, and additions. Following the session, the teacher totaled the number of correctly and incorrectly read words and divided by five, the number of minutes the pupil read. She then graphed the rate of correctly and incorrectly read words per minute.

By studying the graphed data after a few days, the teacher learned that the pupil's correct rates were rather low (on the average, about forty words per minute). During the baseline period, she also learned that the boy's correct rates were quite variable: they ranged from thirty to fifty words per minute. Like many other performance styles, variability can sometimes suggest what teaching procedure should be used. (More will be said about this in a later chapter, Reinforcement Contingencies.)

The teacher decided to tell the child to improve. Each day during a remediation phase, prior to his reading from the book, the teacher said, "Paul, try to read a little faster today." This phase ran for about two weeks. When those data were evaluated it was evident that he had improved, for, on the average, his correct rate was fifty-six words per minute, a gain of sixteen words per minute. What was even more gratifying, his average incorrect rate fell to three words per minute and his day-to-day performance was much less variable than it had been in the first condition.

SO WAS DESCRIBING PICTURES

In this project, the manager worked with a young man who appeared to have a very limited vocabulary. For one thing, it was noted that his responses to questions were very short. During a diagnostic phase, the manager showed the boy a number of cards from various Peabody Language Development Kits and asked him to tell about the pictures. Data were kept on the average response length per session (total words divided by total responses) and on the ratio of different sentence beginnings (different beginnings divided by total beginnings). The data from this period revealed that his average ratio of beginnings and average response length were very low (see figures 2 and 3). Generally, the length of his responses was four words, and each response began with *this*. If, for example, he was shown a picture of a cup, his response would probably be "This is a cup."

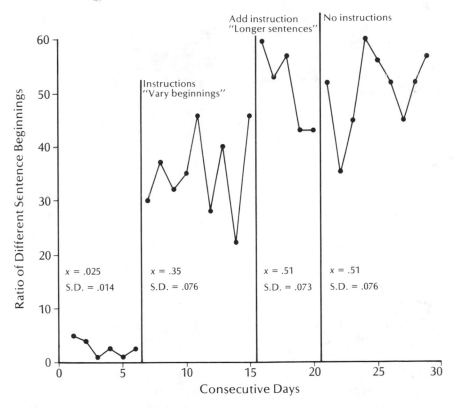

Figure 2. Ratio of different sentence beginnings throughout four experimental phases.

In the next condition of the study, he was requested simply to vary the way in which he began his responses. The data indicated that he did just this; he used several different words to begin sentences instead of always starting with *this*. As a result, his mean ratio of beginnings increased greatly during this phase.

During the third condition, he was asked to use more words to describe the pictures. Once again instructions influenced his behavior. When the data from that phase were compared to his baseline rates, it was apparent that his average number of responses tripled when instructions were used. His average num-

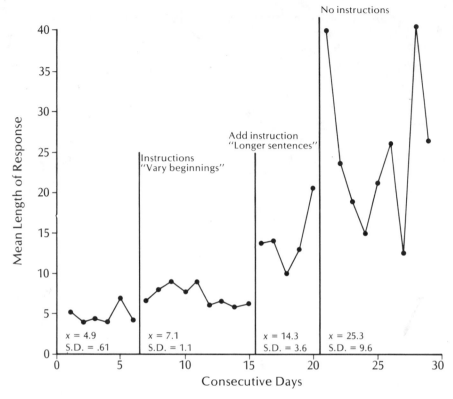

Figure 3. Mean response length throughout four experimental phases.

ber of words during the baseline condition was five, whereas his average frequency in the intervention phase was fifteen. This young man was unusually sensitive to instructions, since two verbal behaviors—using varied sentence beginnings and more words—were immediately and significantly influenced by his being told what to do (Lovitt & J. Smith, 1972).

MATH: PLEASE WORK FASTER

Encouraged by the success of the preceding projects, where the abilities to read orally and to describe pictures were so significantly improved by simple instructions, we decided to try the same technique with another pupil, this time in arithmetic.

Throughout a baseline phase, this youngster was required to work on borrowing facts for one minute. During this condition no instruction, feedback, or reinforcement was scheduled. The data from that period indicated his incorrect rates were generally zero, and his correct rates were about twenty-two problems per minute. But although his accuracy was excellent, he answered the problems very slowly. To be as proficient as his peers in responding to this type of problem, he should have been able to work about forty problems per minute.

During the next phase, the pupil was instructed daily. Prior to setting him to work on the subtraction problems, the teacher told him to "please work faster." The data during this period indicated his compliance; his mean rate rose to thirty-four problems per minute, an increase of about twelve problems per minute over the preceding condition. He was now almost as proficient as his peers. It should also be pointed out that although his correct rate increased considerably, his incorrect rate remained at zero. Thus, his improved proficiency was not at the expense of reduced accuracy.

INSTRUCTIONS AND WRITING

The pupil in this report was an eleven-year-old girl. Each day she was asked to write a story. Throughout the project, several aspects of writing were measured: total words written, number of sentences, correct and incorrect uses of punctuation, correct and incorrect uses of capitals, correctly and incorrectly spelled words, and legible and illegible letters.

During the first condition, which lasted about a week, the girl was asked to write a story on a topic that interested her. She was allowed to write for as long as she wished. No further instructions were scheduled.

Throughout the second phase of the study, she continued to write on a topic of her choosing, but now attention was focused on her primary writing problem, legibility. Each day, during this second condition, the manager of the study said to the girl, "Please write more carefully, because your writing is often difficult to read." This instruction had an immediate and rather significant effect on her penmanship. On the first day it was given, and throughout the condition, her handwriting greatly improved. Throughout this period, the teacher was able to read her stories without asking for assistance.

It was also noted during this condition that, although legibility improved, the other aspects of her writing remained unchanged. She continued to write the same number of words and sentences each day, her ability to use punctuation and capitals remained the same, and her spelling proficiency was unaltered. I will comment at some length about the generalization of behaviors, or the lack of it, in the chapters entitled Direct Teaching, More on Direct Teaching, and Generalization.

Following the instructions-for-penmanship condition, a third phase was scheduled. The reason for this phase was that the teacher had noted during the second phase that the girl often neglected to use capitals, making it difficult to determine when one sentence ended and the next one began. Since her legibility had improved during the second phase, the inappropriate use of capitals was judged to be the most serious weakness in her writing. The instructional focus therefore shifted to capitals.

Throughout this period, the girl received the following instruction: "Your stories would be easier to read if you used capitals to begin each of your sentences." During this phase, her use of capitals greatly improved. Prior to instruction, they were correctly used only about 50 percent of the time. During this phase, she used them correctly from 75 to 100 percent of the time.

In regard to most of the other elements of writing that were measured, her performance remained unaltered. Her writing was about the same in respect to number of words and sentences per day and to spelling accuracy, and her penmanship continued to be satisfactory, even though no instruction was directed toward it.

The only feature of writing that improved with the use of capitals during this condition was the correct use of punctuation marks. Because she was now beginning most of her sentences with capitals, she ended most of her sentences with a mark of some type, usually the correct one.

What may we postulate, then, from these findings? Simply that clear, direct instructions, when properly given, can prove highly effective, in home or school. But often they are neither simple nor clear. One has only to check on the types of instruction children are expected to process and respond to, both at home and at school, to see the dangers that lurk.

Often a child is given several commands at the same time; while he is complying with one instruction, he is given another. Orders are often simultaneously given, one from dad and one from mom. Many times children are requested, in quite different ways, to do the same thing; different words, word orders, and inflections can be confusing. As a result, children are hopelessly baffled by the noise and simply turn it off. They give up; they cease to listen. Little wonder, then, that some teachers and parents have little faith in the function of instructions.

In all four of our projects—reading orally, describing pictures, working math problems, and writing stories—simple instructions were used. They were brief and to the point and were given in the same way every day. The children responded favorably to those instructions in every case.

Admittedly, instructions will not always promote the desired results. But they should certainly be tried initially when behavior change is desired. Telling a child what is expected of him is an inexpensive, simple way to alter behavior, less nerve wracking and time consuming than many involved remediation routines. Teachers and parents can easily learn to give precise instructions consistently if they will just take a few moments to think them through. Certainly no vast library, workshop, or array of degrees and credentials is required to develop the art of giving instructions. And they *will*, more often than you might think, do the job.

Common
Teaching Procedures

SOME teaching procedures that have been used for a long time seem to be okay, others aren't too great.

Some teaching procedures have been around for years; they have been passed on from one generation of teachers to another, like commandments. In my introduction, I pointed out some reasons why certain educational practices persist. It should be added now that the internship model that has been traditionally used to train future teachers perpetuates the handing down of certain favored teaching procedures.

Many of these procedures are specific to certain subject matter areas. In spelling, for example, the practice of requiring students to write their misspelled words several times as a remedial exercise has been a standard technique for many years. I know from experience that it was a common practice in the 1940s when I was being "taught" to spell—many a late afternoon after school did I spend writing on the blackboard the words I had missed during that day's spelling test.

In arithmetic, who has not been exposed to flash-card drills to teach accurate computation? Teachers many years ago were unable to purchase commercially printed flash cards, but many of them developed their own sets; I can remember vividly the dog-eared set of cards my fourth grade teacher used to teach division. Flash cards have also been used for years to teach children to identify certain sounds and words. Almost every primary level teacher has several sets of such cards, some containing the long and short vowels, others featuring color words, the names of animals, and rhyming words. Various modifications of the modeling procedure have been used for years to teach manuscript and cursive writing. One favored technique is for the teacher to write several letters on the board, then to require the students to copy these models many, many times.

Teaching techniques are passed on from teacher to pupil like beliefs about learning or development. Just like the learning notions that pertain to acquisition, discrimination, generalization, retention, and motivation, ideas about how to teach various skills are transmitted from one teacher to the next.

This acquisition and transmission of teaching notions from our teachers is apparent in the play of children. One of the favorite games of youngsters is to play school; little girls and boys love to be the teacher. They seat all their friends in a circle, give them a series of stern directions such as "be nice" and "pay attention," then lecture their "students" or require them to read or to cipher. Youngsters are able to model very accurately many of the teaching practices they have been exposed to.

That children model quite accurately the teaching styles of their teachers was vividly pointed out to me a few years ago when we arranged a penmanship project with two boys. In that study, an older boy was assigned to teach a younger lad. The older boy, the tutor, had received remedial instruction in many subject areas, including penmanship, from a number of special tutors. As a result of this exposure to many teachers, he had amassed a large collection of teaching techniques.

When asked to assist the younger boy in penmanship, the older boy was told to use a teaching procedure of his own selection. The tutor had no problem choosing a technique; in fact, he selected several from his vast repertory. Each day he required the young man to do many familiar things, among them to trace certain letters, to perform a number of letter-formation drills, and to copy several letters and words from models prepared by the tutor. Furthermore, the tutor required his protégé to walk on a rail several minutes each day! Just why, one can easily surmise; apparently he himself had, at one time, been subjected to this teaching technique, and he now passed it on, for whatever it might be worth, to his student of penmanship. He had indeed been amply and diversely tutored and was now the classic example of the eclectic teacher who, without much discrimination, tries everything he has ever heard of. Since he knew several tricks, why not try them all? If one technique was good for a pupil, perhaps ten would be even better. More will be said about the combining of techniques in the next chapter.

Trumpet teachers have passed on the same teaching techniques from one generation to the next, and a student who went from one teaching studio to another could only be amazed at the similarity of teaching approaches. All trumpet teachers require their pupils to practice scales, lip slur, arpeggios, double tonguing exercises, and long tones; in fact, most of them in the United States use the same method book, the classic Joseph J. Arban text.

Hundreds of teaching procedures have been passed on like folk songs. The latter have persisted because for some reason they have been reinforcing to receiving generations and so have not faded into oblivion. Apparently, teaching techniques are similarly transmitted: the reinforcing ones continue to be used, and the nonreinforcing ones fade away or are greatly modified. However, it may not always be quite that simple; a technique may be reinforcing to a teacher, but ineffective for the pupil. And since so few teachers use data to assess the effectiveness of their procedures, many of them make the mistake of believing a procedure to be effective when it is not. Or it may work the other way; a technique may be thought ineffective when it is actually sound. So it is possible that some teaching procedures have been deservedly perpetuated, while others have been transmitted from teacher to teacher when they should have been scrapped.

Following are three examples of the use of these common teaching procedures. In two of the projects, the time-tried methods proved to be effective. In the third example, however, an established procedure was used with several pupils and found to be consistently ineffective.

THINK BEFORE YOU DO

This experiment comprised three studies with an eleven-year-old boy. Experiment 1 consisted of three conditions (throughout, the boy was required to perform twenty problems of the type [ ] - 2 = 6.) In the baseline or first phase he received no teaching, feedback, or reinforcement; when he finished the twenty problems, he was thanked and sent on to another academic activity (Lovitt & Curtiss, 1968).

During the second condition, he was required to verbalize each problem before he wrote the answer. He said, for instance, "Some number minus two equals six," then said and wrote the answer. The teacher monitored his behavior during this phase and occasionally reminded him to verbalize each response. During a third phase, he was asked to refrain from verbalizing the problems and answers.

The data from this experiment indicated that the pupil's performance was better in the condition where verbalization was required than during the baseline phase when no verbalization was demanded. It also showed that his performance was maintained, even improved, in the final condition, when verbalization was no longer practiced (see figure 4).

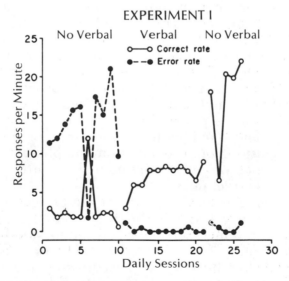

Figure 4. Correct and incorrect rates during the three phases of Experiment I, where the arithmetic problems were of the class [ ] - 2 = 6.

Two other experiments like the first were carried out. In one, problems of the type [ ] - 20 = 40 were used; in the other, the patterns were 4 - 3 = 9 - [ ]. Both of these experiments comprised the same three phases used in the first: in the first phase, no verbalization was required; in the second phase, the pupil verbalized each problem and answer throughout; and, in the final phase, he no longer verbalized the problems at all.

The results of these experiments were identical to those of Experiment 1. During the baseline phase, the boy's correct rate and accuracy were low; in the second phase, they were much improved; in the third phase, the behavior of subtracting was maintained, in spite of the removal of the cue.

This experiment demonstrated that a technique that has been used for many years by teachers and parents can still be effective. Many teachers have encouraged their pupils to think before they make a response. Presumably, the technique of requiring a verbalization of the problem and its answer would be especially effective with pupils who failed to study all the elements of a problem before making a response. It would circumvent rushing through a problem and, as a consequence, making inaccurate responses.

EVERY GOOD "GIRL" DOES FINE

In this project, another ancient teaching technique was used. The topic of the project was music, and the pupil was a six-year-old girl. Her teacher wanted her to learn to name the treble clef notes when they were printed on regular music paper. The sessions throughout the project lasted for exactly one minute. Daily, the teacher counted the number of correctly and incorrectly named notes and recorded each frequency on a graph.

During a baseline phase, the teacher merely gave the girl a sheet of music and asked her to say the names of the notes; she was given no instruction. The data from this phase indicated the girl's performance was extremely poor: her correct rates were low and her incorrect rates high.

Throughout the second phase of the project, the teacher wrote the letters e, g, b, d, f on the five lines of the top staff. She told the child to remember that those letters stood for "every good boy does fine." The girl was also told to use those words to help her remember the letters which corresponded to the musical notes. This mnemonic facilitator proved beneficial, for her correct rates increased significantly, and her incorrect rates approached zero. Her ability to name treble clef notes improved greatly when this technique was used.

Throughout a final phase, the letter names were no longer written on the top staff. Data continued to be gathered, however, to ascertain whether the writing of the letters on the staff was still required. These data indicated that the prop was no longer necessary; the girl could name the notes as rapidly and accurately during this phase as she did in the second condition. Once again, an old technique was proven effective.

FEEDBACK SERVED NO FUNCTION

A few years ago, we investigated the effects of several interventions that are commonly used to teach computation. One of the interventions was modeling; the pupils were shown how to solve the problems. Another was simply to tell the pupils to respond more accurately or to work faster. A third was feedback.

In the first feedback study, the percentage of correct scores of the pupils during a baseline condition was generally zero; they could not correctly answer any of the arithmetic problems. During this study, the students were assigned problems of different types: some were asked to add, some to subtract, and others to multiply.

Following a baseline period, a feedback intervention was scheduled for all of the pupils. During this period, the teacher planned to mark a C alongside each correctly answered problem and a ✓ by each incorrect answer.

This procedure proved to be ineffective for all pupils: none of their performances changed. Not only was the procedure ineffective; it was the cause of considerable anxiety. Most of the boys cried the first day their papers were returned with all their answers marked with a ✓ . Apparently they had, in the past, been punished for making errors, and the high number of checks on their papers was extremely aversive.

In a second study, another type of feedback was used. A baseline phase was initially scheduled, and once again the percentage of correct scores of the boys was generally zero. Throughout the next phase, a changed type of feedback was provided the boys. Marks for correct and incorrect responses as described before were given, and, in addition, the correct answer for each mistaken response was written on the pupil's paper. If the child's answer to the problem 4 + 3 = [ ] was 6, the teacher checked the response (✓), and placed a 7 by the child's answer.

The data from this phase revealed that this form of feedback was effective for only one pupil, whose scores improved somewhat during the feedback condition. The performances of six other boys, however, did not change.

In a third feedback study, we provided students with even more information. During the baseline phase of this study, we again determined that the pupils' accuracy was very low on certain types of arithmetic problems. Throughout this period, they received no feedback. During the next phase, they received three pieces of instruction. As in the first two studies, their correct and incorrect answers were checked. Also, as in the second study, they were provided with the correct answer if they erred on a problem. In addition, they were told, throughout the feedback portion of this study, how to calculate the missed problems. The results from this phase indicated that this third form of feedback was as ineffective as the two preceding efforts; the effects on performance were negligible.

In summary, most of the boys who received feedback in these three studies were not assisted. In fact, some were punished. This evidence that a technique so favored by so many arithmetic teachers was so ineffective can only raise some alarm, for if this technique continues to be passed on from teacher to teacher and remains so nonfunctional, a vast amount of teacher and pupil time is going to be wasted.

I have not intended, in this chapter, to leave the impression that some old-fashioned teaching techniques are always effective while others are always futile. Rather, the point I would like to make here, and a point that has been stressed throughout the book, is that measurement of pupil performance is vitally important. In the context of this chapter, measurement is important because it enables the teacher to determine scientifically whether or not a particular technique is or is not effective.

A second point I have sought to make in this chapter is that teachers must understand the learning styles of children and their stages of development if they are to select teaching techniques wisely. In reference to learning styles, some children quite obviously learn better from some techniques, modeling, for example, than from others. Perhaps their experiences with the effective techniques were favorable in the past and these remembrances have generalized to other circumstances. But, whatever the reason, teachers must try to obtain more precise information as to these personal preferences. One method, of course, is for teachers to measure pupil performance as fully and as accurately as possible and to pass on the data from these measurements to other teachers.

Of equal importance, when it comes to selecting teaching techniques, is the ascertaining of the pupil's level of development. There appear to be at least four stages of development: initial acquisition, advanced acquisition, initial proficiency, and proficiency. During the initial acquisition stage, the pupil has little or none of the behavior he is trying to develop in his current repertory. He is a true beginner. During the advanced acquisition stage, the pupil has mastered about half of the fundamentals, either words or problems. Generally, his scores are about 50 percent correct. During the next stage, initial proficiency, the pupil can respond correctly to almost all the items, though generally he has to think a great deal before responding—his answers are not automatic. During the proficiency stage, the pupil is adept at performing the behavior.

During the first stage, modeling, giving verbal instructions, and providing mediating or mnemonic devices can be effective techniques. However, it might well be that certain types of feedback are ineffective during the initial acquisition stage. Apparently, when a person receives only negative feedback, the effects are negative. In all probability, it would be equally ineffective to use reinforcement procedures during the initial acquisition stage, for there is generally nothing to reinforce during this developmental period.

During the advanced acquisition stage, feedback may prove to be an effective technique. It may be that when even some of the feedback is positive, the technique will be effective. Certain types of drill may also be useful techniques during this period.

One of the most appropriate techniques to use during the initial proficiency stage is some type of reinforcement. During this period, the pupil has demonstrated his accuracy. His problem is one of rate; his responses should be more evenly spaced and more rapid. Since the pupil needs a great deal of practice during this stage, reinforcement procedures can often be used advantageously to maintain that practice.

When all the data are in regarding the comparative effects of techniques with many types of children, it will probably be revealed that (a) most techniques are effective for certain children during certain stages of development, (b) no technique is always effective for all children or all stages of development, and (c) some techniques, for some children at various developmental levels, are more effective than others.

Teaching techniques, like favorite recipes, will be passed on from one teacher to another. The practice should continue, but the decision as to whether or not to participate in this honored line of successsion should be based on data, not whim. Furthermore, when techniques are handed on, certain qualifying statements about the style and stage of development of the sampled youngsters should always accompany the endorsement. New custodians of the techniques should be told that certain techniques were X percent effective when used with children with certain well-specified styles during developmental stages of certain highly specific characteristics.

Some Teaching
Procedures Are Complex

SOME of our teaching procedures are a conglomerate of many techniques; for some kids this amounts to instructional overkill.

Sometimes in our efforts to teach children, we engage in instructional overkill. We attack them with drills, games, homework, and reinforcers. We use filmstrips and overhead projectors, bribes and threats, bromides and homilies.

Consider the approach of some teachers toward the teaching of reading, particularly those who follow the suggestions included in teachers' manuals and who have attended a few inservice classes or workshops devoted to reading instruction. Some of them introduce each story in the text with a discussion of the topic. If the story is about Pete and Marie going to the laundromat, they talk about famous laundromats they have known and ask the children to transport themselves vicariously into a laundromat setting. They then inform the pupils about washing, drying, buying soap, obtaining change from the coin machine, sitting and waiting, reading a magazine, filing nails, and buying a soft drink from a machine.

After they have thus introduced the story, the new words are presented. To continue with our example, let's say these are *dryer* and *washer*, or perhaps *bleach* and *detergent*. This might logically lead to a discussion regarding the derivation and etymology of those words.

Most certainly, then, the teacher would point out the important elements in the words. For example, he would tell the pupils that the *dr* in *dryer* is a blend, and likewise, the *bl* in *bleach*. He would then ask the children to say or list other words that began with *dr* and *bl*. He might require them to look through all their parents' magazines to find pictures of things that begin with *br* and *bl*. The children would cut out these pictures and bring them to school. Then each child would show her pictures to the rest of the class.

After this exercise, the teacher would bring out the workbooks which accompany the basal reader used in the class. The pupils would be required to fill in the blanks, to match items, to define words, and to engage in dozens of other challenging and entertaining activities. Next, not to slight the use of picture cues, the teacher might have the pupils flip through the pages of the story and try to forecast as much as they could about the story before they read it.

No stone would be left unturned, no teaching technique left out, by these earnest souls in their efforts to teach reading. In addition to the techniques and exercises mentioned, they may have learned several phonics games and clever ways to teach suffixes from the *Instructor* or *Grade Teacher*. These aids would also be brought into play. Still undaunted, some teachers would use the lastest tricks they had acquired at reading conventions and regional meetings.

Following this instructional barrage, the pupils would be asked to read their story silently at their desks. After this, they would be called to the reading table in their respective groups—jaguars or cougars—and asked to read. Finally, someone would listen to them read.

Now, it may very well be that such a shotgun approach to the teaching of reading is sometimes effective. In fact, we know that for some children the approach *is* functional, for many do learn to read, presumably at schools and ostensibly because of the type of instruction just outlined.

But my, oh my, look at the time spent. Is it all necessary?

Perhaps all, many, or some of those techniques would be effective in assisting certain difficult-to-teach pupils, but it is doubtful they are all needed for all children. Think of the time wasted for the more rapid learner. Many of them could actually be reading, perhaps writing their own stories, instead of spending their time filling in blanks and cutting out pictures.

If it is true that some pupils do not require the multi-instructional techniques they are subjected to, why then does it happen to them? Why do teachers expose their youngsters to instructional overkill? I believe there are at least two reasons.

One reason that teachers resort to multiple instructional devices and techniques is that they sincerely believe all these strategies are required. They feel they must incorporate all the suggestions received at workshops and in-service meetings, use the techniques suggested by the teachers they admire, and include all the hints from the teacher's manual that accompanies the basal series. They fear that children will either not learn to read at all or will fail to acquire some vital element in the reading process if they are not exposed to the collective mass. To these teachers, teaching is like meal planning: the consumer must eat enough units of proteins, carbohydrates, and fats to thrive.

The second reason for this tendency to overkill is the desire to become unique. Apparently some teachers, in developing their teaching procedures, accept the doctrine that not only the more techniques the better, but also the more expensive, complex, and difficult to obtain these techniques are, the better. By using several instructional devices, techniques, and modes of presentation rather than only one, they feel they can become more elite artists, unique and esteemed in the educational world as creative, inventive, and truly great teachers. The only thing they have to worry about is the competition.

This type of teacher, in order to solidify and maintain his position, must constantly alter his instructional repertory. He must add new techniques, abandon old ones (particularly when too many people begin to use them), rearrange the sequences in which they are used, and vary the amount of time allocated to each.

But enough of that. I want to describe an instance in which some youngsters learned quite satisfactorily when only a part of an instructional technique was used; it was not necessary to expose them to the "whole thing." (Throughout the book, other references and examples about complex teaching are presented.)

EITHER SHOW OR TELL A KID HOW TO DO SOMETHING

Recently, we investigated some techniques that have been used to teach pupils to add, subtract, multiply, and divide. Among those techniques were various types of feedback; the pupils were informed about certain aspects of their performance. This project was briefly explained in the preceding chapter.

Another technique we studied at that time was a form of modeling. Modeling, in that research, consisted of showing a pupil how to do a certain problem, telling him how it should be solved, and leaving the finished product for him to consult once the demonstration was over. For example, if a pupil was assigned problems like 47 − 28 = [   ] (presented vertically to the pupil), the modeling steps were as follows; the instructor first computed the problem on the top left of the page assigned the pupil. As he did so, he explained each step toward the solution of the problem. He mentioned that since the 8 in the bottom number was larger than the number directly above it, borrowing was required. He then explained the borrowing process by saying that the 4 in the tens column should be crossed out and replaced by a 3. Following this, the 1 that was borrowed should be placed to the left of the 7 in the units column. It was then explained that now, since the number 17 was larger than the number below it, subtraction was possible. The teacher next subtracted 8 from 17 and placed a 9 in the units portion of the answer space. Next, the teacher illustrated how the subtracting process shifted from the units column to the tens column. He subtracted the 2 in the bottom number from the 3 in the top number by placing a 1 in the tens portion of the answer space. He finally explained that the correct answer was 19 (see figure 5).

Following this little experiment, we wished to determine whether the entire modeling technique was necessary for all pupils. We suspected that portions of the technique were not necessary for some who would be able to learn just as quickly if only a part of the technique was used.

In order to verify our hunch, we used only certain elements of the technique with selected pupils. With some we simply provided a model and did not verbally explain all the steps toward

STUDY 1

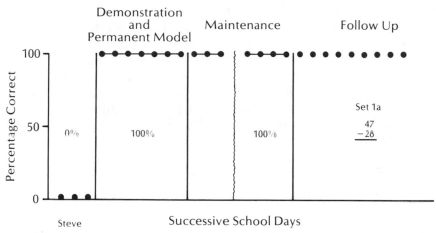

Figure 5. Percentage correct for pupil's set 1a problems. The wavy line indicates a two-week holiday.

solving the problem. The model remained on their papers as they were told to perform the problems. In our example, the following was shown:

$$\begin{array}{r} 31 \\ \cancel{4}7 \\ -28 \\ \hline 19 \end{array}$$

With other children, the process was explained step by step, but once the explanation was finished the model was taken away. The pupils were not able to look back to the sample problem to check their efforts as they worked the remaining problems.

We discovered there were some children who did not need the entire procedure; they learned certain computations when only the model was provided. At the same time, other youngsters learned when only the demonstration aspect was scheduled. Thus, for both of these groups, although the entire procedure required only a minute or so, we would have wasted some of their time had we insisted they go through the complete procedure.

Furthermore, had the teacher not broken up the total modeling procedure into two components and tested their individual effects, he would have continued to use the complete procedure, since this method had always been successful. We also discovered, however, that when the elements of the total procedure were separately tested, some pupils failed to learn particular computations. These were pupils who had previously learned other types of problems when the complete procedure was used. In these cases, when the complete procedure was again scheduled, they learned other types of problems. As I mentioned earlier, there are pupils who need the whole thing (D. Smith & Lovitt, 1975, pp. 283-308).

Pupils are truly unique. In this example, some required the entire technique; others did not. The important feature here is that if only a single, simple instructional technique is required for some pupils in order to learn, only that technique should be used. However, if additional techniques are required, these should by all means be scheduled. The pupil should certainly be given as much assistance in the form of instructional techniques as is required to develop the necessary skills. Teachers, however, must not use instructional overkill; they must not subject their charges to any more instruction than is required.

There are, I believe, two practical reasons for advancing such a caution. (I have commented in an earlier chapter about this.) One is that if pupils are being overinstructed in a specific skill, their time is being wasted. A second reason for the warning is that if teachers unnecessarily spend their time and energy with a certain pupil in providing instruction that is not required, they are stealing time from a more needy student. Such a practice is particularly distressing, since one of the loudest complaints of teachers is that they are expected to teach so many things to so many pupils in such a limited time. Teachers must carefully and judiciously allocate their time if they are to be as efficient as possible.

The Benefits
of Practice

PRACTICE, in itself, probably won't make perfect, but it sometimes helps.

We have all heard the old educational bromide, "Practice makes perfect." It means that if we want to learn something, we must repeat the behavior over and over. The music student, especially, has often been given this advice.

In order to become proficient in some skills, a great deal of practice is required. Often, practice, in itself, is not enough. It must be practice *in the right things.* Take the trumpet player who constantly plays a sour note and believes it is a good sound. He could practice that note till doomsday and, unless he is given some corrective feedback, he would not improve. Perhaps as he blows through the horn he has one lip above the mouthpiece and one below it. Unless he is shown how a trumpet should be played and hears some good player perform, he may never improve, for all of his hours of practice.

What about the person who constantly misuses words, the Mr. or Ms. Malaprop? He will continue in his ways unless he is provided with some informative feedback or instruction that will help him acquire different, more correct speech patterns. Several examples come to mind illustrating that practice will not necessarily make perfect.

I believe the bromide "Practice makes perfect" should be separated into at least two subbromides. One should read, "If you're totally unable to perform the behavior, practice alone will not help." The other should be, "If you're slightly able to perform the behavior, practice alone might help, but it probably won't be enough to assist you to reach proficiency." Let me amplify these subbromides with a couple of examples.

NO ABILITY; PRACTICE WON'T HELP MUCH

Recently, we sought in an arithmetic study to ascertain the effects of various interventions such as modeling and feedback on computational accuracy. These studies have been referred to in the preceding two chapters. Prior to the baseline phases of these studies, we found specific types of problems that each pupil could not perform.

Once these problems were identified, a baseline condition was conducted. Throughout that period, each pupil was given sheets containing problems of the type identified and asked to respond to them for one minute. No instruction, reinforcement, or feedback was scheduled during this condition. Invariably the answers of the pupils to all of the problems were incorrect. Even though they responded to as many as twenty problems a day for as many as five consecutive days, they did not improve from one day to the next. Conceivably, if they had been assigned these same problems for several more days, their accuracy would still have continued to be poor.

We also conducted a spelling study a few years ago, the data from which illustrated again that pupils will not improve without some instruction, no matter how much they "practiced." In that study, throughout several conditions extending over many days, the pupils were required to spell three lists of words each day. All the words contained the /s/ sound. On two of the lists, the s always made the /s/ sound--words like *suburb* and *disturb*. Words on the third list were the exceptions. These contained elements that made the /s/ sound with letters other than a single s—words like *embarrass, century,* and *science*.

During that study, following a baseline period, instruction was focused on the words in the first list. When those were mastered, instruction shifted to the second list of words. Throughout these two instructional periods, the pupils' scores on the third list of words were generally zero. Many of their scores were zero at the outset of the study and continued to be zero throughout the baseline and the two instructional phases. Several pupils scored zero on the third list of words for as long as twenty consecutive days. As with the arithmetic study just described, it is probable that even had the same circumstances continued for many more days, the scores would have remained at zero, since the pupils received neither instruction nor feedback.

In both these instances, arithmetic and spelling, when the initial ability to perform the task was zero, an extended practice period did not help at all. It is significant, however, that when the students were provided with some assistance, their performances quickly improved.

SOME ABILITY; PRACTICE ALONE HELPS (TO A POINT)

Many times, when a person has some proficiency in a task, his performance in that task improves from day to day, even though no apparent instruction, feedback, or reinforcement is provided. Following are a couple of instances that illustrate this point.

Prior to placing the children in our class in one reading level or another for instructional purposes, we had them read from several texts. Our intent was to place them in the highest level reader where their correct rates were from 45 to 65 words per minute and their errors between 2 and 6 words per minute.

Once the appropriate reader was determined for each pupil, the baseline condition commenced. Throughout that phase, the pupils read 500 words each day from their newly assigned book, during which time they received no feedback. Often, throughout that condition, their correct rates improved. Many of them began the baseline phase reading at rates less than 65 words per minute and improved as much as 10 words per minute during the seven- or eight-day baseline period.

In an arithmetic project we conducted some time ago, similar improvement was noted throughout a baseline phase, although no feedback was provided. At that time, we required the pupils to respond to problems they were able to compute, but only at very slow rates. These students were in the initial proficiency stage. The purpose of the study was to analyze the effects on accuracy and correct rate of several interventions. Our ultimate objective was to increase the pupils' correct rates until they reached proficiency levels.

Throughout the baseline condition, before any instruction began, many of the pupils improved. One, for example, whose correct rate was fifteen problems per minute the first day of baseline, accelerated to a correct rate of twenty-one on the twelfth day. Another progressed from eleven to twenty correct problems per minute in a sixteen-day baseline. A third moved from a correct rate of three problems per minute to a rate of nine within a five-day baseline.

We have also observed similar instances of baseline improvement in penmanship and creative writing. Based on these observations, our conclusion is that when a pupil has a substantial portion of the behavior in his repertory, improvement will apparently result from practice alone.

A few years ago, Harold Kunzelmann, then with the Washington State Department of Public Instruction, began a lengthy study to appraise the basic skill proficiencies of youngsters in grades K through 3 in Washington's three largest cities, Seattle, Spokane, and Tacoma. Basic skills, in the context of this program, were certain behaviors believed to be necessary for the acquisition of more complex skills such as computing, reading, and writing.

One of the basic skills was a writing-numbers task, in which the pupils were asked to copy a series of numbers, one through ten. A second skill was that of writing letters; for this, the pupils were required to print the letters of the alphabet in order. A third task required them to say the numbers in order from one to ten. A fourth was to read randomly ordered numbers from a printed script, and in a fifth they were required to read randomly and sequentially printed letters. A sixth involved the printing, from a model, of lowercase, randomly sequenced letters. For another task, the pupils were required to pronounce certain sounds as they referred to the printed symbol and also to write the sounds as they heard them. The sounds for both these tasks ranged from short vowels and single consonants to vowel-consonant blends and consonant-vowel-consonant words. An additional task required the pupils to write a number of short words that were dictated to them. Several arithmetic tasks were also arranged, each pertaining to a specific process: addition, subtraction, multiplication, or division.

To administer these tasks, work sheets were developed which corresponded to each basic skill. For example, the sheet for obtaining information about writing numbers in order had the digits one through ten printed on the page eight times. Underneath each digit was a blank. It was the child's task to write numbers serially in those blanks. Similar sheets were developed for the other basic skills. The pupils worked on a specific, basic skill for one minute. Their correct and incorrect rates were calculated for the minute sessions and then graphed.

The important feature to note here, in the context of practice without instruction, is that the pupils responded to their assigned work sheets for about five days in a row, during which time there was no instruction. Neither was a reinforcement contingency nor a type of feedback arranged for any of the pupils.

These data, as I have indicated, were graphed daily. Invariably, when these graphs of the five-day baselines were inspected, it was apparent that the correct rates were going up, an indication that the pupils were improving in speed; they were becoming more and more proficient. This development was noted on every basic skill for children of all ages.

In that project, progress was made in spite of the lack of instruction. I hasten to add, however, that the progress of the children during this period was not highly significant. Generally, their correct rates increased for a few days, then leveled off. During this period, those whose rates were furthest from proficiency improved the most; the students whose initial performances were nearest the proficiency limits gained the least.

Based on the data from the studies just described and from other observations over the past few years, certain conclusions on practice may be drawn. First of all, as I have outlined in a preceding chapter, I believe it is necessary to consider four stages of learning, or development: initial acquisition, advanced acquisition, initial proficiency, and proficiency. Whether or not practice will be effective in assisting the pupil to master a skill depends, like other instructional techniques, on the pupil's stage of development.

During the initial acquisition stage, the person is exposed to a new skill. He has perhaps developed his requisite skills, but has none of the new behavior in his repertory. During this stage, I believe practice is important; but if only practice is scheduled, without some form of instruction, it is unlikely any improvement will be noted.

In regard to practice alone, even Thorndike, the noted psychologist, changed his mind. At one point in his career he announced the Law of Exercise, which proclaimed, in essence, that practice made perfect. Although he later changed his opinion and qualified the law by saying that probably some instruction is required along with practice before learning can occur, many educators continued to subscribe to Thorndike's original notion.

During the third learning stage—initial proficiency—practice can well be more important than in the preceding two stages. When the pupil is in this period, he knows all the rules and principles that pertain to a specific skill, but he cannot respond fluently. Therefore, practice, in itself, can be helpful in assisting him to increase his rate. He will not require much instruction during this period. It appears, then, that the closer the person approaches proficiency, the less will be the instruction required, and the more helpful will judicious practice become.

When the student reaches the fourth learning stage, or proficiency, it is sometimes important to maintain the newly acquired level of performance by developing a maintenance plan. In respect to certain skills, the matter of planned maintenance, once proficiency is reached, is not a prime concern. An example of such an instance would be a person who moved to Mexico and bit by bit became fluent in the Spanish language. Although he might require study and practice to develop fluency, it would not be necessary to plan a maintenance strategy once proficiency was reached, for the natural contingencies of the culture would maintain the behavior.

There are other times, however, when planned maintenance might be very important. These would be instances in which the person became proficient in the use of some behavior, and his environment then changed to the extent that he no longer used that behavior. If he then wished to maintain that skill, programmed contingencies would have to be arranged. In other words, he should set up a systematic practice program so that he regularly rehearsed parts or all of the formerly developed behavior.

An example of an instance in which maintenance should have been programmed can be taken from my own experience. I received instruction and practiced the trumpet for several years before reaching a fair degree of proficiency. Later, when I played in orchestras and gave lessons, those contingencies maintained my behavior. Throughout that period, I maintained whatever degree of proficiency I had when I began that career (I may even have improved a bit). Later, however, when I left the music business, those natural contingencies disappeared. I no longer had to keep in shape for concerts and students and, therefore, stopped practicing. As a result, I became less and less proficient. After a few years of little or no practice, when I did try to play something, it sounded as if I were playing a kazoo.

Since abandoning practice, I have lost many of my former trumpet skills. My tone is not as good as it once was, my technique is less adequate, my breathing is worse, and my endurance is nonexistent. I could possibly resurrect those skills, though to do so would probably require more time than I have. But it is quite likely that had I arranged a regular practice schedule a few years ago to maintain what proficiency I had, I would still be able to play the trumpet.

So instead of saying, "Practice makes perfect," we should say, as I have pointed out earlier, "If you're totally unable to perform the skill, practice alone will not help," or "If you're slightly able to perform the behavior, practice alone might help, but probably won't be enough to assist you to reach proficiency." We may also add, "After you've reached proficiency, practice in itself will probably be enough to maintain the skill."

Teaching Youngsters
and Oldsters

YOU can teach a young pup old tricks and an old dog new tricks if you want to.

Most of us have some rather strange ideas about learning and development. For one thing, we speak of developmental epochs, assuming that people behave the way they do because they are of a certain age. In schools, this alleged relationship between age and development is apparent. Children are taught to read when they are six; they shift from manuscript to cursive writing at about the third grade. Division and multiplication exercises are scheduled for the third grade, fractions for the fourth, and decimals for the fifth. This type of scheduling intimates that people should be taught certain skills only when they have reached the appropriate age and that to jump the gun would be, at the very least, a waste of time.

A corollary notion, sometimes attached to such a belief, is that once the appropriate time for learning a behavior is passed, it is nearly impossible for a person to learn the skill. Illustrative of this belief is the saying, "You can't teach an old dog new tricks." How discouraging (or perhaps comforting) it must be for people who share this belief and yet desire (at least they say so) to learn some skill that should have been learned earlier.

It is a mystery how such a notion concerning development came to be acquired. To some extent, we learn about such things from magazines and newspapers that feature articles or columns by child development experts. Other notions on the subject have been passed on to us by parents and teachers. And we have, of course, acquired many of these beliefs from our own experiences. For example, if we could not learn something at one age (*before* we were supposed to), then later developed that skill (*when* we were supposed to), or failed to learn something at a later age (*after* we were supposed to), we were inclined to translate those isolated experiences into behavioral laws.

Whatever the factors are that have shaped our notions about development, these ideas are generally deeply imbedded. Most of us would rather change our politics or religion, possibly our spouses, than alter our developmental beliefs.

However, implications of entertaining such erroneous concepts about young and old learners are serious. Unlike the consequences of adhering to other obtuse ideas that affect only the individual himself, the person who is in a state of confusion about the developmental processes can adversely influence the behaviors of many others. It is tragic when parents are dim of wit regarding development, for their children will suffer. It is doubly tragic, however, when teachers are possessed by such superstitions, for they can transmit the consequences of their ignorance to countless future citizens.

DON'T SELL THE OLD DOGS SHORT

One of the university classes I teach deals with classroom management. I try to present the idea that if we are to educate children, we must first pinpoint the areas for instruction. Then we talk about identifying the elements of arithmetic, spelling, reading, and writing that can be taught.

In this class I try also to instill the notion that when a decision has been made about what to teach, the child's ability to perform those tasks must first be ascertained. In other words, a baseline, or diagnostic, condition must be scheduled. If the data from that condition reveal that the pupil is incapable of performing that skill, some instructional technique must be arranged, and measurement must be gathered continually in order to monitor individual progress. It is of primary concern in this class that behaviors must be measured, first, during the baseline phase to confirm whether instruction is necessary, second, during the instructional condition to determine whether the instructional technique is effective, and, third, during a maintenance phase to learn whether the behavior continues to be adequate when the instructional technique is removed.

Other activities are scheduled for this class. The students review a number of Applied Behavior Analysis studies with children. They study definitions and examples of various techniques used to alter pupil behavior: reinforcement, time out, extinction, punishment, response cost, modeling, and cueing.

In addition to these exercises, students are required to conduct three teaching projects with children. The students are asked to: (1) identify an area of instruction (from bead stringing to calculus), (2) obtain baseline data, (3) schedule an instructional procedure, (4) remove the procedure once mastery is obtained, and (5) report their findings.

One of the more difficult instructional problems I have in this class is to teach the pupils how to obtain data, particularly rate per minute data. Since our primary recourse for reporting pupil progress is correct and incorrect response rate per minute, it is crucial that the students learn to calculate it.

As has been noted earlier in the book, two pieces of information are required in order to derive rate per minute: the number of answers of a certain type and the number of minutes the session lasted. With this information, rate is calculated by dividing the number of answers, either correct or incorrect, by the number of minutes. For example, if a pupil read fifty correct words in two minutes, his correct rate was twenty-five.

The pupils in my university class can generally understand calculations of this simpler type and, therefore, rapidly realize a number of success experiences. That is, until the time arrives, as it does every quarter, for them to divide with decimals. Then the pained question often comes: "What is the pupil's correct rate if she answered twenty problems in 2.5 minutes?"

One evening a few years ago I posed this problem and asked the students to answer the question. I then walked around the room and peered over the shoulders of several to see how they approached the problem. Apparently, about twenty of the thirty had correctly performed the task. The rest, confessing their inability to arrive at the solution, admitted that they simply did not remember how to divide using decimals.

We therefore carefully analyzed their response patterns. Some had transformed the 2.5 to a fraction and tried unsuccessfully to arrive at the answer. Some did not shift the decimal in either the divisor or the dividend before they divided. Others knew they were supposed to shift the decimal in the 2.5, but were not sure just where. (Some simply estimated the answer.) Still others divided 20 by 2 and 3, then split the difference.

We talked about this problem. Most of the students who were unable to perform the task remembered that in the fourth, fifth, perhaps the sixth grade, their teachers had shown them how to divide with decimals, but for some reason the instruction did not take. They also admitted to being extremely anxious and embarrassed whenever a situation arose in which they were expected to divide by a decimal. They confessed to all sorts of avoidance behaviors: telling others they were slow at dividing, saying they did not have pencils, asking someone else to calculate the problem for them, or changing the subject.

Many of the students, when asked why they did not request help at some time during their lives, confessed that they were too embarrassed to do so. They knew they would lose face if they admitted not knowing how to perform a task that most fifth graders would regard as a breeze.

We then had a remediation phase. I told them to place the 20 in the box ($\lceil\quad\rceil$) and the 2.5 to the left of the box. I then told the class members to shift the decimal in 2.5 to the right, until a whole number was formed. In this instance, it was necessary to shift the decimal one space. They were then told to add as many zeros to the right of the number in the box as spaces covered in the number outside the box. Since one space was covered in the 2.5, one zero was placed to the right of 20. The transformed problem was now 25 $\lceil\overline{200}$.

Now they were ready to divide 25 $\lceil\overline{200}$. Almost everyone was able to do this. Some had a few other division problems that had to be corrected, but, in time, everyone understood how to divide with decimals. All expressed relief; it was as though some deep, dark secret had been unlocked. They realized it *was* possible after all to learn, just like fifth graders.

This was a memorable moment in my teaching career. I was reinforced, first by the fact that some of the students admitted to having a deficit, then by the fact that the remedial students and the rest of the class were willing to take the time to develop the response. The entire lesson lasted about twenty minutes.

This exercise diverted us from the scheduled topic for the night; after learning to divide, we shared other instances of not having learned something when we were supposed to and of later being too embarrassed to ask for help. We recalled buying books and secretly searching for the answers, often to no avail. We agreed that the primary reason we were afraid to ask for help was that we, as adults, believed that only children should ask why and how. We also agreed that apparently we regarded adults as above making errors, and as a result we would rather not perform than risk making a mistake.

As to the old dogs and new tricks proverb, it has been my belief (and I hold the conviction more firmly the older I get) that one *can* teach oldsters new tricks if first it is determined whether they have the requisite skills and, second, if they can be motivated to make the effort. To illustrate, let me once again draw upon my past.

At one time in my life, as I have previously mentioned, I had many trumpet students, and there were always some adults among my flock of pupils. Generally, it was more difficult for me to teach the oldsters than the children. In retrospect, I have tried to discover why this was true. Perhaps they were less able to achieve than the children because of the two conditions mentioned earlier: requisite skills and motivation. Many of these adults had heard Doc Severinson or Al Hirt and wanted to play like them. But after a few weeks of practicing and attempting to imitate their idols, many of them realized they were a long, long way from ever playing club dates in New Orleans or fronting the Tonight Show Orchestra. Consequently, many of them quit and converted their trumpets to lamps and spittoons.

In contrast, although many young trumpet students have also heard Al Hirt perform, they have also listened to Pete Jones, the third chair trumpeter in the grade school band. When these children first began to play, their skills more closely resembled their real perceptions of trumpet playing than was true with the adults. Furthermore, they know that Pete Jones began playing only eight months ago. These youngsters who aspired to learn the trumpet had, therefore, the requisite behaviors to become as proficient as Pete Jones in as short a period of time. The adults, however, were many steps and many years removed from Al Hirt and any real thought (after that second lesson) of ever playing like him. Because of the closer distance between their current level and their anticipated goal, the children continued with their lessons.

Motivation is another ingredient that affects learning; it is as important a factor in adult learning as it is in children's. Several reinforcers are available for children who are studying trumpet. For one, they will probably receive abundant praise from parents and relatives (along with the nagging and pleading). They may be reinforced by playing in the school band, particularly if it takes a few trips, or by receiving new silver bell King trumpets or Mugsy Spanier straight mutes. Often, students who practice are awarded several fringe benefits in the home like being relieved from housecleaning and from lawn or gardening chores.

On the other hand, reinforcement for aspiring adults is rather lean. Who is going to tell adults forlornly fumbling with "Old Folks at Home" or "My Bonnie Lies Over the Ocean" that they are really doing a great job? Usually when adults practice, their spouses or children tell them to cool it because the noise is interfering with their television viewing. The would-be artists' friends and family callously and constantly remind them that they do not sound one bit like Al Hirt or Doc Severinson.

SOME YOUNG PUPS CAN LEARN A BUNCH

I have mentioned earlier that some people apparently believe there is an inviolable sequence of skills corresponding to rather specific ages; that a skill can be learned only when the appropriate age is reached. One obvious consequence of such a belief is that no attempt will be made to teach children certain skills until they have reached the appropriate age.

When children do learn skills "before they should," or before most other youngsters do, adults are amazed. We often hear awed comments about precocious children who can read at three or four years of age. I suppose that most of us are, indeed, at least mildly impressed by a child who reads before going to school, for she has learned something not only before she was supposed to, but in a place where she was not supposed to learn it.

All of us too, are impressed by the child prodigy who is able to do something better at an age when she should not be able to do it, than others are at ages when they should be able to do it. I recently read a feature story in the *New York Times* about a young lady who, at the age of thirteen, was the musical sensation of the year. Her violin virtuosity has impressed concert goers around the world. She is perhaps unaware of the fact that a great share of her success, charm, and ability to draw huge crowds must be attributed to the fact that she is only thirteen. Violinists are not supposed to be as good as she is when they are only thirteen. But what about her success and charm when she is fourteen or fifteen; will the audiences be as large? It is possible that her popularity will diminish each year unless, of course, her ability steadily improves. But the point is, all of us are impressed by children who develop a behavior to a high degree of expertness before they are supposed to. And the younger the prodigy the more are we impressed.

In our class at the Experimental Education Unit (EEU), we taught a skill out of sequence. Although our pupils were certainly not being groomed for roles as child prodigies, we taught them a skill that is characteristically not offered until secondary school. They were taught to type.

Normally, pupils begin typing instruction when they are in the tenth, eleventh, or twelfth grades; from about fifteen years of age. Our pupils were nine- to twelve-year-old boys in grades three to six. They were therefore beginning typing instruction several years before they were supposed to. Furthermore, our pupils had had problems in the language arts and other academic activities; they had often, in fact, been described as learning disabled.

In spite of their ages and educational classifications, however, they thrived on the instruction. The typing period was the high point of the day for most of the boys. Not only did they enjoy the typing period, but they learned to type in the process.

Our decision to teach typing was based largely on our attitude toward our penmanship program. In the past, we had spent many hours teaching our pupils to write legibly and at proficient rates. Although we were generally successful, it appeared to us that a great amount of time had been spent in the development of penmanship skills that could have been devoted to instruction in other behaviors. (Some of the comments in an earlier chapter, Behavioral Objectives, in reference to specifying the cost of teaching a skill are pertinent here.)

We thought about the need in our present world for handwriting and decided that perhaps we were teaching a skill no longer as important as it once was. Although people must be able to write in order to sign checks, compose shopping lists, fill out questionnaires, and apply for jobs, handwriting is currently not needed in many other types of communication.

When it comes to composing—for example, writing letters or reports—it is generally more efficient to use a typewriter than a pen or pencil. First, typing eliminates the problem of legibility so often presented by handwriting. When a person strikes an a, that letter consistently appears, whereas when he writes an a, it may be almost anything.

A second advantage of typing over writing is speed. My normal handwriting rate is from ten to twenty words per minute over a thirty-minute period. When I type for the same period of time my rate is in excess of fifty words per minute. Although I am neither a rapid writer nor a speedy typist, I imagine the rate differential is about the same for many individuals: more than twice as fast for the typing.

The typing program with our boys began the first month of a school year. Each day they received from two to five minutes of instruction. Our instructional procedures were the exact suggestions outlined by a typing workbook. The only innovations we incorporated throughout the year were the addition of a few instructional techniques designed to overcome specific typing problems of some of the students. For example, some pupils looked at their keys when they typed rather than at the book. Obviously such a habit slowed them down; therefore, they were given points for so many seconds of typing while looking only at the book. These points could be exchanged for minutes of free time. Other students had difficulty typing certain letter combinations like *fr* or *ju;* these required additional practice.

Daily, several pieces of data were kept: (a) correct and incorrect rates for typing the various lines; (b) number of lines and lessons passed; and (c) number of days required to pass each line. At the end of the year most of the boys had learned the keyboard. Their correct rates ranged from twelve to twenty words per minute.

After several weeks of instruction their typing rates were about the same as their writing rates. The legibility of their typing, however, even when erasures and strikeovers were considered, was much better than that of their writing.

Even though these boys began typing before they were supposed to, they did quite well. They were able to learn to type because they had the requisite skills. They knew the letters of the alphabet, they could read and spell a large number of words, and their fingers were big enough to cover the keys. Furthermore, these youngsters were motivated. They liked to type, believed it was an adult behavior, and received large doses of reinforcement from adults for this very reason.

The teachers of the class were also reinforced for this program. Invariably, when we explained our total research program to visitors, they were most impressed by the typing study. They asked many more questions about the instruction of typing than about our reading, arithmetic, or spelling activities.

So much for the typing program. But one more word on the subject of teaching a skill "out of sequence." It appears to me that if children are being taught something before they are supposed to learn it, they are rarely punished for making mistakes. It also seems that children in such circumstances receive more reinforcement than they ordinarily would for learning a behavior that was theoretically appropriate to their particular age.

Perhaps this disproportionate amount of reinforcement accounts for some of the child prodigies who have so often impressed us. Perhaps they received great amounts of reinforcement for developing a skill they were not supposed to learn, and received lesser amounts of reinforcement for the skills they were expected to develop. Continuing with such a hypothesis, since the prodigies were reinforced for performing behaviors out of sequence, they spent even more time developing them, hence received even more reinforcement, hence . . . . Pardon my conjectures.

Perhaps with the advent of nongraded schools and adult education classes, the notions of age and skill congruence will be tempered. Conceivably, as more people learn that reading can be taught at age three, thirteen, thirty, or sixty, they will change their ideas about the ideal periods at which certain skills, reading at least, can be learned. Such a recasting of developmental beliefs might offer welcome encouragement to certain individuals who always wanted to learn to ride a bike or speak Spanish but feared they had passed the time for such longed-for achievements.

If more people shared the notion that human beings could develop skills regardless of age, granted only that they had the requisite basic skills and were motivated, how different our schools and homes might well become! Imagine the happy, productive atmosphere if all kinds of people, young and old, were encouraged to develop skills together. Would not the youngsters be strongly reinforced by being allowed to study "adult" behaviors and the adults experience veritable waves of self-renewal by learning new skills?

Those who subscribe to the belief that time, in itself, is an irrelevant variable so far as learning is concerned would be entirely comfortable when being taught certain behaviors with students both younger and older than themselves. Furthermore, they would not mind being instructed in these new behaviors by teachers both younger and older than themselves. As it is, most of us do not object to being taught by older folks (particularly if they have more credentials than we do), but many of us shy away from situations where the instructor is younger than we are.

If age is an irrelevant factor for teaching and learning, what *are* the essential ingredients? Earlier, I discussed two important ingredients for learning: basic requisites for developing the new behaviors and motivation to learn the task. If the learner does not bring to the learning situation sufficient motivation, the teacher must alter the reinforcement system. (More will be said about altering motivational levels in the next four chapters.)

So much for the learner. What about the teacher; what are the requisite behaviors for teaching? For one thing, the teacher must have the ability (the more the better) to do or know the things that he purports to teach. He must be able to play tennis, ride a bike, read, write, plant crops, sing, make coffee, jump hurdles, philosophize, legislate, build houses. In addition, he must have some information or skill that he wants to transmit to the one who, in turn, wants to acquire it. Furthermore, the teacher must be able to evaluate the learner's efforts at performing the task; he must also provide feedback of some effective sort to the learner. If the learner does not accurately perform the task, the teacher must provide a model. He must reinforce successive approximations to the desired goal. He must, when necessary, schedule remedial exercises.

If we accept these definitions of learners and teachers, it follows that virtually everyone can be both. As a professional teacher, I have often bridled at the snide expression we have all heard, "Those who can, do; those who can't, teach." I suppose this is in reference to people who have few negotiable skills. But the allegation is a contradiction of terms, for teaching is, and can only be, doing. However, there are many behaviors I do not have. I cannot speak Spanish, fix a carburetor or a fuel pump, fly an airplane, make a shirt, or cook spaghetti—these are among the thousands of skills I do not have in my behavioral portfolio. But, as it happens, some of my children have these skills. One of my boys is a fair mechanic; he can repair fuel pumps and carburetors. Another of my sons is a good cook; he can fix spaghetti and make an excellent sauce. Conceivably, if I wanted to acquire these skills, I could learn from them.

Some of the grade schools in the Seattle area have recently opened up their facilities to the public. After school, throughout the week and on weekends, anyone who wants to teach a class can do so. About the only restriction as to what will be taught is finding a teacher and enough people to take the course. Some of these classes are taught by teenagers, others by adults of all ages. The enrollment in most classes is diverse in every respect, including age.

This type of teaching should be widely considered. For if people are able to interact with other people at the specific skill level rather than at the age level, their notions regarding inferiority, superiority, individual differences, and developmental characteristics are certain to be modified. If, for example, a man is teaching his two-year-old daughter to talk, a teenager is teaching him to dance, he is teaching a mentally retarded child to read, and a professor is teaching him all about philosophy, he should be well aware of the fact that he is neither universally superior nor wholly inferior to others. When we allow ourselves to appreciate the many behavioral dimensions of others, we cannot fail to regard them as individuals far more unique than we had initially imagined. Many people, however, have not faced this reality. There are many individuals like the top executive of a big corporation who regards himself as totally superior to his secretary. He has arrived at this conclusion because at the office he commands respect, people call him sir, he has been wined and dined by all the big-wigs. Meanwhile his secretary has merely typed and filed. But away from the job, his secretary has traveled widely, is an expert linguist, has skied, and is a respectable amateur archaeologist. The executive's interests, away from his business, are martinis, Sunday afternoon football, and napping.

Evaluating
Curriculum and Teachers

WE don't need to use expensive techniques to evaluate curriculum materials or teacher effectiveness; the data from kids will do these jobs for us.

We often hear the expression, "You must match the curriculum materials with the needs of the child." Who can disagree when teachers, publishers of curricula, and other educational specialists express this plea? Certainly no one wants to say, "Don't match the materials with the needs of the child."

The rationale for such a plea is obvious. If the pupil needs X, then material that supplies X should be scheduled; if he needs Y, a certain amount of Y material should be arranged. Such a rationale was probably furnished us by our medical brethren. In medical practice, if a malfunction of the body is diagnosed, a corresponding shot, pill, or therapy is prescribed. Many times (apparently often enough to maintain a fairly high degree of credibility) the treatments recommended match the needs of the patient, and behold, he is cured.

As is the case with many other medical analogies, however, when attempts are made to bring medical wisdom to education, the system breaks down. Perhaps the reason this particular analogy is not applicable to education is that the determination of need and material, not to mention their match-up, is less valid in education than is the determination of need and therapy in medicine. Because educational needs are often imprecisely defined, the attempt to actualize the saying, "Match the materials with the pupil," often results in failure.

Another reason for the failure to match pupils and materials is that, generally, materials and pupils are evaluated separately. The pupil is evaluated by one set of examiners in one setting; the materials, by another in a different setting; then perhaps a third person, in yet another setting, is expected to fit the two together. Pretty—isn't it!

Pupils and materials must be evaluated as one; the interaction between passive materials and active pupils is the all-important factor. Before I elaborate further regarding the necessity for evaluating such an interaction, let me make a few more comments on the current method of evaluating pupils and materials.

The truth is that all too often the needs of pupils are determined by indirect means. Many times, at the beginning of the school year, children are required to take an achievement test. Some of these tests have items from several academic areas such as reading, arithmetic, and spelling. If a pupil's score in a certain area is a great deal lower than the average score for the other pupils his age, the determination is made that he has a need in that area.

The difficulty with this is that achievement tests often require pupils to respond to problems or words they have not studied. Conversely, they are often *not* asked to respond to situations they *have* studied. For example, if a pupil is currently being instructed to add and subtract simple facts and is given an achievement test that assesses his ability to borrow and carry, he might do poorly on the arithmetic subtest of the achievement test. He would therefore receive a score which indicated his arithmetic score was lower than the scores for most other pupils his age, and a recommendation would be made to provide him extra assistance in arithmetic.

But it could well be that the pupil does not need remedial assistance. Perhaps he is learning what he is supposed to learn or at least what he is being taught. He is developing proficiencies with addition and subtraction facts. Yet, because he received a low score on the achievement test, the decision was made to provide him with extra help in arithmetic. He might even be sent to a special or remedial class, all because the test did not directly measure his ability to perform simple addition and subtraction facts, problems of the type he was being currently assigned. Had such an assessment been made, it might have turned out that he was doing quite well.

The manner in which curriculum materials are evaluated might well be described as topographic and subjective. Topographic, in that curriculum designers generally explain such details as number of pages, number of color prints, number of stories, number of moving parts. Designers also specify the dimensions and colors of the kit or box that houses the materials. Other characteristics of the materials are vividly described, depending on the type of material, whether a book, kit, film, or a mixture.

Subjective descriptions of the materials in the form of testimonials are also provided. For some, the claim is glowingly made that many diverse aspects of the communicative process will be enhanced if this does-it-all is used. An arithmetic package has claimed that, if it is used, the pupils will learn not only how to compute and all about the distributive and associative processes, but will also develop an awareness of the logic of numbers. Recently, a spelling text was advertised as "the answer to the dilemma of orthographic illiteracy." Many of the claims for and about curriculum materials read like the raves for detergents and deodorants or like the excerpts on the covers of paperback books. Like many television commercials that promote various soaps, denture cements, and beers, curriculum claims are supported by spurious, limited, or no data at all. The claims made for household products are at least, to some extent, monitored by various consumer agencies that profess to protect the public from buying faulty items. But no such agency exists to protect pupils and teachers from the high-powered tactics of the educational market hucksters.

In the world of special education, there has long been a cry to "match the materials to the needs of the child." The reason this bromide is bantered about so much is perhaps that, by definition, special education youngsters have many unique needs. Some have obvious physical problems; others cannot read, write, or cipher. And they also have many urgent social needs.

Another reason for the prevalence of the cliché is that special education has been besieged by a plethora of materials. Many publishers have responded, even capitalized, on these deviations of our young people. Materials have been designed for every need. In fact, materials have been designed for needs that have yet to be pointed out.

This superabundance of materials prompted influential government officials some eight to ten years ago to fund regional Instructional Materials Centers. Originally there were about six of these centers, distributed geographically throughout the United States. Their primary purpose was to evaluate materials and thus be in a better position to assist school teachers in this very problem of matching materials with the needs of special children.

These centers set out to evaluate materials by employing essentially the methods just described. They became libraries where teachers could see new materials and make their own judgments about student match-ups. Some displayed materials via traveling Conestoga wagons that went from one deprived area to another. Interestingly enough, even though few educators have provided positive testimony (certainly no data) as to the worth of these centers (or wagons), there are more of them today than a decade ago. In Washington State, for example, there are four special education Instructional Materials Centers—and a clamoring for more. Those cities which do not have one want one.

So you have it: pupil needs have been largely determined by indirect and imprecise tests, and curriculum materials have been described more often than evaluated. Amidst this confusion, teachers have attempted to match pupil needs with materials. Small wonder that they must often try several types of curricula before finding the right one. The divorce rate between pupils and materials has been scandalously high.

A guarantee that a pupil will get along with his materials cannot be made unless the pair are evaluated together. As has been observed, data must be obtained in regard to the interaction between pupil and his program. A teacher who separately evaluated a pupil and certain materials would be like a conductor who did likewise with a trumpet player and his horn. Considering them separately, the conductor could say that the individual was able to describe the characteristics of many composers and knew all the Beethoven opus numbers and that the trumpet was made from high quality brass and had no dents, but nothing would be known about the individual as a trumpet player unless he and his instrument were evaluated together.

The same argument can be made when it comes to evaluating teachers. They cannot be judged functionally apart from their pupils any more than students can be evaluated apart from the instruction received from teachers.

Three projects are presented regarding the evaluation of materials and teachers. The first illustrates how pupil data can be used to match the student with the right material. The second illustrates how the data from pupil performance can be used to evaluate reading materials. The third project describes how pupil data can be used to evaluate teacher effectiveness.

USING PUPIL DATA TO MATCH PUPILS AND MATERIALS

At the beginning of every school year, one of the initial problems confronting the teacher is reading placement—she must decide which book, from an array of many, is the right one for each pupil. Different teachers use different approaches to the problem. Some, those who take no great stock in theories of individualized instruction, place all their pupils in the reader that carries the label of their grade: third grade students will read from a third grade reader and no nonsense about it. Others use achievement test scores, reading diagnostic tests, or informal reading inventories to place pupils.

I would like to describe the method we have used for the past few years to deal with this very important problem. As you might guess, it utilizes pupil data for placement. The approach is based on the interaction between pupils and materials and goes like this:

Throughout our reading placement sessions, the pupils are required to read orally from eight readers of the same basal series. For the past few years, they have read orally for one minute each day from books D, E, F, G, H, I, J, and K of the Lippincott series. Following each reading, they are required to answer a series of comprehension questions. Every day, during placement, correct and incorrect rate data for oral reading and percentage correct data for answering comprehension questions are plotted in respect to each of the eight books. This process lasts for five days (Lovitt & Hansen, 1976).

Following the fifth day, the teacher calculates a median score for each of the three measures for all eight books. First, she notes the books in which the correct rates were within forty-five to sixty-five words per minute. Then she notes the books in which the incorrect rates were within three to seven words per minute. Next, she notes the books in which the correct percentage comprehension scores are between 50 and 75 percent. Finally, she notes the highest ranking reader in which all three of the above conditions are indicated. The pupils are then placed in those books for purposes of initial instruction (see figure 6).

We have been extremely pleased with this method of placement, for our pupils have, over a school year, usually improved a great deal. By using this method of placement, that is, employing pupil data to determine placement, we have generally avoided all serious mismatches between pupils and materials. We have significantly reduced the pupil-curriculum divorce rate.

USING PUPIL DATA TO COMPARE PROGRAMS

In this project, three reading books were compared, based on pupil data. Daily, for six weeks, a boy read orally for five minutes from three different books. According to the publishers, the reading levels of the three were 2^2, 3^1, and 3^1. The first two books were basal readers; the third was a high interest, low vocabulary book. Readability indexes of 4.5, 4.0, and 3.5 were obtained. These indexes reflected word complexity and sentence length (Lovitt, Schaaf, & Sayre, 1970).

As the boy read, the teacher followed along in another reader. If he mispronounced or could not pronounce a word he was told that word and encouraged to continue reading. At the end of each session, after he had read from all three books, the teacher totaled the correctly and incorrectly read words from each book. She then divided each correct and incorrect total by five (minutes) to obtain correct and incorrect rates. These data were then plotted on three graphs, one for each book.

When the data were studied, it was evident that the pupil's performance was about the same in all three books, with a slight advantage noted in the high interest, low vocabulary text. Similar performance was noted in the three books in spite of the fact that the grade levels and the readability indexes differed. The method described here for comparing reading texts has also been used in comparing first-aid manuals, science books, and social studies texts.

PUPIL DATA CAN EVALUATE TEACHERS

The certification of teachers has long been an issue. Although some critics advocate the elimination of certificates, believing

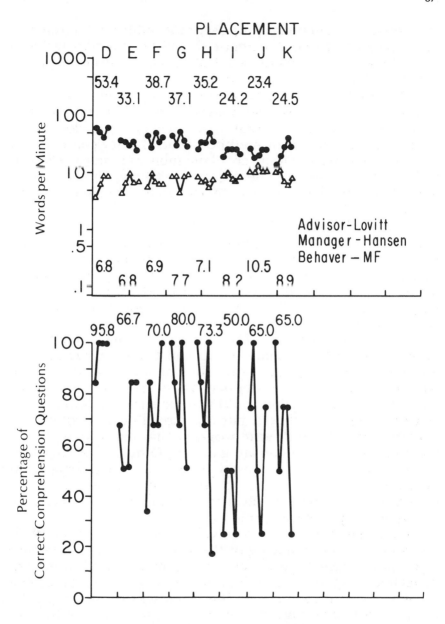

Figure 6. The top figure shows a pupil's correct and incorrect rates while reading orally from eight Lippincott readers. The numerals above and below the data are the median correct and incorrect rates for all the readers. The bottom figure shows the pupil's comprehension scores from the readers. The numerals are the median scores.

they serve no functional purpose, most educators agree that some type of official document should be given to teachers when they have completed a set of courses or experiences, as evidence that they are ready to teach.

Historically, there has been a great deal of controversy as to just what courses or experiences should be required for certification. Many authorities argue that teachers in the elementary grades should take mostly methods courses. They contend that if a person is expected to teach all the subjects to third or fourth grade children, she sould be required to take methods courses in reading, arithmetic, science, social studies, language arts, and music.

Others argue as vehemently that teachers should spend more time taking courses about learning. They concede that teachers should know something about content areas such as reading and arithmetic, but maintain that they should also know a great deal about theories of learning, child development, sociology, personality development, human interactions, and social relationships.

Trainers and certifiers of teachers argue over still other aspects of the teacher-training curriculum. Some believe that the entire period of training should be conducted in the public schools, much like the apprentice system used to train carpenters and bricklayers. Others hold that some training should take place in the public schools, but this should be scheduled only near the end of the four-year program. They conceive of the intern experience as a culminating activity. Others, as usual, take a moderate position and suggest that prospective teachers should be given experience with children throughout their four-year program, but that they should also take course work at a college throughout their degree program.

From one year to the next and from one college to another, the content and sequencing of the teacher-training curriculum varies widely. One time, the emphasis is on early and continued educational experiences in the public schools. Other times, the emphasis is on certain specified courses. Current popular courses bear such engaging titles as: "How to Relate to/with Your Pupils," "Teaching the Dyslexic Child," "Teaching in the Open Classroom," "How to Start and Operate Your Own Free School," "Thoughts and Ideas of Current Educational Critics," and "Unteaching Modern Math." In a year or so, I am certain the best-seller lists will change drastically.

Whatever the trend, whether the emphasis of a teacher-training program is on course work or on teaching experiences, it continues to be true that prospective teachers are sent into the market when they have completed the experiences required at a particular place and time. But whenever or wherever they obtained these experiences, the evaluation of their skills is all too often based on regrettably irrelevant factors.

In their course work, prospective teachers are often evaluated on the basis of the size of the notebooks they submit to their reading and science teachers; the bigger the better. During their internship, they are often evaluated on equally irrelevant considerations. They are given A's if they show up on time every day at their assigned school, if they interact just enough with the faculty before and after school, if they prepare novel and interesting lessons (but not too), if their pupils are fairly well behaved and interested in their teaching (but not too), if they watch their master teachers a lot, if they reinforce their master teachers for their teaching expertise, if they ask enough questions of master teachers about procedures, materials, and policy matters (but not too many), if, when master teachers reinforce them, they are humble, and if, when master teachers admonish them, they show penance and accept criticism.

Teachers should not be evaluated and granted their credentials on such subjective criteria. If a teacher imparts many skills to many children, she is good; if not, she is not good. Other things being equal—length of instructional time, type of child, adequacy of supplies—if one teacher helps her pupils gain two years in reading and another advances her pupils only one year, the first teacher is twice as good as the second. Accordingly, teachers should be sent out to jobs *when they have demonstrated they can teach,* not when they have taken certain courses or have interned for a given period of time.

Occasionally, an intern was assigned to the class I worked with at the EEU. During one quarter, our intern was an exceptionally fine young woman. She had all the attributes of a good teacher: she asked the right questions, seemed to be pleased with the responses she was given, showed up for work on time, stayed late, and complimented the head teacher. But in addition to her excellence in these behaviors, we knew that she could teach. Let me explain how we knew this.

As I have said before, we kept daily data for the children in our class in every subject matter area. Furthermore, these data were obtained by the head teacher and her assistant under conditions that were carefully controlled.

At the beginning of the quarter during which the intern was with us, the head teacher familiarized her with all the pupils and the subjects they were assigned. She was told what was being measured, how the data were gathered, and what instructional procedures were in effect. After a short indoctrination period, each subject matter area was successively turned over to her. First, she took over our typing class, then composition, then arithmetic. For a while she handled only one area at a time, that is, typing or composition. Later, she was given the responsibility of managing several subjects throughout the day.

Since we had data from all the pupils in all their subjects prior to the intern's taking over, we were able to compare their performances after she managed the class with their progress before her arrival. To our delight, we found that the rate of student progress was maintained. Although the performances of some children changed more when the regular teacher was in charge, the performances of other children were better when the intern ran the classroom.

Although this is but a single illustration of how pupil data can be used to evaluate a teacher, specifically one in training, it should serve to point out a method that can be used with great certainty to assess the effectiveness of all teachers. I must say it again: it would be far better, from the pupils' standpoint, if teachers were allowed to teach whenever they had demonstrated their ability to teach, rather than given a stamp of approval only after they had sat dutifully through a certain number of prescribed courses and experiences.

In reference to teacher training, I have often thought that perhaps the prospective teacher should amass a portfolio much like that of a photographer or commercial artist. Individuals in those professions collect a number of their best or representative photos or drawings, and when they seek employment, show their portfolios to prospective employers. Granted, employers will want to ask about where they were trained and for whom they have worked, but the employers would also have the immense advantage of evaluating the artists objectively since the evidence of their talents was before them.

A prospective teacher's portfolio might well consist of a number of descriptions of her ability to teach, among them some graphs and write-ups about what she has taught and to whom. If, for example, she had taught ten learning disabled boys to read, she could provide graphs illustrating their progress together with a brief but thorough write-up explaining the procedures and materials used and interpreting the data from the project. She could also include in the portfolio evidence of other teaching efforts, such as the materials or teaching aids which she had developed.

Portfolios of some teachers, like some photographers', would be more specialized than others. As some photographers are particularly skilled with personality shots, their portfolios would be heavily weighted with portraits and human interest scenes. The interests of others are more diversified; their portfolios would include a wider range of pictures—news photos, landscapes, nature studies, commercial art, or whatever.

The same diversity would appear among teachers. The portfolios of some applicants might include only summaries of reading studies—data from first graders through sixth graders, from severely retarded, normal, and gifted readers. Some of the projects might have focused on the development of sounds, on letter names, on oral and silent reading, or on various comprehension projects. In such a folder the teacher would attempt to convince the evaluator—her prospective employer—that she could deal with many types of reading performance and with many types of individuals.

The portfolios of other teachers might include a wider range of projects. For example, that of the teacher seeking a fourth grade position should indicate her ability to teach many skills to boys and girls nine or ten years old. Her dossier would include projects relating to her ability to teach several types of math skills, penmanship, various reading components, various social studies elements, many scientific concepts, creative writing, art, music, and physical education. It should also include some evidence that she had managed and changed several behaviors of the kind that would interfere with learning, such as fighting or quarreling with others.

All this would be very different, indeed, from current interviewing procedures. With these evidences of applicants' skills as teachers before them, prospective employers would know what they were hiring. As it is, employers ordinarily try to obtain information by interviewing candidates, by asking questions of former employers, or by scanning college transcripts. And all too often, none of these methods accurately describe applicants' abilities to teach. When people are hired today it is often for reasons other than their teaching excellence, or because they are recognized as potentially great teachers through "gut level" reactions on the part of the interviewers.

ANOTHER TYPE OF PUPIL DATA
USED TO EVALUATE TEACHERS

The preceding project demonstrated how pupil performance can be a meaningful measure of teacher competence. The implication of such a system is that the more children learn or produce, the better the teacher. To a great extent few would deny that, other things being equal, a teacher who assists her children to learn many skills is better than one who imparts only a few skills.

But perhaps another dimension of the teacher must be considered—how her pupils feel about her. A good teacher should be one who not only teaches her children, but teaches them in such a way that they "feel" good about themselves and the learning situation, and, therefore, develop a "love for learning." Although it is a large order, the effective teacher must be one who instructs many skills and pleases children in the process.

A few years ago a young man in one of my classes did a project concerning teachers and their responsiveness to children's expectations. He surmised that if the teacher's style fulfilled the expectations of the children, they would be happy and would perhaps learn more.

The project took place in two intermediate classes. One was headed by a young woman, a first-year teacher. The other class was directed by an older man who had taught for twelve years. The sixty children in these situations were asked to list the behaviors they thought good teachers should exhibit. In response, they turned in a total of 266 items. These statements were read by the project manager, who boiled them down to a list of 15 behaviors that included most of the children's suggestions and that could be easily observed. These behaviors were then presented to the classes for their final approval. Although a few slight modifications were made, the children agreed that the list fairly well described a good teacher.

Following are the 15 behaviors: (1) compliment children, (2) enforce rules the same for all, (3) let children come to you for help, (4) help each child, (5) listen to both sides of the story, (6) give homework, (7) set example by using good manners, (8) do experiments, (9) give study time, (10) show trust for children, (11) keep room quiet, (12) have children clean room, (13) join in class humor, (14) explain more than once, and (15) ask children for help.

It is interesting to study the list. Obviously, the pupils were concerned about fair play. They also wanted the teacher to be a real person with a sense of humor. They wanted to be included in the action, as is evidenced by the last suggestion. And apparently they also wanted to get some work done, as they believed they should have study time and the room should be quiet.

Once the 15 behaviors were listed, the manager came into both rooms and counted the frequency with which the teacher engaged in the specified behaviors. The manager had a sheet with 15 columns, one for each behavior, and several rows, one for each day of the baseline period. During the observation period, each time the teacher displayed one of the behaviors a tally was entered on the recording sheet alongside the label of that behavior.

Generally, the manager observed each teacher for about twenty minutes each day. At the end of an observation period, the frequency of the behaviors was tallied and plotted on a graph.

Throughout this project, the two teachers also kept some pupil data. The male teacher measured the arithmetic performance of one boy. These data were obtained at the same time data were being gathered regarding the teacher. The female teacher recorded total daily assignments handed in by all her pupils.

Throughout this project, no intervention was arranged for the pupils. Rather, the intervention was directed toward the teachers. The project manager wanted to know if, when the teachers began to behave more appropriately (according to the children), the children would be more productive.

The project was conducted in two parts. Throughout the baseline phase, which ran for eleven days, the teachers received no feedback. Throughout the next condition of the project, which lasted for twelve days, they were shown which of their behaviors were being observed. At the end of each day, they were provided feedback regarding their performance.

The teachers' data during this second phase indicated that they were responsive to feedback. During the first condition, they both engaged in the listed behaviors on the average of ten times per session. Throughout the feedback condition, they engaged in these behaviors on the average of fourteen times per session. Interestingly, both teachers were equally responsive. The older teacher was just "as good a teacher" as the younger and changed his behavior just as much, apparently because of feedback, as did she. (You *can* teach an old dog new tricks.)

The change on the part of the two teachers was the result of their engaging in the same teacher behaviors throughout the project, but *more* of the behaviors occurred in the feedback phase. They did not exhibit behaviors in the second phase that they had not exhibited during the baseline phase.

The two behaviors both teachers exhibited the most frequently throughout the study were to "compliment children" and to "let children come to you for help." The two they engaged in the least were to "listen to both sides of the story" and to "enforce rules the same for all." The probable explanation for the low frequency of these latter behaviors was that they were very difficult to detect.

When the pupils' data were studied, it was discovered that they improved in both classes from first to second condition. In the male's class, the accuracy and speed of the boy who worked on arithmetic problems improved. In the female's class, her students handed in twice as many assignments during the feedback-to-teacher phase as they did during the baseline.

It might be concluded from this project that teacher improvement is directly related to pupil improvement. As the teacher behaved more appropriately (according to the children), the children behaved more appropriately (according to the teachers). Fair is fair. But the important message from this study is that, as the teacher did more things that pleased the students, they did more to please the teacher. Apparently, then, happiness and production are related. They at least do not appear to be reciprocal; as one goes up the other does too.

Motivation

CHILDREN are often good motivation analysts.

As I have indicated in a previous section, the systematic arrangement of a reinforcer can be a powerful learning variable. It may be a bit strong to suggest that unless children are motivated, they will not learn a particular skill. A more conservative statement would be, "Learning will, in all probability, occur more quickly when people are motivated to learn than when they are not motivated." Whichever statement is more accurate, most people would agree that motivation is an important learning factor.

Some children, when asked to do something, will not comply. We know they could perform the behavior if they tried, but they will not respond. In such instances, they must be motivated to perform. (An instance is offered in the next chapter to illustrate this fact.) Therefore, the teacher must find a reinforcer and then must arrange it contingent on the desired behavior. In other words, the only way the student can obtain the reinforcer is by performing the desired task.

Finding reinforcers for most children is not a problem; they are turned on by so many things. The teacher needs only to select a properly tempting reward and arrange it contingent on performance.

For some youngsters, it is very difficult to find effective reinforcers. They simply do not enjoy the usual things. They aren't turned on by teacher praise, which is for many pupils an effective reinforcer, couldn't care less about playing with toys or games that most children enjoy, and aren't even motivated by seeing their daily scores or charting their own performance scores, as most other children are.

To help a teacher find the elusive motivators for some of these children, several strategies are available. First, the teacher can try to recall other situations in which he experienced difficulty in finding a reinforcer for a pupil, but somehow finally managed to come up with one. (Such a memory-searching strategy would be greatly facilitated for the teacher who had kept data.) Second, he can ask his fellow teachers what they did when they encountered "motivationless" children. Third, he can consult the literature and look for reports of cases in which unique reinforcers were successfully used. Fourth, he can ask the child's parents and friends to suggest potential reinforcers. Fifth, he can ask the child herself what she does like or enjoy.

All of these techniques have been used successfully in the past to identify potential reinforcers. An alternative strategy, one I strongly recommend, is just to watch children; often, they are excellent motivation analysts. When we watch them as they work or play and keep anecdotal records of what we see, we can learn about what they naturally like to do.

In order to do this it is sometimes necessary, with some children, to create situations in which they can be watched. One way to do this is to take a child from one setting to another and monitor her behavior. She might be taken to a park, a supermarket, a laundromat, or a car wash, and her reactions to these new situations studied. Most of the time, however, it is not practical to move the child about in this fashion.

We can also try changing the classroom or setting in which she normally operates. On one day, some new games, activities, pictures, or books might be brought in; on another, still different items could be arranged. The routine of the classroom could also be varied from day to day. It is quite possible that such a cafeteria approach to reinforcer sampling would be required, that either the child or her surrounding circumstances would need to be shifted periodically.

But this children-watching and recording technique need not necessarily involve moving them about or altering the classroom environment. Children will reveal what they prefer to do, even in normal surroundings, to the attentive observer.

We must discover these motivations and observe the full range of their preferences, without judging their likes and dislikes. Remember the old adage, "Different strokes for different folks." People are different, not only in their differing capabilities to read, write, and run, but also in their differing interests, tastes, and styles. Each one of us has a unique reinforcement system.

We must also keep in mind that what is reinforcing for one person may be meaningless or perhaps even aversive to another. Some are turned on by M & M's, some are nauseated at the very mention of them. Some are reinforced by teacher praise; for others, teacher praise is meaningless and, for some few, even punishing.

Although there is probably no single reinforcer, or motivator, that works for everyone, there is probably one (if not several) for everyone, if only it can be found. Everyone *is* reinforced by something.

Preschoolers, kindergartners, and first graders are generally easily motivated by their teachers, much more so than older children. Typically, the first thing these kiddies do in the morning when they see their teachers is to surround them. They want to touch, chatter, and wave their arms; anything to get their teachers' attention. They are saying, in effect, "Teachers, you are very motivating. If you arrange yourselves (praise, attention) contingent on certain of our behaviors, we will run off a high rate of those behaviors to obtain your attention." These youngsters are their own motivation analysts; they are showing their teachers what is, for them, reinforcing. Older children, in other ways, "tell" teachers the same thing.

Following are two examples of children who were difficult to teach. That is, they exhibited learning problems in certain skills and were not motivated to perform those skills. Attempts had been made previously to motivate the pupils in rather traditional ways but to no avail. Praise and other classroom "reinforcers" were used. After these failures, the teachers decided to "watch" the children to determine potential reinforcers.

JOHN AND THE COUNTERS

A few years ago we brought a new lad into our Curriculum Research Classroom. He came in several days after the other children had been admitted. John, our late arrival, had been identified at his regular school as a learning disabled child who had particular problems in reading and who also displayed certain bizarre behaviors from time to time.

The day he joined our class was memorable. His first act was to pick up a hand counter—used by our teachers to record the number of correct and incorrect words read by pupils—and punch away! These were double counters with two levers to press and two banks of digits. Naturally, this erasing activity nullified the accumulated data from the reading situation. He then ran around the room shutting off stopwatches that were running and starting watches that were not running. This created further confusion for the teachers who were timing or preparing to time the performances of various children in reading, arithmetic, or penmanship. In between starting and stopping watches, John came back to the double counter and punched away some more.

All the while, John was enormously delighted. Either he had never experienced the thrill of playing with counters and stopwatches, or this had been an activity of long-standing interest. No one knew; but the fact that he was so intent on the apparatus, so gleeful and so oblivious to everyone and everything around him, indicated that he was, indeed, turned on by turning off counters and clocks.

Finally, when John was coaxed away from the counters and watches, he was given some assignments. He was required to do some reading, writing, and arithmetic. The teachers believed it more important for John to develop skills in those areas than to punch counters. It should be mentioned at this point that the incidents of the first day were not recorded. The teachers simply interpreted his rampage as an example of bizarre behavior, for which he had been referred to them.

In a few days, John had settled into a routine and was given assignments in several activites. In reading, for example, he was expected to work in the Sullivan programmed materials for thirty minutes each day. He performed very well for a few days after entering the class; his correct rates were high enough and steadily increasing, and his incorrect rates were generally low. Then, after a few days, his performance began to deteriorate;

his correct rates dropped, he began making careless errors, and of course his incorrect rates increased. Day by day, John's performance grew steadily worse.

The teachers, in their attempt to explain his poor performance, thought that perhaps he had reached a difficult part of the book. They therefore studied carefully each item John had been required to answer. The analysis revealed that from the time the young man began the program through the period when his performance had begun to deteriorate, the material had not changed drastically. The format was the same from his "good" to his "bad" period; not even a new or different vowel or consonant sound had suddenly been introduced.

The teachers then decided that the explanation for John's poor performance lay in motivational reasons. Working on that premise, they began to search for a means of changing his motivation system; they needed to find a reinforcer. This need led to a teacher conference where the collective wit would be assembled. The first suggestion to come from these deliberations was to use contingent teacher praise, but both teachers agreed that the success of this strategy was highly improbable, since John did not react to teachers as did the others in the class. Sometimes when they complimented him for good performance, he hardly seemed to hear them. The next suggestion was to use toys. The option was likewise ruled out because John had never been seen playing with any toy. The third suggestion, that peer reinforcement of some type be arranged, was also dismissed because John was not particularly attached to any of his classmates nor they to him.

After the meeting had gone on for several minutes, one of the teachers recalled the first day that John came to the class and how he ran from counter to counter, from stopwatch to stopwatch. Although his behavior that particular day had been judged as bizarre and was certainly disruptive (he ruined the data from six or seven projects), it was possible that those bizarre and disruptive acts could be used to everyone's advantage. This idea stimulated the teachers to devise ways for establishing a situation in which John could use the treasured counters and watches, and his reading would improve.

Such a contingency was agreed upon. The next day it was explained to John that at the end of thirty-minute reading period a teacher would count his correct and incorrect answers. If he found that John had correctly answered more than a certain number, and had made fewer than a certain number of errors, then he would be allowed to use the counter to go back over his assignment and recount the number of correct and incorrect responses.

John was delighted, the teachers were delighted, and thus the dilemma was solved. For the data, by showing great improvement in both correct and incorrect rates, further substantiated the fact that John was pleased, hence motivated, by punching away at his beloved counter.

DANNY AND THE STOCK MARKET

Each day as Danny entered his class at the EEU he quoted excerpts from that morning's stock market report. Before he came to school, he watched a television show, beginning about 7:30 A.M., which gave the stock market quotations for the day. After his briefing, Danny would come to school and announce that General Motors was down two points, Bell Telephone was up three, Industrials had risen four, Utilities were off two points. Although Danny had difficulty remembering how to pronounce some of the words he read, he had little difficulty in remembering these stock market facts.

At first, when Danny rattled off this information, his teachers suspected that he had merely learned the language of the stock exchange—General Motors, Bell Telephone, down a point, up two points—and spouted these terms at random.

However, when his reports were checked with those of the stock exchange, they were found to be surprisingly accurate.

Midway through a quarter, when it became apparent that Danny had problems in reading, his teacher decided to make use of his affinity for the stock market and arranged the following contingency: the teacher talked the matter over with Danny and they agreed that on those days when his correct oral reading rate was higher and his incorrect oral reading rate was lower than previously specified, he could watch the TV show that broadcast stock market information for fifteen minutes. Throughout this period of contingent TV, his reading was much improved, as indicated by correct and incorrect rates.

To illustrate further the potency of reinforcers, a story about a girl in a sixth grade class near Seattle comes to mind. Peggy had at least two consistent behaviors: she enjoyed cleaning tables following lunch, and she was habitually late for school. The sixth grade teacher arranged these events as a contingency; Peggy was allowed to clean the tables *if* she came to school on time. As a result of this arrangement, her promptness improved, the tables were cleaner, and the girl, her parents, and the teacher were all greatly pleased.

In these examples, rather unusual reinforcers were arranged contingent on acceptable academic performance. Being allowed to use a counter, to watch the stock market quotations, and to clean tables are not generally regarded as highly reinforcing events. Nevertheless, for the children described here, they were precisely that, as indicated by the fact that their academic performances improved markedly when the reinforcers were contingently arranged.

Each of these three reinforcers was located by merely watching and listening to the youngsters. If we take the time to observe and record the things children like to do, there will be no reason for sending them to motivational specialists, for they are often their own best motivation analysts.

Reinforcement Contingencies

REINFORCEMENT contingencies can shape up some kids who are erratic performers.

When it comes to doing their work, some children seem to play games with their teachers. When asked to do their assignments, they just don't do them, even though they are quite capable of responding. These children are thus particularly frustrating to work with.

There are, for example, children who, during recess, play such elaborate games as Monopoly and who are able to arrive at rather complex solutions in short order. If they land on Atlantic Avenue, which is owned by someone else who has two houses on the property, and if they give the owner $500, they can quickly calculate how much change they should receive. Yet the next day, during arithmetic period, when the teacher asks them to solve problems of the type $42 + 8 = [\quad]$ or $76 - 9 = [\quad]$, they say they cannot do the calculating and turn in their assignments without answers or with incorrect answers.

Then there are the children who write letters to stamp companies asking that approvals be sent to them. The penmanship, grammar, and syntax of these letters may be close to perfect. Yet in their penmanship or creative writing classes, their writing is barely legible, and the content of the stories is woefully sketchy and illogical.

These children are different from those who can't compute accurately or write legibly. These children choose not to do something simply because they do not want to. Obviously, if a child does not do something because he cannot do it, the teacher should show or tell him how to do it. He needs some form of instruction, perhaps a lot of it.

However, the teacher must arrange other conditions for the child who, though he is capable, refuses to perform a task. First, she must determine whether or not the pupil is proficient in the skill he balks at doing. If, for example, a boy is asked every day to do problems like 6 + 2 = [ ] and refuses to respond, she should arrange a few sessions where he can be persuaded to do them, then study his rates. If the goal or desired correct rate for these problems is twenty per minute, and the child can do them at or beyond that rate, he should be advanced to more difficult, or at least different, problems. It may well be that the reason some children will not perform certain tasks is simply that they see no point in doing them. If it is discovered that they are, in fact, proficient in the skill, then they are quite right—they have behaved appropriately by going on strike. There is no reason to require proficient youngsters to respond to the same problems day after day. If the maintenance of the behavior is of concern, they should, of course, be required to practice the problems intermittently to retain the skill. But this will certainly not be every day.

As an aside, may I note that the strategy of using desired correct rates should always be explained to the pupils. They should be told that they are expected to continue to work on one type of problem until a desired correct rate is reached, after which they will be advanced to other material. In fact, teachers should make the effort generally to explain the whole process of teaching to their pupils.

But back to the topic at hand. Although there are some children who do not perform the problems, but can, and who in fact should not be asked to do them (those who are proficient), there are others who do not do the problems, but can, who *should* continue doing them. These latter children are the ones who, although they can do the work, do so very slowly. These children, as I have indicated earlier, are in the initial proficiency stage of development.

These are the children who are able to read, write, or compute, but their rates are inadequate. They have not practiced those skills enough so that their responses are automatic. They are the ones who, although their responses are perfect (when they want them to be), have to think a great deal or use some crutch before they can respond. With them, it is necessary to arrange conditions under which their initial responses become more accurate over a period of time (not just when they feel like it) and, ultimately, occur at rates that are proficient.

Some teachers, when confronted with these children, give up and pass them on to more difficult or different material, only to discover later that they are incapable of performing the new skill. The teachers then bring in all types of instruction, reinforcement, and feedback in their attempts to teach the new skill, and the cost in such situations can be great. In many instances, the reason the pupils have difficulty performing the new task is simply that they did not reach proficiency in the skills prerequisite to this new behavior.

But what to do with these children? How should teachers assist them and convince them that proficiency should be reached on each skill before an advanced one is scheduled? My recommendation is that mild reinforcement contingencies be arranged. The motivational system must be altered to such an extent that the pupil will decide it is worth his effort to respond accurately, consistently, and at an acceptable rate to these problems.

Following are three cases where reinforcement contingencies were scheduled. In the first example, such a strategy was instrumental in modifying a girl's pattern of responding to arithmetic problems. In the second project, a contingency assisted a boy to read orally with great accuracy. In the third project, a reinforcement contingency helped a twelve year old to improve his spelling accuracy after several previous instructional procedures had failed. In all three projects, reinforcement contingencies helped the pupils attain the first step leading toward proficiency; they learned to respond with consistent accuracy. The next stage, although it is not discussed here, was to increase their rates so that they became highly proficient.

WITHDRAWAL OF RECESS TIME

A twelve-year-old girl was the subject of this project, and the behavior of concern was subtraction. The teacher had observed that, on occasion, when the pupil was asked to do subtraction problems her performance was excellent. At other times she answered most of the problems incorrectly (Lovitt & D. Smith, 1974).

In order to determine the exact nature and extent of the problem, the teacher scheduled a baseline phase. Three classes of subtraction problems were identified. The Class 1 (S1) problems were of the type 18 − 9 = [　]; S2 of the type 24 − 6 = [　]; and S3, similar to 34 − 16 = [　]. Each day, during the baseline phase, the pupil was required to complete a sheet of twenty-five problems of each class. Different arrangements of the problems were assigned from day to day. The data were plotted on three percentage charts, one for each class (see figure 7).

During the baseline period, her scores were generally poor. On the first day, her score on the S1 problems was 100 percent, but thereafter the percentage scores were low. On the S2 problems, she scored 68 percent one day; the other scores were from zero to 24 percent. Most of her scores on the S3 problems were zero.

In the next phase of the project, a contingency was put into effect; for each S1 problem that was incorrect she lost one minute of recess time. This contingency was not arranged for the other two sheets of problems. The results were immediate and dramatic. Her average score on the S1 problems during this phase was 94 percent. Meanwhile, her accuracy on the two other classes of problems, where the contingency was not in effect, remained low.

In the next phase, the contingency continued to be scheduled for the S1 problems and was also arranged for the S2 problems. Her performance was again affected. Now, her accuracy was high on the S1 and S2 problems, but it continued to be low for the S3 problems.

In the following phase, the withdrawal contingency was arranged for all three classes. Once again her performance was immediately influenced. Throughout this phase, her accuracy was excellent for all three classes.

During subsequent phases, the contingency was removed from the various classes; she was not penalized for making errors. The data in these conditions revealed that her performance continued to be satisfactory.

Thus did a withdrawal contingency result in improved accuracy—our twelve year old loved her recesses. In this instance, performance improved even though no instruction was provided. Since the child could do the problems when she chose to

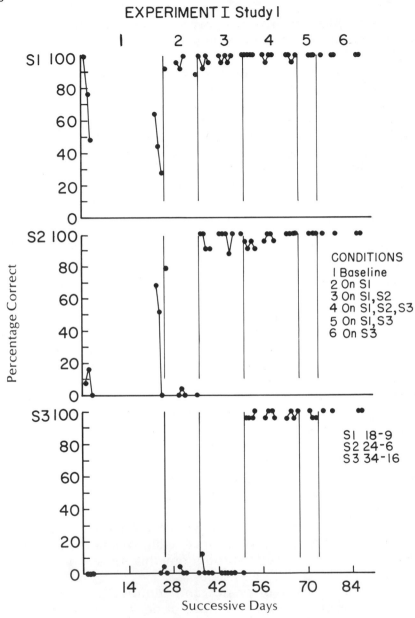

Figure 7. A pupil's correct percentage scores on three types of subtraction problems throughout six conditions of a study.

do so, the contingency simply motivated her to want to do them. It is unlikely that such instructional procedures as drill or modeling would have been as effective in her case.

A CONTINGENCY ON ERRORS

This example is much like the preceding, a reinforcement contingency arranged for errors. Contingent on each error, points—redeemable for minutes of recess time—were withdrawn. The differences between the two examples, however, were that now the topic was reading rather than arithmetic, and the measure was rate rather than percentage.

In this report, a boy read orally for five minutes each day. Throughout the project, if he needed assistance with a word, the teacher said it for him. No other form of feedback or instruction was provided. The project comprised two phases: a baseline period and a contingency period.

During the baseline phase, the teacher noted that most of the child's errors were careless ones. On several occasions, he simply skipped words that he knew, while at other times he erred on simple words like a, an, and the.

Throughout the second condition, a withdrawal contingency was arranged. Each day the pupil was given, noncontingently, fifteen points. The points were then taken away on a 2:1 ratio; for every two errors, one point was withdrawn. This withdrawal process took place after the five-minute reading session, not immediately following incorrect responses.

In the first phase of the project, the boy's average correct and incorrect rates were sixty and six words per minute; his average percentage of correctly read words was 91 percent. During the withdrawal condition his average correct and incorrect rates were fifty-nine and three. His mean percentage correct score was 96 percent. Although his correct rates went down slightly, presumably because he was being more cautious about making errors than he had been, his errors were significantly reduced. When accuracy was compared across conditions, as indicated by the average correct percentage scores, the scores were better in the second condition.

As was the case in the preceding study, a withdrawal contingency helped eliminate careless errors. The performances of both children throughout the contingency phases were much less erratic than during the baseline conditions.

SPELLING AND THE "PERFECT CONTINGENCY"

The topic of this project was spelling, and the pupil was a twelve-year-old boy. Daily, three lists of spelling words were assigned; there were ten words per list. The words on the first and second lists were alike in that they all contained the ea digraph, as in *peach* and *reach*. The words on the third list had the same long e sound but contained the ee digraph.

The purpose of this project was to determine whether or not generalizations would occur when instruction focused on certain lists but not on others. More precisely, we wanted to know what would happen to this pupil's performances on the second and third lists of words when teaching was directed only to the words on the first list. We theorized that the pupil would be able to generalize to both the second list of words, which were spelled similarly to those of the first list, and to the third list of words, which sounded alike but were spelled differently.

The lists and the words within each list were dictated to the pupil in an order that changed from day to day. During the baseline period, neither instruction nor reinforcement was provided. His percentage scores on all the lists were generally zero.

During the next phase, teaching focused on the first list of words. Prior to the daily measurement, the pupil was given a copy of the words and told that they all contained the long e sound and that this sound was made by the letters ea. He was then allowed to look over the word list for a few minutes. This technique was successful, for only seven days were required before he reached criterion (in this project, three successive 100 percent days).

Throughout the next phase, teaching focused on the second list of words. Teaching consisted of the same steps used for the first list. Criterion was reached on this list in the same number of days required to master the first list of words. Next, teaching of the same type was directed toward the third list of words. Criterion was reached on this list in four days. Meanwhile, however, as perfection was reached on the third list *(ee)*, accuracy deteriorated on the first and second lists. The pupil had overgeneralized; he had substituted the ee digraph for the ea digraph. *Peach* was now spelled *peech*.

Now the task was to teach the student to discriminate between the ee and ea words. Therefore, in the next phase, instruction was directed toward words on all lists. Instruction consisted of the teacher's pointing out that some words with the long e sound were spelled ee, others with ea. Examples of both forms were then given. The boy quickly regained his proficiency for words on the first two lists during this phase, but his performance was poor for the words on the third list.

During the next phase, instruction, as has been previously explained, was continued, and in addition the boy received feedback on all his answers; he was told which ones were correct and which were incorrect. Although his performance improved, criterion was not reached for all lists.

In the next phase, teaching as described was continued, and the pupil was also required to write each incorrectly spelled word five times following the spelling session. His performance still did not reach criterion.

In the following phase, all the above-mentioned procedures were continued; in addition, the pupil was required to spell orally each misspelled word. During this period, he reached criterion on the first two lists, but not for the third list.

By this time, the end of school was rapidly approaching, and criterion was yet to be achieved on all three lists. In an attempt to obtain mastery, a "perfect contingency" was put into effect. The day before this contingency was arranged, the teacher took the boy into the supply room and asked him to pick out three items. He selected a box of paper clips, a felt-tip pencil, and an eraser. The teacher then explained the contingency to him: "If you score 100 percent on all lists for three days in a row, you will win all the prizes!"

His scores the next day were perfect on the first two lists, and he missed only one word on the third list. His next day's scores were identical. Then, on the third day of this contingency, his scores were perfect, and they continued to be perfect for two more days. Criterion was reached!

Prior to the involvement of this contingency, four teaching procedures were arranged over a period of seventy-four days. When the "perfect contingency" was put into operation, only five days were required to reach criterion.

This project, apart from the fact that it illustrates how contingencies are often effective in stabilizing performance, is also a good example of poor teaching. It had been determined early in this study that the pupil could spell all the words on the three lists, provided they were presented one list at a time. He simply was unable to discriminate between ee and ea words when presented together. It is very likely that learning would have been speeded up if, as in the cases of the girl and subtraction and the boy and reading, a contingency had been involved earlier.

The futile search for an effective teaching procedure in this project is an example of the instructional strategy used by many classroom teachers who often resort to first one procedure and then another, aimlessly searching for an effective method. Such a strategy will often lead to frustration, particularly if the pupil can already do the required task, but will not perform on cue.

In the projects described here, contingencies were used in two ways to effect behavior change. In the first two projects, the contingency focused on errors; contingent on making errors, points were withdrawn. In the third project, the contingency was arranged for correct responses. In all three instances, accuracy increased. In addition to these contingency options, the manager might choose to use contingencies for both types of responding simultaneously; points, or whatever, being taken away for incorrect responses and given for correct answers.

A Hierarchy
of Reinforcers

SOMETIMES it is necessary to arrange reinforcers, but don't give away the store.

A teacher should go through several careful steps before attempting to teach a given pupil a specific skill and before using reinforcers. Before making any decision, he should satisfy himself that the pupil involved should indeed learn the behavior. Having determined this, the teacher should then decide if the pupil has the required behaviors. He should then discuss how long the process will take. And when all this is accomplished, he should then arrange a teaching atmosphere that is as efficient and attractive as it can be.

The next major step, of course, is to measure pupil development. If the teacher discovers that the pupil does not learn under the initial conditions and is reasonably assured that the pupil has the requisite behaviors to perform the task and that the learning environment seems appropriate, he should then analyze the pupil's performance. If she is consistently making a certain type of error or does not seem to know how to perform a particular type of problem, perhaps some instructional intervention like modeling should be scheduled. If, however, the child is like the ones described in the preceding chapter, one who *can* perform a given task but will not do so, then perhaps a reinforcement contingency of some type should be arranged.

Teachers should be very careful, however, about arranging reinforcers, particularly those that are expensive, improper in themselves, or habit forming . Ordinarily, once a reinforcer is used to change behavior, it should be removed as soon as the behavior has changed. Like a medicine or any other therapy, it can, if used unwisely, effect a cure that is worse than the problem. With these cautions in mind, then, let me rank, in order of use, different types of reinforcers, together with several principles that should guide us in their selection.

Whether or not a reinforcer needs to be arranged, the manager should make the effort to schedule contingencies that, in themselves, contribute to learning. If he can arrange a situation where the pupil develops a negotiable skill from the reinforcing situation, and that situation at the same time assists the pupil to learn some other behavior, he will doubly contribute to the pupil's behavioral repertoire.

ARRANGING TWO SIMULTANEOUS BEHAVIORS

One strategy of this type to consider would be to arrange one academic activity contingent on another, a strategy than can be approached in either a positive or negative manner. In the former, a situation may be devised whereby the pupil earns the privilege of engaging in one academic activity if she performs up to standards in another. For example, if she naturally enjoys reading but her arithmetic is poor, an arrangement may be provided whereby she will be allowed to read from a favorite book if her arithmetic performance is accurate or surpasses a prescribed rate. If it is the negative approach, a nonfavored activity may be scheduled contingent on performance of another nonfavored activity. If, for example, the pupil is a poor speller and her correct reading rate is low, an arrangement might be scheduled which specifies that unless her correct oral reading rate exceeds a certain level she will be required to practice spelling for so many minutes.

Another strategy for building two behaviors simultaneously would be to arrange some pupil management activity contingent on academic performance. For example, if the pupil's reading or arithmetic performance reached a certain level, then she would be permitted to see or make her own daily plot on her graph. Several other pupil-management components could be contingently arranged: pupil scheduling, counting, -specifying objectives, and -specifying contingencies. In instances such as these, the pupil would acquire proficiency in some basic skill and learn about graphing techniques, measurement, and the development of independence at the same time.

A third strategy for developing two behaviors simultaneously is to schedule some task (preferably one that needs to be done) contingent on academic performance. There are many routine tasks about the school that someone must do, ranging from cleaning the rooms and carrying messages from one teacher to another to filing papers and typing reports. Many times these activities are reinforcing for children, though they may be considered onerous for adults. And the pupils can learn happily from these tasks.

A fourth strategy for developing two behaviors simultaneously is to use contingent teaching. Many children love to play school, and just as often teachers may need help—they cannot give their assistance to all their pupils. One way to arrange such a situation would be to permit a pupil who is having trouble with a skill to teach a younger child that same skill. If, for example, a fourth grader who is having trouble with her reading would like to teach a first grader, it could be arranged so that if the older girl's performance was acceptable, she could then work with the younger child for a few minutes a day.

If all of these strategies prove nonfunctional, that is, if situations cannot be arranged whereby the student develops two behaviors at the same time, still other approaches must be considered. The manager must now arrange some socially acceptable, if not gainful, behavior contingent on performance.

ARRANGING SOCIALLY ACCEPTABLE BEHAVIORS

One such strategy would be to give increased recognition to the child of concern. Several examples of this approach may be cited. One would be to allow the student to talk with a favorite person contingent on performance. Another would be to allow the child to display a graph of her performance, a picture she has drawn, or her arithmetic sheet in a favorite place contingent on performance. Still another approach would be to give the pupil notes or send notes home contingent, again, on her performance.

A second strategy of this type would be to allow the student to do certain things in the classroom, contingent on performance, earning such privileges as erasing the chalkboard, being first in line for recess, choosing a song during music class, selecting the game during recess, being a team captain, or distributing papers.

A third recourse would be to grant leisure time contingent on performance. There are at least two ways in which this can be done. One is to allow the pupil to do almost anything she wants at her desk when she has completed the prescribed task. If she has completed her arithmetic assignment satisfactorily, she can remain at her desk and draw, read, or color. An alternate approach is to arrange, in the classroom, a leisure-time area, in which there may be games, toys, and records that are appealing to various children. The pupil can gain access to this area only by performing some academic behavior at a specified level of acceptance. (More will be said about leisure time in the next chapter.)

ARRANGING APPROVAL-BASED CONTINGENCIES

The third class of reinforcers are those which must be approved by others. Although the manager may have reason to believe that certain items or circumstances will effect change if they are arranged contingently, some of these should be checked out with other observers. One example would be contingent rest. Perhaps a child consistently comes to school tired and is also a poor reader. Conceivably, a situation could be arranged whereby she could rest contingent on acceptable reading performance. Although the youngster, as a result of this arrangement, might very well improve her reading and catch up on her sleep, the teacher would be ill-advised to use such a contingency without first consulting with the parents on the matter. Otherwise, unless informed of the arrangement, they might take a rather dim view of a school that allowed children to sleep during the day.

CONSIDERING THE TOKEN ECONOMY

The fourth class of reinforcement contingencies is the token economy. There are many variations on this theme, but the basic elements are that pupils are first given something—a mark or an actual token—contingent on performance, and then later these awards are redeemable for articles, free time, toys, or whatever. Some of these systems do, in fact, help students learn, but they are invariably costly. Furthermore, the research to date is discouraging in regard to subsequent maintenance of performance, once the token economy is removed.

ARRANGING TANGIBLE REWARDS

The fifth type of reinforcement, and the most expensive to operate and difficult to remove, is the direct granting of some tangible reward item contingent on performance. In the early days of behavior modification, the favored "reinforcer" was M & M candies. These were fed to children contingent on all types of behaviors, from walking to reading. Many other rewards, such as cookies, soda pop, and model airplanes, have also been contingently arranged in efforts to modify behaviors.

What, then, is my final advice as to the selection of reinforcers? Basically, it is that the manager should begin with the first type and move up. To begin with the most expensive and most difficult to remove reinforcer would be foolish. If it is ultimately determined, however, that a pupil will not develop a desired behavior unless an expensive system is used, that system should, by all means, be scheduled.

Contingent
FreeTime

LEISURE time is as big a reinforcer for youngsters as it is for adults.

Several chapters in this book have dealt with motivation, the selection and arrangement of reinforcers for children. The next chapter, devoted to pupil management, provides examples of children who were motivated to learn various skills when they were allowed to control various features of the learning environment. In a previous chapter, Motivation, an argument was offered to the effect that children are their own best motivation analysts; projects were described in which effective, albeit unusual, reinforcers were identified by watching and listening to the youngsters in action.

This chapter also focuses on motivation, but not on a specific event such as teacher praise, candies, or toys. The concern here is with a host of events or nonevents that are classified under the category of leisure time.

It has been my experience, in dealing with dozens of children, that leisure time is generally reinforcing. That is, when children are allowed to do what they want, contingent on academic performance, those performances improve. For instance, when leisure time is granted contingent on completed assignments, more assignments are completed. Similarly, when leisure time has been given for assignments accurately or swiftly completed, more assignments are accurately and swiftly completed.

That children are often motivated by leisure-time pursuits should not be too surprising; for most children (during certain parts of the day, at least) simply like to goof off. They enjoy sitting and dreaming, doodling with a pencil, staring at a bug, twirling the knobs of a TV set, or flipping through the pages of a magazine. Children, like adults, also enjoy doing as they wish; they are turned on by being able to elect whether to build model airplanes, color pictures, work puzzles, or play cards. And that is just the point. Leisure-time periods allow children the opportunity to goof off and to pursue the activity of their own choosing.

Adults run off a lot of activity in order to obtain leisure time. Many of them work very hard throughout the year for a two- or three-week vacation. Weekends are also reinforcing for most workers; for on Saturdays and Sundays they can (theoretically) engage in leisure-time pursuits, either goofing off or enjoying pleasurable activites.

That leisure time is reinforcing to workers is also indicated by the short workweek many businesses are adopting, down to even the four-day week which, coupled with the many holidays that have been legislated recently, provides workers with increased periods of leisure. No doubt about it, many workers stay with jobs that they do not really like because of the leisure time—vacations, weekends, and holidays—anticipated.

Students of all ages are notoriously motivated by weekends. They, too, count the days until the end of the week; they eagerly anticipate the freedom and leisure of Saturdays and Sundays. The frequency with which the expression TGIF is spoken on Friday mornings indicates unmistakably the reinforcing power of the forthcoming weekend.

Although I support the idea of more leisure time for workers (adults and children), I also maintain that work situations themselves should be made as reinforcing as possible. There are numerous aspects of most work environments that may be altered to make work a more interesting, if not exactly a pleasurable, experience, and much has been written on this topic of late.

In situations where the work environment is really bad, contingent leisure time will certainly be effective; workers will do anything to escape, even momentarily, their surroundings. In such instances leisure time, or for that matter any other kind of time, would be reinforcing, for one situation is relative to another. Admittedly, there are many instances in which individuals are enticed into performing in situations that are nothing short of demoralizing, by the use of such powerful reinforcers as leisure time. But I consider such abuses to be tragic and dehumanizing.

Just as industrialists should not use reinforcers to maintain workers in menial posts, neither should teachers or others responsible for the development of children use reinforcers, including leisure time, to influence pupils to perform dull, mean, or irrelevant tasks. Certainly teachers should do everything possible to make learning situations as palatable as they can be made.

Following are examples of instances in which leisure time was arranged contingent on academic performance. In the reading examples, leisure time was granted to one pupil for correct reading rate and to another for correct rate and quality. In the arithmetic example, leisure time was contingent on correct rate. In the third project, free time was awarded for accurate spelling.

LEISURE TIME AND READING

Two situations will be discussed in this section. In the first, an eleven-year-old boy was assigned to a Bank Street 2^2 reader. For five minutes each day, he read orally from the book. As he read, the teacher counted each correct and incorrect response. Incorrect responses were words that were added, omitted, and substituted (Lovitt, Eaton, Kirkwood, & Pelander, 1971, pp. 54-71).

Two conditions, each lasting about twelve days, comprised the project. During the first condition, no contingencies were in effect. Throughout the second phase, a point contingency was instituted. The requirements of the contingency were that if, after the five-minute reading period, the boy's correct rate was equal to or exceeded fifty words per minute and his incorrect rate was less than two words per minute, he would be granted points on a 25:1 ratio; that is, he received one point for each twenty-five correctly read words. If his correct and incorrect rates were not better than the established requirements, he received no points.

Each point was redeemable for one minute of free time following the reading session. During that time, he could sit at his desk and draw, read, stare, or sleep, or he could go to another area in the classroom and play with models, games, or puzzles.

When his rates in the two conditions were compared, it was obvious that leisure time was motivating. His average correct rate was twelve words per minute higher in the second condition than in the first, and his average incorrect rate in the second condition was one word per minute lower. Throughout the second phase, his correct rates were between fifty and sixty words on most days. He earned, on the average, only two minutes of free time each day.

The next reading project was similar. In this example an eleven-year-old girl read daily from a MacMillan reader. Like the boy, she read orally for five minutes, and data were kept on correct and incorrect words per minute. This project differed from the first in that it contained four conditions rather than two. During the first condition, no contingency was arranged. Throughout the second phase, a 30.1 point contingency was scheduled: she received one point for each thirty correctly read words, each point being redeemable for a minute of free time. The third condition was the same as the first, while the fourth was like the second (see figure 8).

During the free-time period, the same choices offered the boy were available to the girl; she could either stay at her desk or go to another part of the room. The only restrictions during free time were that she could not leave the room for the entire period, and she could not talk with anyone who was working on an assignment.

The results from this project were as impressive as those for the boy. Her correct rates were higher during those conditions when leisure time was available than when it was not. In addition, her incorrect rates were lower during the conditions of contingent leisure time.

On most days during the leisure-time periods, her correct rates were between sixty and seventy words per minute. Ordinarily, she earned two minutes of free time each day. This project, like the preceding findings, indicated that even a small amount of leisure time was measurably reinforcing.

MULTIPLE RATIOS AND ARITHMETIC PERFORMANCE

In the last two examples, single reinforcement ratios were used, the ratio in the first project being 25:1, and that in the second, 30:1. A few years ago, however, we conducted an experiment

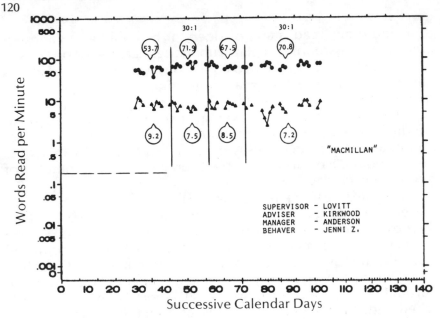

Figure 8. Correct and incorrect rates while reading from a Macmillan reader. The reinforcement contingency was in effect during the second and fourth phases. Median scores are shown in the teardrops.

which dealt with multiple ratios; we were interested in determining the comparative effects on performance of single and multiple ratios. Two studies comprised this experiment, the subject of which was a twelve-year-old boy (Lovitt & Esveldt, 1970).

Each day, in the first study, the pupil worked for fifteen minutes on problems of the type 49 + 23 = [   ]. Throughout the first condition, he received neither feedback nor teaching. He was, however, granted points from a single-ratio schedule, receiving one point for twenty correctly answered problems (20:1). Each point was redeemable for a minute of free time.

In the second phase, multiple ratios were established, with four ratios being arranged. If he responded below a certain rate, he received no points; above that rate he was granted points on the lowest ratio; above another rate he received points on a higher ratio; above yet another rate he was awarded points from the highest ratio. In the third phase, points were awarded from only the single ratio. In the fourth condition, multiple ratios were again instituted.

The results from this study revealed that the boy's correct rates were twice as high during the multiple-ratio conditions as they were during the single-ratio phases. Incorrect rates throughout all conditions were very low (see figure 9).

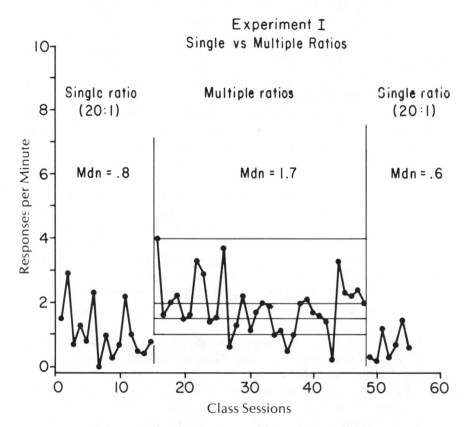

Figure 9. Correct arithmetic response rate throughout Experiment I where single and multiple ratios were manipulated. The horizontal lines through the multiple-ratio phase indicate the four contingency bands.

A second study, identical to the first, was then conducted. Once again, the pupil was required to respond to addition facts for fifteen minutes each day, and the study was made up of four conditions. During the first and third conditions, a single ratio was in effect; during the second and fourth conditions, multiple ratios were arranged.

The results of this study were like those of the first. The boy's correct rates were much higher during multiple-ratio conditions than during single-ratio phases.

During the leisure-time period in both studies, the boy went to a separate area of the classroom, where he could play with various games, toys, or puzzles. He was free to switch from one activity to another (which he usually did). Throughout the last study, he generally responded fast enough to be paid off from the highest ratio level (10:1) during the multiple-ratio conditions. Ordinarily, he was awarded about twelve minutes of free time each day.

LEISURE TIME AND SPELLING

This study took place in a regular fourth grade class of thirty-two pupils. The project was conducted by the classroom teacher; he administered the spelling program, calculated and graphed the pupils' scores, and managed the contingency system (Lovitt, Guppy, & Blattner, 1969).

During the baseline condition of the study, spelling was administered in a traditional manner. On Monday the new words were introduced and the children read a story containing those words. On Wednesday a trial test was given. On Thursday the pupils were assigned workbook exercises which pertained to the spelling assignment and wrote each spelling word several times. On Friday (of course) the final spelling test was given. Each pupil's Friday score was graphed as a correct percentage score.

During the second phase, the pupils were presented the lists of words and given the same type of spelling assignments as before. Throughout this period, the pupils were simply required to hand in their work; no specific time was scheduled for completing the various activities as during the first phase. The major difference between this condition and the former, however, was that spelling tests were scheduled four days a week, rather than only once. The pupils were through with spelling for the week if they received a 100 percent score. If on Tuesday, the day of the first test, a pupil scored 100 percent and had handed in the spelling assignments, he was finished with spelling for a week. During the spelling period throughout the remainder of the week, he was free to engage in a number of leisure-time pursuits; he could read comic books, work on puzzles, or draw pictures. A pupil continued to take spelling tests until his score was perfect or through Friday.

Throughout this second phase, the teacher recorded the pupil's score as 100 percent if he returned a perfect paper on Tuesday, Wednesday, Thursday, or Friday; otherwise, if the pupil never achieved 100 percent, his Friday score was recorded. The teacher also entered on each pupil's graph a numeral which corresponded to the day the score was obtained: 1 for Tuesday, 2 for Wednesday, and so forth.

As a result of being able to earn free time (or to escape from spelling) the performances of most children improved. Twice as many 100 percent papers were recorded in the second condition as during the first. Many children obtained 100 percent scores in the second phase who had never before done so.

The third condition was a group contingency. If all students scored 100 percent on the same day, they could listen to the radio for a few minutes. (see figure 10).

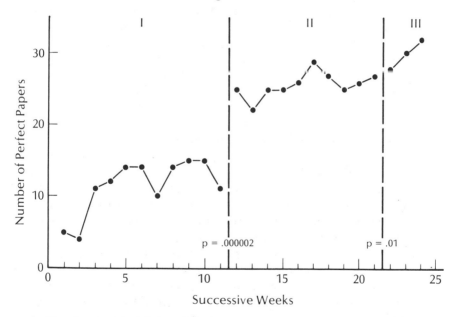

Figure 10. Number of 100 percent papers recorded each successive week throughout the three experimental conditions. The *p* values reflect the degree of significance between adjacent conditions.

Bill Hopkins, a staff member of the Department of Human Development at the University of Kansas, designed a penmanship study, with first and second graders, using free time as a contingency. Each day, the first graders were required to copy a story in manuscript form; the second graders were given a cursive writing assignment. Data were kept on correctly and incorrectly formed letters.

During a baseline period, when a pupil finished his assignments, he remained at his desk until everyone in the class had finished. Throughout the next phase, a free-time contingency was scheduled. When a student had finished with his assignment, he could go to a special area and play with toys and games. During subsequent conditions in the study, free time was alternately available and unavailable. Hopkins reported that during the conditions in which leisure time could be earned, the pupil's rates and accuracies were far better than during those in which leisure time was not available.

Arranging leisure time contingent on academic performance is a relatively simple matter for teachers or parents. For one thing, no extra equipment is required. Although a special leisure-time area was already available in some of the studies discussed here, such a location, if not at hand, could easily be arranged in most schools. In the spelling study, there was no special place provided; the pupils remained at their desks during leisure-time periods.

Some teachers are reluctant to use contingent free time, believing that free time should be granted freely, not earned. Many consider recess, for example, as an event that should not, under any circumstances, be withheld from a child. As I have made clear in an earlier chapter, I do not believe that reinforcement contingencies or other instructional techniques should be capriciously scheduled. But if the manager has worked through the instructional steps previously discussed and the pupil is still not learning what he should be learning, then certainly reinforcers such as leisure time should be arranged. For a teacher to withhold a technique that stands a good chance of assisting a child to read, compute, spell, or write simply because of some mistaken ethic would be like a doctor withholding penicillin from a patient suffering from strep throat because of some bias against drugs.

The manager who considers the use of free-time contingencies should keep in mind two things: the ratio of points to responses that will be scheduled and just what events will be offered. As to the former, an infinite number of ratios can be arranged—a pupil could be granted one minute of free time for 1, 10, 20, or 100 answers. Or for one correct answer he could be given 1, 10, 20, or 100 minutes. As to the events that can be scheduled, several options are possible. If a free-time area is furnished, the items may range from simple games and toys to sophisticated puzzles and experiments.

An important feature of free-time areas that should be considered has to do with socialization. In some of the experiments discussed here, there was room for several people to be in the free-time area at the same time. It is quite possible that some children are as reinforced by being able to talk and interact with others as they are by having leisure time to play with toys or games.

Another factor that might conceivably account for the increased production of pupils when contingent leisure time is used is escape from school. Perhaps the true motivating factor of free-time arrangements *is* the opportunity to escape work rather than to gain access to leisure-time pursuits. In fact, I would not be at all surprised if this should prove true. More will be said on this point in the Epilogue

Pupil
Management

KIDS are turned on when you give them a piece of the action.

As I have pointed out in the preceding four chapters, motivation can play a very important role in skill development. I have also suggested various methods for locating appropriate reinforcers for given individuals, one of which is the simple device of watching children. Another simple and effective way to motivate pupils is to let them play a part in managing their own affairs—give them a piece of the action.

It's human nature to like to have a say in what we do; to think, at least, that we are the masters of our destinies. Not many people are motivated by the military-type situations where they are told when to get up, what to do every minute of the day, how to spend their leisure time, and when to go to bed.

College students are certainly anxious to have a say in their own affairs. On many campuses they have been quite vocal—stridently vocal at times—in their demands for representation. They want a voice as to what courses should be taught and how they themselves should be graded; they want to be represented on various university committees and boards of regents and are telling the administration in no uncertain terms that self-management is indeed motivating. Implicit, perhaps, in their demands is the insistence that if they are granted more responsibility for their actions they will be more productive.

In most school situations, however, teachers call all the shots. They decide what subjects will be studied, when these activities will be scheduled, how materials should be presented, how performances will be evaluated, how feedback or confirmation will be given, and what reinforcers, if any, will be arranged. Rarely are pupils, particularly those in elementary schools, given any options as to their own learning and development. This situation is somewhat paradoxical when we read educational objectives that espouse the fostering of independence and self-control.

To indicate how certain self-management components can be reinforcing, I will present four projects. Two of them pertain to self-scheduling, one to the self-specification of contingencies, and one to the self-selection of a remediation technique.

HE LIKED TO ARRANGE HIS SCHEDULE

The pupil in this project was enrolled in the Curriculum Research Classroom. Every day, he was required to complete assignments in phonics, reading, penmanship, arithmetic, and spelling. Midway through one academic quarter, his performances in all subjects, except phonics, were quite satisfactory. In this area, however, he made several careless errors, more than the teacher believed were necessary (Lovitt, 1973).

The teacher thought that, since his phonics errors were random and probably due to carelessness, his behavior would improve if a reinforcement contingency were arranged. At this same time, we had also been talking about various self-management components and how academic performance might be influenced if certain of those elements were contingently arranged.

It was decided, therefore, to arrange self-scheduling contingent on performance in phonics. Specifically, the arrangement was that if the pupil completed his phonics assignment with four errors or less he would be permitted to schedule the next four subjects; he could decide when to work on math, reading, spelling, and penmanship.

The data following the involvement of the contingency revealed that, generally speaking, he not only made fewer than four errors, but he also finished his phonics task more quickly than at any time prior to the contingency phase. This boy, then, was motivated by being able to earn the right to schedule his own time, even though he still had to complete five assignments each day.

EVEN CONTINGENCY SPECIFICATION CAN BE REINFORCING

A few years ago in our Curriculum Research Classroom we were investigating the effects of free time on academic performance. The children could earn minutes of free time by responding to academic materials. One boy, for example, was given one minute of free time for every five correctly answered math problems (5:1). In a reading program he was given one minute of free time for each ten correctly answered items (10:1). Similar ratios were established for his other activities: penmanship, phonics, and social studies. Several days of data were obtained during which time the teacher specified all the contingencies (Lovitt & Curtiss, 1969).

Prior to the next condition, the teacher discussed these various ratios with the pupil. She wanted to determine how well the boy understood them. When asked how many minutes of free time he would earn if he answered ten math problems correctly (the ratio was 5:1), he said two. When asked how many minutes he would receive if he correctly answered thirty items in his reading program (the ratio was 10:1), he said three. Similar questions were asked about the other ratios. When the teacher was satisfied that the pupil understood the ratios and could transform the number of items to minutes of free time, she asked him to specify his own ratios, explaining that now he would be allowed to determine the ratios in each of his subjects for himself. This he did, and the teacher wrote the ratios on a card which she taped to his desk.

Data continued to be gathered for several days under pupil-specification conditions. Then, after a period of time, the teacher told the boy that he would be given points from *her* ratio system. The same ratios that were in effect during the first teacher-specification phase of the study were specified and again taped on his desk.

When the data from this project were analyzed, it was apparent that the pupil performed better when *he* specified the contingencies than when they were arranged by the teacher. His correct rates during the pupil-specification phase of the project were higher than his rates during the teacher-specification phases (see figure 11).

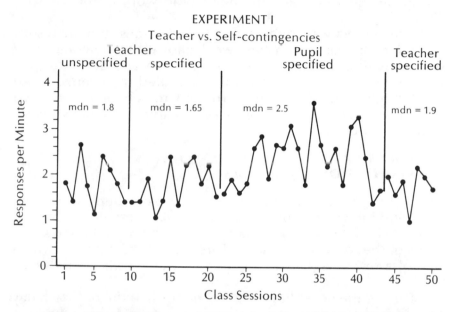

Figure 11. Daily correct response rate throughout Experiment I. The pupil specified the contingencies during the third condition.

Throughout the next academic quarter, an identical project was conducted with the same boy. Once again, during the second and fourth phases, the teacher specified all the ratios, and throughout the third phase the ratios were determined by the pupil. The data once again revealed that the pupil performed better when he specified the contingencies than when they were established by the teacher.

WHEN ALLOWED TO SCHEDULE, WORK IMPROVES

This project was like the first one in that we were interested in determining what would happen to a pupil's performance when allowed to schedule his own activities. Throughout the project, we monitored pupils' performances in math and reading.

The responsibility for scheduling was alternated throughout this project. During some conditions, the teacher scheduled the activities; at other times, the pupils scheduled them. In either event, the pupils had to work just as long, in both reading and math. The only difference throughout the project was that during the periods scheduled by the pupil, he and the teacher would decide which activity they would work on first (Lovitt, 1973).

This project was conducted with two pupils, and the results were very similar; when they were allowed to schedule their own activities, they were more productive and accurate than during periods when the teacher scheduled the events. These results indicated that being permitted to schedule even two such relatively low-motivating tasks as reading and math was reinforcing to both pupils.

PUPILS CAN EVEN SELECT THEIR OWN REMEDIATION TECHNIQUES

In this project, the teacher sought to assist a pupil to say the short and long vowel sounds. Daily, he was presented a sheet of vowels with long and short markings, and he was asked to say as many of the sounds as possible. Throughout the baseline, which ran for a few days, he was unable to say any of the sounds correctly.

During the next phase, the teacher drilled the boy each day for a few minutes on various sounds. She talked about the long and short symbols and gave several examples of each sound. Following the drill, the boy's performance was measured. Great improvement was noted throughout this condition; his average correct rate was sixty-five sounds per minute. Although his incorrect rate improved, he still made, on the average, three errors per minute.

After a few days, the pupil correctly diagnosed his performance by saying that he had the most difficulty with the short e sound. On the basis of this self-analysis, he decided to write the word *ten* on each sheet. When his daily performance was measured, this notation served as a cue; he could look at the word *ten* as a reminder of the pronunciation of the short e. Throughout this condition his performance improved significantly; his correct rate nearly doubled, and his incorrect rate fell to zero.

After a few days, he was told to remove the cue from the sound sheets in order to determine whether his newly acquired accuracy and speed of saying the sounds would continue. Much to the pupil's and the teacher's delight, it did.

So much for the evidence of the four projects. There are many other elements of the teaching process that might prove to be reinforcing if turned over to pupils. These include self-correcting, giving pupils answer keys to use for correcting their own work; self-graphing, teaching pupils to graph a record of their performance; self-selecting, allowing pupils to determine what they should learn; self-goal specification, allowing pupils to establish their own performance objectives; and self-evaluating, allowing pupils to judge the worth of their performances and perhaps even assign their own grades.

Apart from the major purpose of teaching self-management behaviors (so that pupils will become more independent), at least three other reasons for considering such a strategy should be noted. One important factor is that when pupils handle certain of their affairs they can, to that extent, assist their teachers. Obviously, if teachers are required to obtain, without outside help, measurements from thirty children in several academic areas, their patience, zeal, and ingenuity will soon be seriously depleted.

Another reason for instructing children to manage their own affairs relates to the academic curriculum. When children are taught to correct, count, chart, and evaluate their own performances, they are learning in highly functional ways to add, divide, tell time, and compare. The amount of pupil involvement and the extent to which this involvement is incorporated into the math and science curriculum is limited only by the creativity of the teacher.

The third reason for arranging pupil-management activities is that often children are highly motivated when allowed to assume portions of their instructional responsibility. The four projects described in this section are certainly illustrative of this phenomenon.

Relationship Between
Errors and Learning

SOME children, even when they've made the same mistake over and over again, can still learn to do it right.

Many developmental concepts have been advanced in reference to committing errors. Some people believe that learning will not occur unless a few mistakes are made. Others maintain that incorrect responses should be rigorously minimized.

The belief that some errors are necessary before learning can occur has many advocates whose slogans include, "The only way to learn is by doing" and "Sink or swim." A majority of those who subscribe to the middle-class work ethic support this notion. They are rather blunt in their approach and unsympathetic toward those who have problems. They do not believe in too much mollycoddling or too many frills, preferring to hold that there is no easy road to learning; learning is hard work, and hard work is good for you. They also have many favorite ways of stating their theories about work that are freely passed on, and on, and on. They believe that if a learner is to be taught to ride a bike, to swim, or to conjugate verbs, he must be immersed in those situations. They insist that he will "learn from his mistakes."

There are other people, however, who take a rather dim view of such a rigorous attitude toward the committing of errors. They subscribe to the belief that if a pupil makes the same mistake over and over again, he may never learn to perform the task correctly. They argue that if a pupil consistently responds to the problem 2 + 2 = [ ] by saying or writing 5, repeatedly calls a *b* a *d*, or reads the word *bed* as *bid*, it will be impossible to correct those errors. They are convinced that if a person consistently does something incorrectly a habit will be formed that becomes so strong nothing can later be done to change that pattern.

A third group concerned with errors and retention are those who support the notion of overlearning. Their belief is that all learners, particularly the mentally retarded, should correctly practice a skill many times *after* the behavior has been "learned." They believe, apparently, that the correct response can thus be thoroughly stamped into the cerebellum and will always be executed correctly thereafter.

Some psychologists also share the notion that errors should be zealously avoided. They support the concept of errorless learning. Their primary effort is to design programs that pupils can react to without making errors, believing that when a pupil makes an error his progress is greatly retarded. They contend that when errors are made a great amount of time must be spent in an effort to eliminate them, then still more time is needed to replace the error with an appropriate response. In some respects, such a belief cannot be contested, for if a certain number of correct responses are required before a skill is mastered, then time is indeed wasted each time an error is made. However, whether it takes *additional* time to eliminate such errors is still subject to much conjecture.

I shall not attempt, in this chapter, to cite projects that illustrate all of these varied notions regarding errors. Although a significant amount of research in reference to overlearning and errorless learning has been published, we have not ourselves conducted such investigations. Neither have we thrown children to the lions by plunging them in learning situations where they will certainly fail. We have been careful to determine the requisite tasks for a particular behavior and to judge whether or not the pupil possesses these requisite behaviors before subjecting him to a new learning situation.

This chapter has to do with the reality that pupils do make errors. Although we try, in the situation where I work, to assign children to tasks they can be expected to accomplish, they still make errors) sometimes several. I am certain that even the "errorless learning" people have been frustrated from time to time by children who, in spite of the most elaborate precautions, still make errors.

This chapter is addressed to those teachers who are extremely pessimistic about trying to teach children who have in the past committed many errors and who may even have been tempted to give up with such children. Perhaps they have tried four techniques for teaching a pupil to spell certain words, but he still made mistakes. As a result, their teaching behaviors were extinguished. Perhaps they have been assigned a boy who had failed kindergarten and first grade and who was rejected by various remedial centers. Knowing this, a pessimistic teacher might well refuse even to begin teaching.

This chapter is also directed to those teachers who believe that it is possible to save a child who has failed repeatedly in a certain skill, but who also are convinced that massive rehabilitation will be required. They, unlike the teachers without hope, will begin instruction, but they will commence only when they have amassed a huge repertory of techniques and are prepared for a long instructional siege. These are the teachers who practice instructional overkill.

As to those pupils with a long history of failure, I maintain that they *can* succeed and succeed without massive rehabilitation. Following are instances of pupils who erred repeatedly on academic behaviors, but who were quickly able to adjust their responses, *once teaching was directly focused on a specific skill.*

A DIVIDING BY ZERO HANG UP

In this example a boy was presented a sheet of division facts to work each day. On it were problems like $6 + 1 = [\quad]$ and $4 \div 2 = [\quad]$. About half the problems included zeros; problems like $0 \div 1 = [\quad]$ and $0 \div 4 = [\quad]$. This assignment, however, was only a part of his daily computation tasks. He was also given sheets that contained addition and multiplication problems. Throughout a baseline period, he received no feedback or instruction on any of the sheets.

During this condition, it was apparent that he could add simple facts; consequently, that portion of the program was dropped. His accuracy in performing multiplication and division problems, however, was poor. In a few days his accuracy improved significantly in multiplication, and that program also was dropped from the schedule.

Throughout the baseline phase during which three sheets were presented, and throughout the next period when instruction focused on multiplication, the pupil's scores on the division sheets were about 50 percent correct each day. Although he answered correctly the nonzero problems, he consistently missed *all* of the zero problems, bringing his overall percentage scores down to 50 percent. This pattern of missing all the zero problems (about twenty a day) continued for fifteen consecutive days. During that period, he committed about 300 errors on those problems.

When accuracy was reached on the multiplication problems, instruction was shifted to the division sheets. This instruction was very simple; the teacher merely placed a check alongside his errors. On the day following this procedure, his answers for the zero, as well as the nonzero problems, were all correct. Throughout the next twelve days, he missed only four problems, none of which were zero problems.

Although this boy had erred on the zero problems for many days, once instruction—minimal instruction at that—was scheduled, his learning was immediate. In this case, obviously, feedback was extremely effective; a lengthy acquisition period was not required.

FLASH CARDS PULLED HIM THROUGH

In this situation, a boy was assigned two sheets of multiplication problems daily. Simple facts were included on one sheet: problems like 3 x 1 = [ ] and 4 x 2 = [ ]. The second sheet contained harder facts like 8 x 3 = [ ] and 7 x 4 = [ ].

Throughout a baseline condition, no instruction was given for either sheet. During this period, the pupil's accuracy on the easy sheet was low, and he usually missed all the problems on the second sheet. During the next phase, instruction was directed toward the easy sheet; no instruction was provided for the hard facts. This instruction consisted of a five-minute flashcard drill prior to the measurement.

Sixteen days were required until performance on the easy facts reached a satisfactory level. Throughout that time, he obtained a score of zero for the hard facts on twelve of the sixteen days.

When criterion was reached on the easy facts, instruction shifted to the hard facts. On the first day following instruction, his scores were perfect. Throughout the next eighteen-day condition, when instruction was focused on the hard facts, his scores were perfect for twelve of those days. Only on one occasion did he miss as many as two problems. As was illustrated in the preceding example, learning here was immediate once teaching was scheduled for the troublesome behavior.

Projects such as these should be encouraging to teachers who have been assigned children with long histories of failure. It is entirely possible that many children who have performed inappropriately for long periods of time can be assisted to behave satisfactorily if their response patterns are carefully studied and if instructional techniques are arranged in accordance with those diagnoses.

Whether or not the research evidence of the future will prove the "sink or swim," "overlearning," or "errorless learning" proponents to be correct, I would like to make a final suggestion in regard to errors. I recommend that teachers do everything possible to deemphasize incorrect responses.

Some children are so nervous, so afraid of making a mistake, that they will not respond. If they do respond incorrectly, many times they are scolded and threatened. Teachers should very seriously consider how they react to these pupils who have erred. If they make fun of, scold, or punish such a youngster, he will quickly learn to avoid all potential learning situations. As a consequence of this curtailing of his responses, such a pupil will have no opportunities to adjust slightly mistaken responses. There are several approaches that may be considered as aids in reducing the tension of making errors, one of which is discussed at some length in the Epilogue.

Direct
Teaching

IF you want to teach kids to crawl, do it; if you want to teach them to read, do that. Just don't expect that when you teach kids to crawl, they'll learn to read.

For years in the world of education there have been advocates of indirect teaching. They have promoted the idea that if you want pupils to learn something, you should teach them something else. Long ago, people called sensationalists believed that the senses should be trained, and when they were developed to a high degree, other cognitive skills would emerge.

Itard, for example, was an early advocate of sensory stimulation. His major objective was to activate the nervous system of pupils by educating each of their separate senses. He developed a systematic sensory discrimination program that focused on the senses of taste, touch, temperature, and smell. This program was most conspicuously pursued in his long-term effort to teach Victor, his celebrated pupil. Itard apparently believed that once the senses were developed, other, more practical behaviors would either emerge on their own or could be taught rather simply.

137

Seguin, a student of Itard's, continued to advocate sensory instruction. In accordance with these theories, his first task in instructing pupils, particularly the mentally retarded, was to focus attention on their muscular systems. He believed it was most important to train the hand muscles and therefore encouraged teachers to foster the tactile curiosity of children initially. He recommended that the senses of taste and smell be emphasized next, followed by training and developing of the auditory sense. Finally, he turned to the development of visual abilities.

Maria Montessori was another believer in training the senses and muscles. Her original teaching materials, which consisted of twenty-six items, stressed the training of all the senses except those of taste and smell.

If the senses were highly developed in various didactic situations, early educators assumed that transfer of training to practical life situations would then occur. In other words, if children's senses of touch, vision, and hearing were trained to become more acute, they would be better able to learn to read, write, and cipher than if these senses had been less acutely developed.

The influence of these educational pioneers, particularly that of Montessori, is today widespread. Private schools which bear her name can be found in most cities of the world, some more authentic than others. Although some of these schools stress the notion of muscular and sensory development as prerequisites to cognitive development, many have diluted this emphasis and are reminiscent of other schools.

Currently, the most widespread practitioners of sensory training are Doman's and Delacato's disciples, who insist that muscular training is vital to the development of cognitive skills. When dealing with children with reading problems, for example, they hypothesize that such difficulties stem from the fact that some muscle or set of muscles was not fully developed at some time along the growth continuum. They advocate, therefore, that such children be developmentally reprogrammed, that they be retaught to creep and crawl and to generally engage in early muscular activities. They insist on the notion that if children are motorically reprogrammed and, as a result, become proficient in the use of complex motor skills, they will, in turn, be better able to read and write.

There are Doman-Delacato training camps throughout the

United States. Many learning disabled children are sent to these locations, where they receive the recommended exercise program. As I have said, among the most important of these drills are the creeping and crawling exercises. When a child is initially assigned to this regimen, several assistants aid in manipulating his limbs; in fact, several manipulative cadres alternate in the work, each one taking its turn for several minutes. The staff-to-client ratio in these camps is extremely high. Children here are also encouraged to participate in solo activities and are required to engage in other types of muscle and coordination exercises.

Another popular school of muscle development and body coordination was developed by Newell Kephart. He hypothesized that children must first become aware of their bodily parts and be able to coordinate their gross muscle movements before they develop more sophisticated cognitive skills. One of Kephart's favored techniques for developing muscle coordination is the Angels in the Snow routine. In order to carry out this training, the children are shown, as they are lying on the floor, a series of cards which depict the arms and legs in various positions. The children are then expected to arrange their bodies in positions matching the figures on the cards.

As to the effects of these sensory programs, it is likely that when children are taught to discriminate certain sounds, shapes, or movements the senses involved do develop. Furthermore, it is quite likely that if children are taught to move their bodies into positions that match a series of stick figures on placards, they will become adept at that skill. Finally, it is altogether possible that if children are to become proficient creepers or crawlers, instructional time can profitably be devoted toward those skills.

However, basing my judgment on my experience with children, particularly on the data I have scrutinized regarding transfer of training, I cannot support the strategy of developing the proficiencies of one skill by teaching another. Instead, I strongly recommend a more direct approach to instruction. That is, if a teacher wants to teach a certain behavior, that behavior should be taught, not another one.

In the past few years, we have arranged a few studies to inquire into this notion of transfer from one skill to another. In most of these experiments, the behaviors we taught and the ones we monitored for possible transfer were closely related, much closer than crawling and reading. Nevertheless, in most of our studies transfer did not occur. Following is a brief description of three such projects.

WE TAUGHT PART WORDS;
WHOLE WORDS DIDN'T DEVELOP

In this project, we were concerned about transfer of training from one reading element to another. Throughout, we measured the abilities of two pupils to say part words (certain letters or letter combinations), whole words, and to read in context. The whole words were from a basal reader and the part words were taken from them. For example, one of the whole words was *plate,* and one of the part words was *pl.*

During the next condition, instruction focused on whole any of the three skills. Following this phase, instruction was focused on only the part words. For a few minutes prior to the measurement of a particular skill, the teacher drilled the pupils on the various sounds. She also asked them to think of the words that began with these part words. Two or three part words were stressed each day.

Following a few days of instruction, the boys' performance on the part words greatly improved. During this time, however, their abilities to say whole words or to read in context did not show any change.

During the next condition, instruction focused on whole words. Before the daily measurement, the teacher drilled the boys on several words from the list. Following a few days' instruction, their performance improved significantly on the whole words. Once again, however, transfer did not take place. Even though their abilities to identify whole words improved, their abilities to read in context were unchanged. To summarize: when teaching was first directed toward part words, and then toward whole words, those skills successively improved. The indirect effects of instruction, however, were not observable on the whole words or words read in context.

Occasionally, however, under similar circumstances, transfer of training does occur—or seems to. A few years ago we ran a project very similar to the one just described. In it we obtained measurements in several part-word skills (discriminating short vowels, initial consonants, consonant blends, vowel digraphs) and in oral reading. During the baseline phase, no instruction was provided; throughout the next condition, teaching focused on the part words. The instructional effects were immediately noted on the part words, and the pupil also improved in oral reading, presumably because his part-word proficiency had improved. However it is possible that, even in this project, transfer did not take place. The boy's increased oral reading performance may have been the function of some variable still unaccounted for (Lovitt & Hurlbut, 1974).

WE TAUGHT WHOLE WORDS; PART WORDS DIDN'T DEVELOP

This project began about the same time as the preceding one. Throughout the study, we were curious about the possible retro-sequential effects of teaching whole words. The purpose was to find out whether or not training on whole words would generalize to part words. This objective is the reverse of that sought in the preceding study, where the concern was to measure the transfer effects from part words to whole words.

Throughout the project, we obtained daily measures regarding a pupil's ability to (a) identify part words, (b) identify whole words (say the words), and (c) read orally from a text.

Each day the pupil was asked to read from lists the sounds of twenty letters or letter combinations and twenty words. He was also required to read words orally in context. The words on the list were taken from the reader, and the part words were initial elements from those words; all the components were related.

As usual, a baseline phase was scheduled. Throughout this period, neither instruction nor feedback was arranged. Data from this phase revealed that the pupil's accuracy in all three areas was poor. He was very inept when required to say sounds and isolated words and to read in context. During the next condition, teaching was directed toward whole words. Each day, for about ten minutes before the measurements were obtained, the teacher drilled the pupil. She showed him, one at a time, flash cards on which were printed the same words that would subsequently appear on the test. If he correctly pronounced a word, she said "good" and advanced to the next card. If he did not know the word, she pronounced it for him and asked him to repeat it.

The effects of this drill were immediate and impressive. From the first day following instruction, the pupil showed improvement; in a few days, he correctly said all twenty words.

Meanwhile, measurement continued in the nontaught behaviors: saying part words and reading in context. The pupil did not improve in either of these skills. Later, however, when teaching focused directly on first saying part words and then on reading in context, the pupil's performance improved on the first behavior, then on the other.

This project illustrated once again that a simple teaching procedure was proved effective—but only on the behavior that was taught. Indirect effects, or transfer of teaching, were not indicated, even though the behaviors were closely related.

WE TAUGHT A CHILD TO MULTIPLY; IT DIDN'T HELP HIM DIVIDE

With this pupil, a fourteen-year-old educationally handicapped youngster, instruction focused on division. He knew the basic division facts like 6 ÷ 3 = [ ] and 18 ÷ 2 = [ ] but he had difficulty with problems like 396 ÷ 3 = [ ].

During a baseline period, he was required to solve 19 problems of the latter type. This baseline ran for about a week, and the data indicated that his performance was generally from 80 to 85 percent accurate. These data further revealed that the boy's rate of computing the problems was very slow. On the average, he worked the 19 problems at a correct rate of 1.5 problems per minute. In other words, it took him about 12.5 minutes to compute all of them. We had data which indicated that in order to be proficient with this type of problem, he should have been able to compute 19 of them in less than one minute.

It was the teacher's belief that the boy's lack of accuracy and speed was due to his inability to recall quickly the answers to the basic multiplication facts. She hypothesized that if he were more adept with those facts, he would be better able to divide. Therefore, she scheduled a ten-minute instructional period which preceded the daily measurement of the division problems. Each day during this period, the boy flipped through a set of multiplication flash cards as quickly as he could give the answers. During this time, the teacher monitored his responses to the cards and noted that, with few exceptions, his answers were correct. She also counted the number of correct answers during these sessions and divided that frequency by ten to determine his rate per minute for reciting answers to flash cards.

On the first day of the intervention, his correct rate for saying multiplication facts was seven per minute. On each succeeding day, his rate was faster; the last day of the intervention, some twenty-three days later, his correct rate was seventeen per minute. Thus, throughout the intervention phase, his rate more than doubled for saying multiplication facts. A rather substantial improvement, certainly.

Meanwhile, daily measures continued to be obtained as he

computed the 19 division facts, to determine whether the multiplication drill would influence his ability to divide. These data indicated there was no effect. Throughout the twenty-three days when the pupil practiced multiplication facts, neither his accuracy nor his correct rate increased for the division facts. His accuracy scores continued to be from 80 to 85 percent, and his correct rates continued to be about 1.5 problems per minute.

These three examples—two in reading, one in arithmetic—illustrated that when two or more behaviors were measured and teaching was directed toward only one, only the behavior taught improved. It should also be pointed out that the three projects differed in terms of sequencing. In the first example, part words, whole words, and reading in context were measured, and teaching was focused on part words, the element which was presumed to be the simplest In the second project, when the same behaviors were measured, teaching was scheduled for whole words, presumably a more advanced skill. In neither case, however, was transfer noted, either up or down the sequential path.

In the third project, a pupil's ability to compute two problem types—division and multiplication—was the topic. According to most mathematicians and teachers, both processes are of equal difficulty. In that project, when teaching was directed toward multiplication, no improvement in division was noted. Thus, generalization across processes did not occur.

At first glance, the case made in this chapter might appear to be contradictory to the subject matter of a later chapter, Generalization, where studies indicating that transfer actually took place are described. This apparent contradiction, however, should not be disturbing; it simply reinforces the fact that just as some pupils acquire individual behaviors at rates faster than those of other students, so are some pupils better able to generalize than others. Since we are well aware of the capricious nature of generalization, we should be greatly reinforced when generalization *does* occur; but when it does not occur, we must program for it. And, finally, when we realize that generalization, from even one closely related skill to another, is a "sometime thing," we should focus our teaching on what we want developed, not on something related to what we want developed. The next chapter is also concerned with this matter of directness.

More on
Direct Teaching

FOCUS on the behavior you want to develop, not on the
one you don't want.

Strange as it may seem, there are great numbers of teachers
who spend as much time trying to eliminate children's behaviors they do not want as they do attempting to develop the behaviors they do want. I have known many, for instance, who devote a large amount of time trying to eliminate the talk-outs and
out-of-seats of their youngsters. (Talk-outs are generally defined
as unsolicited outbursts, while out-of-seats refer to the times
children pop out of their chairs without asking permission.)

Ask any group of teachers what their major problems with
children are, and these two behaviors—talk-outs and out-of-
seats—will invariably make the top ten. They demand more
classroom time, for some teachers, than instruction in reading,
training in listening, or the development of creative writing
skills.

Many teachers admit that they devote too much time to
curtailing behaviors and resent the fact that these duties take
time from their teaching. Some do not like to be the heavies, or

144

wardens, of the school. They would rather promote a calm, pleasant atmosphere where everyone is quiet and eager to learn.

Many teachers, however, although they agree that more time should be spent developing behaviors than trying to eliminate them, believe it is first necessary to reduce behaviors like talk-outs and out-of-seats before they begin teaching. They insist that instruction can begin only when all the pupils are sitting quietly and are never talking out of turn. They fondly hope that when pupils reach this passive state their little minds will be so open and receptive that teaching them will be a thing of beauty and a joy forever.

I would have to agree in part with some of these worries about noise and other disturbances. I am strongly convinced, however, that when a teacher becomes obsessively concerned over one of these so-called interfering behaviors, she should take a sober, second thought and ask herself to assess her reasons for being so concerned.

Let us examine some of these exacerbating situations. A boy gets up from his chair several times a day and roams around the room. This can certainly annoy a teacher. Perhaps she fears that his walking around will interfere with his work—an entirely legitimate concern. What she should do, however, rather than merely attempt to curtail the walking, is to verify her hypothesis. She should measure the walker's performance during conditions in which he does and does not roam about the room. If his work is just as satisfactory when he roams as when he doesn't roam, then that reason for concern is out.

But there is another, even more obvious, reason for her concern. She may believe that his walking about the room bothers others. This hypothesis should also checked out by obtaining data from the other members of the class. If it is determined that he is indeed annoying others, his ambulatory activities should be curtailed. But if others are not troubled by his wanderings, the concern again is groundless.

Or the teacher may have a third concern over this behavior. She might reasonably fear that when one boy walks around the room others are going to imitate his actions. Once again, she should verify her suspicions with data—data revealing that others either do or do not imitate his behaviors. If they do begin to roam about, she should once again give thought to her concerns and subject them to analysis. Even if others were to imitate the erratic behavior, and the roaming was, in fact, harmful to them and to others, there still remains the possibility that certain pupils in the room *should* be allowed to roam freely, if they are reliable and independent enough to do so with propriety. Just as it would be ridiculous to teach all the children in the class using the lowest level reader or the easiest math problems, it is foolish to treat all pupils the same way regarding other behaviors. Even the most reactionary teacher professes some ideas and concerns about individualization.

But the point I am trying to make here is that some teachers are overconcerned about nonproblems. One of the primary features of the measurement system advocated throughout this text is that by invoking its aid a teacher can discover when a concern is, in fact, a problem and when it is not. When hard data are obtained, she is reliably informed as to whether out-of-seat or some other "interfering" behavior is hindering the work of others. If it is harmful, than appropriate action can be taken.

There is another matter arising from these disturbing behaviors in a classroom. If the teacher has first determined that such actions are deleterious, that some pupil's production is low because of them, she should candidly examine her own behavior and the general atmosphere of her classroom. She may discover that she required the children to work on childish, dumb, or repetitious programs. If she is sensitive to the results of her self-study, she might well wish to alter certain aspects of her program and to determine how this change influences the behavioral problems and the production of the class.

Other factors may conceivably account for low production and behavioral problems. Maybe the teacher is a crab; all she does is nag and reprimand. Maybe she is nonreinforcing: she never praises her children; all she does is threaten and find fault. If such a teacher were to begin to nag less, to ignore certain inappropriate behaviors, and to praise certain good behaviors, the atmosphere of the class might improve mightily. The behavior problems would be reduced and the production level increased.

In many instances only very minor alterations, such as those just mentioned, will alter the mood of the class dramatically. It isn't at all necessary to rebuild a classroom system totally by instituting dozens of complicated techniques in order to attenuate the naughty behaviors. A minor tune-up can bring about positive changes.

Still another strategy the teacher beleaguered with behavioral problems should consider is to focus on reciprocal behaviors. Suppose there is a child in the class who has a high rate of uttering inappropriate words or phrases or a boy who, for no apparent reason, swears or uses language that is generally offensive. Let's assume that the language of both children *is* annoying to the privacy or productivity of others. The teacher obviously would want to curtail such speech. She does not want, however, to eliminate all speech; she has worked hard to increase her pupils' verbalizations and to allow them to express their needs and communicate with others over a wide range of topics. But, at the same time, she feels duty-bound to reduce the type of verbalizations that are annoying and nonproductive.

In such instances, teachers should focus more on developing the behavior they want developed, than on eliminating the one they want eliminated. A situation of this type is explained in some detail in a later chapter, Children as Managers. In that example, a boy let forth some highly inappropriate phrases from time to time. The teacher's concern in the project was to eliminate the inappropriate verbalizations and to develop a more appropriate verbal repertory. Techniques were incorporated to decrease one form of verbalization and increase another. In general, these efforts, as will be noted, were successful.

Several examples come to mind of instances in which teachers were able to focus on the reciprocal of the naughty behavior. For example, adults are often disturbed by children who are impolite, and a common strategy used to improve their manners is to punish impoliteness and ignore politeness. I would suggest the opposite approach; the teacher should reinforce politeness and perhaps ignore impoliteness. The pupil would be praised or reinforced in some other way for being polite, rather than being scolded or reprimanded for being impolite. Another situation in which a reciprocal intervention would be appropriate arises with the pupil who is a chronic latecomer to school. He should be reinforced for prompt attendance, rather than punished for his tardiness.

Another strategy for dealing with misbehavior is to develop behaviors that are incompatible with the behaviors of concern. This approach is somewhat similar, but not exactly so, to the strategy just described, that of developing a reciprocal behavior. An instance of focusing on an incompatible behavior would arise if the behavior of concern was stealing. To be sure, there is no single reciprocal behavior to stealing; "not stealing" is not a specific behavior. And nonstealing might well be sleeping, writing, killing, praying—anything but stealing. However, a behavior that *is* incompatible with stealing is guarding. Let us examine the case of a boy who is suspected of being the head thief of the watermelon patch. One rehabilitation approach some adults might take would be to punish him or to put him in time out (prison). If, however, the incompatible behavior approach was used, the boy would be appointed to be the guardian of the watermelon patch. His ability to perform as an effective guard would then have to be reinforced.

This approach has a lot going for it. For one thing, who knows more about stealing watermelons than the head thief? He would know all the tricks and would, therefore, be wise to all the techniques of pilferers who were less competent. This strategy, of course, has been widely used and often very successfully. Witness the highly effective work of former alcoholics with current alcoholics, of former drug addicts with current addicts.

Obviously, this strategy, like any other, can be overdone. It appears to me, however, that those individuals who developed "competencies" in regard to certain inappropriate behaviors, then decided not to use those behaviors and developed other, more negotiable behaviors, have many of the credentials for being excellent teachers. Not only would they know how to deal with problem behaviors, but if they have developed alternative responses, they have evidence that they are capable of change—an important ingredient for being a teacher, one that most teachers do not have.

Whatever strategy the teacher uses to assist children—whether she changes the classroom into a more motivating environment, focuses her energies on a reciprocal behavior, or concentrates on creating incompatible behavior—she will indeed find it profitable to spend more time in developing rather than eliminating behaviors. Following are two projects that dealt positively with irksome behaviors.

A RECIPROCAL TECHNIQUE: DEVELOP APPROPRIATE TALK-OUTS

This study extended over a period of sixteen weeks and took place during a group discussion period in an EEU classroom. Two of the boys in the group were eight years old, the other was seven. Several mornings a week, the three boys and their teacher were seated at a table. The topics they discussed were stories from a Lippincott reader they had previously read. The period generally lasted for ten minutes.

One of the purposes of the discussion period was to provide the boys with information about the stories they had read. Another objective was to encourage them to raise their hands, be recognized by their teacher, then interact with the group by asking a question, answering a question, or telling about some personal incident related to the day's topic. One of the recorded behaviors throughout this period, and the focus of this report, was the hand raising of the three boys.

During the first phase of the project, the teacher recorded each hand raise, tallying when she acknowledged the pupil and he responded in some way. Throughout this phase, the teacher found the frequencies of this behavior low: for Scott, a median of ten hand raises per session; for Greg, five; and for John, fourteen.

The teacher also observed during this discussion period that there were a number of inappropriate talk-outs. Many times, in the heat of an interchange, the boys blurted out an answer, outbursts which interrupted another youngster who was talking and which resulted in a debate as to who had the floor. Such arguments often spoiled the discussion; it was sometimes quite a problem for the teacher to guide the trio back to the topic at hand.

Since talk-outs appeared to be interfering with an activity the teacher believed to be worthwhile, she wanted to eliminate the disturbance. The most common way of dealing with this problem would be a frontal attack; the teacher would punish the child each time he spoke without raising his hand. In this situation, however, she did not wish to use this method for fear the boys would stop speaking entirely. She simply wanted them to share talking and listening time in better fashion.

Therefore, instead of punishing the children each time they spoke without being recognized, she used a reciprocal technique, that is, she reinforced appropriate hand raises. Throughout the second condition of the project, when this technique was used, she asked two of the boys to record their hand raises. She had reason to believe that self-recording would serve as a reinforcer, since this technique had been successfully emphasized in a number of other projects. Her hypothesis was that if the self-recording of hand raising was reinforcing, the boys would appropriately raise their hands more often, and, in addition, would talk out of turn less often.

During this phase, the rates of the two boys who recorded

their hand raises accelerated; John's to a median of thirty-three per session, and Greg's to twenty-eight. Meanwhile, Scott's rate remained constant. His baseline median was twelve hand raises per session, and his median rate stayed about the same during the two-week period in which the other boys self-recorded.

Throughout the third part of the project, which ran for three weeks, Scott was asked to tally his hand raises. During this time his median number of hand raises increased to a rate of eighteen per session. Routinely, during those periods when the pupils recorded their own behaviors, the teacher checked their accuracies. She reported that her tally agreed closely with theirs.

A fourth phase was then begun at the same time for all the pupils. During this period, they were asked not to tally their hand raises; the teacher, however, continued to record them. During this final phase, the median hand-raising rates for John and Greg were the same as they had been during the pupil-recording phases. John's rate for the two adjacent phases was thirty-three and Greg's was twenty-eight. During this phase, however, Scott's median rate was lower than during the pupil-recording period. His hand raises fell from eighteen per session to thirteen.

During the conditions in which the boys recorded their hand raises, the teacher noticed that there were very few talk-outs. Apparently, since the boys were reinforced by recording their hand raises, they did not want to waste an opportunity to be reinforced by blurting out a statement.

The teacher also observed that the responses from the boys became more sophisticated as the project continued. Although they wanted to speak more often throughout the pupil-recording phases so as to gain recognition, they did not sacrifice quality in order to credit themselves with another tally.

Ellery Phillips, the director of Achievement Place, a home for delinquent boys in Lawrence, Kansas, has conducted a project similar to this one. In his investigation, the concern was the boys' promptness at mealtime. This is a problem faced by every parent, by no means just parents of delinquents! Phillips's technique for solving this problem was somewhat different from ordinary procedures, however, which would be to punish the late child by not giving him his food, lecturing him, or requiring him to perform some onerous task. Phillips used a reciprocal technique of giving points for promptness. If a boy was on time for a meal, he received 100 points. These points were redeemable for privileges about the home, such as staying up late or watching television.

The data from his project indicated the effectiveness of the technique. Throughout a baseline condition the boys were, on the average, ten minutes late. On some days they were as late as sixteen minutes. Throughout the second condition, when Phillips rewarded promptness, there was great improvement. On the average, the boys were only three minutes late to their meals.

AN INCOMPATIBLE TECHNIQUE: DEVELOP COOPERATION

This project involved two second grade boys who fought with each other. The teacher noted that their fights occurred at different times of the day: before school, during recess, as the pupils lined up for various activities, and after school. She decided, therefore, to count the frequency of the fights throughout the day.

A fight was defined as any physical activity the pair engaged in. If one boy struck the other and the second boy retaliated, that was a fight. If one boy hit the other and the victim did not reciprocate, that was not a fight. If the two boys only teased one another, which they often did, or threatened one another, that was not a fight either.

During the baseline phase, which lasted for five days, the teacher discovered that, on the average, the boys fought seven times a day. During the second phase of the project, Etch-A-Sketch was introduced. This is a shallow plastic box which contains a clear slate and graphite. There are two knobs on the box. When one knob is turned, a graphite line moves vertically. When the other knob is dialed, the line moves horizontally. When the two are moved simultaneously, the line moves in different directions depending on the speed with which either knob is turned. Prior to recess each day, the two boys were given the Etch-A-Sketch and told to write on it the word *friends,* each manipulating one of the knobs. When they had written the word, each was then given an ice cream cone, and they were sent out to recess. For the first few days, it took the boys several minutes to complete the task. The data revealed that during this five-day phase the boys generally fought only once per day.

A second intervention phase was then established. Throughout that period, the boys had to write the word *friends* on their slate within ten minutes in order to receive the ice cream and be allowed to go out to recess. The reason this time limit was placed on their writing was that during the preceding phase, although the boys completed the required task, they argued a great deal. The teacher believed that if they were allotted less time to complete the task, they would argue less. The fight rate throughout this phase was nearly zero.

A final phase was instituted during which the ice cream contingency was withdrawn. The boys now continued to write *friends* within ten minutes before going to recess, but they were no longer given ice cream. The data from this phase revealed that the fighting did not recur.

The project was outlined to illustrate the strategy of focusing on an incompatible behavior. In this case, the teacher had identified what she believed was a problem: the fighting of the two boys. She had further decided that she should do something to stop the fights. Instead of punishing the young combatants for fighting, she rewarded them for cooperating, a behavior that is incompatible with fighting.

Usually, when teachers are confronted with similar problems, they design techniques to attack the problem directly, and an ingenious variety of punishment techniques have been used. In this instance, for example, the two boys might have been required to stay after school if they fought; their parents might have been informed of their fights; they might have been sent to the principal. Their teacher, as a matter of fact, had used those techniques and others with children who had engaged in fist fights in the past. Although some of those punishing techniques had been effective in curtailing overt aggression, she did not believe the "fighters" had actually learned to tolerate one another—they merely avoided each other, learning to fight in more discreet ways or when the teacher was not around. These alternatives the teacher wanted to avoid.

She did not necessarily hold the view that everyone in her class should love one another, but neither did she want to stimulate sophisticated sabotage and blackmail by eliminating overt scrimmages. She simply believed that if the boys were forced to perform some cooperative act they would fight less. Since one boy controlled the vertical and the other the horizontal knob of the Etch-A-Sketch, it required the cooperation of both operators to execute the task.

As is indicated by the reduction in fights throughout the project, her technique was successful. By the end of the experiment, the boys were not fighting at all. And they not only stopped fighting—they ceased arguing as well. The teacher could not say at the end of the project that the boys were now close friends, for they were not; but neither were they mortal enemies. They now talked to one another on occasion and spoke of one another with mutual respect.

As is the case with every strategy or hypothesis put forth in this book, the idea just discussed probably has its limitations. I am not certain just what they are, however, because most people have not tried to reduce inappropriate behaviors by building in other, more negotiable, behaviors. I would therefore recommend that more teachers spend more of their time developing rather than eliminating behaviors.

Perhaps one limitation of such a notion would be found in those instances where a naughty behavior was interfering with the development of a behavior, and there was neither an incompatible nor a reciprocal behavior on which to focus, or the teacher was not creative enough to conceive of one. In those instances, other strategies should be attempted for eliminating the misbehavior. One such procedure, described in an earlier chapter, Clarifying Expectations, would be to ask the child not to engage in the inappropriate behavior. As has been shown earlier, when children are consistently and precisely told what to do, they will often comply. Quite possibly, some of them will also *not* do what they are doing if they are told not to do it.

Although the notion described here stressed the idea of an indirect attack on the problem, this approach should not be confused with the method advocated in the previous chapter. There, I chided teachers who taught one thing when they were, in fact, intending to develop something else. I cited instances of teachers who had taught certain behaviors when they wanted others to develop and found that the latter behavior did not always emerge. At that point, however, the issue was whether to focus instruction directly on the behavior of concern or indirectly on a related behavior.

In this chapter, the issue was whether to develop or eliminate behaviors. Should a teacher focus her energies on developing behaviors that are indirect and often incompatible with an "interfering" behavior, or should she design an assault and attack the interfering behavior head on? There are times, of course, when it would be wasteful to develop an incompatible behavior; in such cases, a frontal attack would be a wiser strategy. I would like, however, to reemphasize the major argument of this chapter, if not of the entire book: it is the teacher's primary task to help others *develop* behaviors, not to eliminate them.

Generalization

SOME pupils, when taught something, actually do generalize that skill to different situations (just as they're supposed to).

Generalization, or transfer, is to a great extent what education is all about. We hope that when a student is taught one skill, that act of learning will facilitate the acquisition of other skills. If, for example, a student was taught that when 1 is added to 2 the answer is 3, and was able, in another situation, to respond to the problem 1 plus 3 by answering with a 4, she has generalized the concept of oneness. This type of generalization, when the pupil is taught to do certain problems and can also perform problems of about the same type that have not been taught, is commonly referred to as *response generalization*.

If a youngster is taught to do something in one situation, teachers also anticipate that she will display that same behavior in a different setting. If a pupil, for example, is taught to read certain words during reading class and can also read those words during a social studies assignment, she has evidenced a type of generalization. This type of transfer is referred to as *situational generalization*.

Generalizations do occur frequently, either from one response to another or from one situation to another. There are many times, however, when transfer, even though desired and expected, does not occur. Certainly, the projects cited in an earlier chapter, Direct Teaching, are indicative of the nontransfer phenomenon.

When generalization does not happen, the teacher has at least three options. One, she can scold the pupil for not transferring his learnings. Two, she can lament the fact that generalization has not occurred. Three, she can devise a program that will insure that generalization does happen. Obviously, the third option is the most practical of the three. If generalization does not take place, conditions must be arranged to teach either response or situational transfer.

Occasionally, as I have just noted, generalization does occur. In those instances, the teacher should be reinforced, since his direct teachings have been extended into other areas. He should count his blessings, for he has been spared the tedium of arranging one condition after another until generalization has taken place, until all the responses of a type have been learned or until the response has been built up in all possible situations.

Following are three instances where generalizations were noted. In the first two projects, the pupil generalized from one response to another; in the third, not only did response generalization occur, but situational generalization was also indicated.

A SUBTRACTION SKILL TRANSFERRED

The pupil in this project was an eleven-year-old boy. The behavior of concern was subtraction of the class 18 - 9 = [ ]. From a pool of problems of this type, two subclasses containing different problems were formed. Each day the boy was given two sheets, one from each subclass. Each sheet contained twenty-five problems (Smith, Lovitt, & Kidder, 1972, pp. 342-360).

During the baseline period, which ran two days, no instruction or feedback was provided. His percentage scores each day for both subclasses were zero.

In the next condition, instruction was focused on only one subclass. At this time, he was given eighteen paper clips and shown how to use them to obtain the answers. He was told that if the problem was 18 - 9 = [ ], he should remove nine clips from the total, count the remainder and then write down that number. He was allowed to use the clips as he worked one sheet (subclass) of problems, but not the other.

On the first day of this phase, his score on the sheet where he used the clips was 92 percent. Throughout the phase, which ran for nine days, his average score on the sheet continued to be high. Meanwhile, his score the first day on the sheet not associated with paper clips was also 92 percent; his average score for the entire phase was also quite high (see figure 12).

In the third condition of this project, the paper clips were removed; the pupil was required to do the subtraction problems without them. The data indicated that his average scores for both subclasses remained at nearly 100 percent.

Baseline data were then obtained on another class of problems, problems like 24 - 6 = [ ] which required borrowing. Again, two subclasses of problems were formed. Daily, the pupil was given sheets, one from each subclass, of twenty-five problems each. During the baseline phase, when no instruction was offered, his percentage scores on the two subclasses were very low.

Throughout the instruction phase, the pupil was given an abacus and was instructed on how to use it to solve subtraction problems. He was allowed to use the abacus, however, only when he worked the problems of one subclass. The data indicated that throughout this eight-day condition his average score on the problems where he used the abacus increased from 2 to 100 percent. Meanwhile, his average score on the subclass where he did not use the abacus increased from a baseline mean of 13 to 100 percent. In a condition following the abacus phase, the device was no longer available. His scores throughout this condition remained at nearly 100 percent on both subclasses.

Thus, generalization was noted for two types of subtraction problems. As the boy was taught to use paper clips and an abacus to solve certain subtraction problems, that ability generalized to other problems of the same classes where the devices were not used. Furthermore, in both instances when the devices were withdrawn, the boy's performance was maintained for both the subclasses where the aids were used and the subclasses where the aids were not available.

IDENTIFY LOWER- AND UPPERCASE LETTERS
AND MATCH LETTERS

Three behaviors were measured throughout this project: naming lowercase letters, naming uppercase letters, and matching lower- and uppercase letters. The pupil was a six-year-old boy.

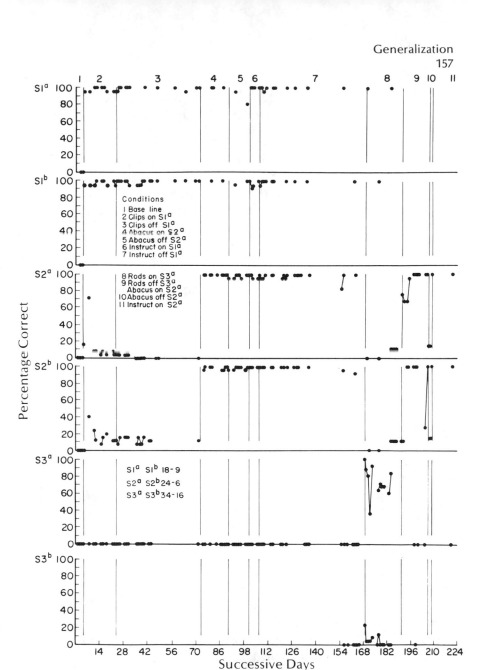

Figure 12. Percentage of correct scores on six subclasses of subtraction problems through the eleven-phase experiment.

One purpose of the project was to determine whether a simple teaching technique would facilitate the identification of lowercase letters. A second purpose was to determine the extent to which learning to identify lowercase letters would generalize to the identification of uppercase letters and to the matching of lower- and uppercase letters.

Each session was composed of three parts; each lasted for one minute. During one part, the pupil was required to name lowercase letters. For this task, cards with lowercase letters were randomly scattered on the floor. The pupil was required to pick up one at a time and name it. If he responded to all the cards within the minute, the process was repeated. The teacher scored all the responses as either correct or incorrect.

For the second part of each session, uppercase cards were placed on the floor. The procedures were identical to those used for the lowercase task. Throughout the third part of the session, the boy was asked to match lower- and uppercase letters. For this exercise, both stacks of letters were placed on a table, and the child matched the pairs.

During the baseline period, neither instruction nor feedback was provided for any of the tasks. Throughout the next condition, some instruction was scheduled which focused on only the lowercase letters. The teacher named some of the letters the pupil had been unable to identify. She then requested that he imitate her labeling, and when he did so, she praised him. This instruction lasted for about five minutes each day. The child was then required to name lowercase and uppercase letters as before.

During the baseline condition, the lad's median correct and incorrect rates for the lowercase identification were thirteen and eight letters per minute. In the instructional phase, his median rates were twenty and six letters per minute.

His correct and incorrect rates in the baseline condition for identifying uppercase letters were eighteen and seven letters per minute. From one day to the next, both rates were moving in a negative direction; the correct rate was going down, and the incorrect rate up. In the second phase, when instruction focused on lowercase letters, his rates improved; both rates moved in a positive direction.

b - d GENERALIZATIONS

A portion of this project was discussed in the first chapter to illustrate the point that when diagnosis is direct, teaching can be simple and immediate. To review, the teacher took baseline data as the pupil wrote words that began and ended with b and *d*. When she determined that his primary reversal problem was with the initial *d*, she focused an intervention on that component. Learning was almost immediate; a few days after instruction began the pupil no longer reversed initial or final *b*'s or *d*'s (D. Smith & Lovitt, 1973).

Following this project, the teacher wanted to know whether this *b* - *d* discrimination had generalized. In order to learn about this, she formed three lists of words: *(a)* a list of single syllable words (similar to those in the initial project); *(b)* a list of words that were longer than those used in the first experiment and that contained a *b* or *d* in initial or final position; and (c) a list of words that had *b* or *d* in medial position. Then, for three or four days, she asked the pupil to write those words as they were dictated to him.

Much to the teacher's delight, his performance was accurate on all three word lists; his initial *b* - *d* training had generalized to words of the same length, to longer words, and from initial-final position to medial position. Thus, response generalization had indeed occurred.

Next, the teacher wanted to determine whether this discrimination had generalized to another academic area. In order to obtain this information, she analyzed all the boy's penmanship papers before and after the *b* - *d* treatment. This analysis disclosed that although several reversals were made prior to the intervention, only a few were made after it. Situation generalization had also occurred; the boy was taught a skill in spelling that generalized to penmanship.

CERTAIN DESCRIPTIVE SKILLS TRANSFERRED

This project was conducted by a speech therapist a few years ago who ran the study to fulfill a requirement in one of my graduate classes. His objective throughout the study was to determine whether transfer would take place in connection with a child's ability to describe objects. The pupil was a three-year-old boy.

In order to obtain information on the direct and generalized effects of training, the speech therapist assembled two sets of objects. One was referred to as the Training Set and the other as the Generalization Set.

There were six objects in each set. In the Training Set were a butter knife, laryngeal mirror, pair of standard pliers, Boy Scout compass, cup hook, and hand magnifying glass. The six objects in the Generalization Set were similar: a rug knife, compact mirror, pointed pliers, center adjusted compass, door hook, and eye magnifying glass. As may be noted, objects selected for the Generalization Set were, in many respects, like those in the Training Set.

Throughout the project, the child was shown the Training Set objects individually and asked to describe them. After he had had an opportunity to describe these, he was asked to tell about the Generalization Set objects.

The pupil could score as many as seven points for each object. One point was given for use of each of the following: naming the object, its color, its shape, its composition, its size, its function, and its major parts. Throughout the project, the manager tallied the number and type of responses to each object.

The project was composed of two phases. Throughout the baseline, no feedback or instruction was offered. During the next phase, before requiring the boy to tell about the objects, some instruction was provided on only the six objects in the Training Set. During this time, the child was shown each item in the Training Set, one at a time, and told its name, color, shape, composition, size, use, and major parts.

Throughout the baseline phase, his ability to describe objects from both sets was severely limited. On several occasions, he could only name the objects and tell something about their function; he was unable to tell anything about other dimensions or features. During this period, his performance on both sets was about equal.

Throughout the second phase, direct and generalized effects of the training were indicated. Although significant change was not noted as the boy described the Training Set objects, improvement in every dimension except reference to size was indicated. The data further indicated that about the same amount and type of change was noted in regard to the Generalization Set. Thus, response generalization had taken place; about as much change was noted for the untaught objects as for those that were taught.

In the three projects just described, two types of generalizations are illustrated: response and situation. In the first project, generalization of a third type was also indicated; that is, when the teaching aids were removed, the boy's accuracy was maintained.

Perhaps the inability to generalize distinguishes learning disabled and mentally retarded children from their normal peers as much as do other learning characteristics. If this is true, surely some emphasis should be devoted to the matter of transfer. Conceivably, instructional programs or strategies can be designed that will promote generalization and maintenance. An argument can be made that it is as vital to develop strategies to foster generalization as it is to design systems to enable pupils to acquire specific skills.

Children
as Managers

SOMETIMES youngsters are better managers of behavior than adults.

Most of the time, adults—teachers and parents—are appropriate child developers. In times past, millions of children have been assisted by adult managers to develop billions of skills.

That children learn from other children, however, cannot be denied. Many of the games youngsters learn, some of their notions about sex, certainly their styles of interacting with others on whatever basis, are learned from other children.

Most parents are fully aware of this truth, particularly when they regard the playmate as being either superior or inferior to their child in reference to certain behaviors. Ordinarily, when the playmate is perceived as superior in some respect, their own child is reinforced for interacting with the peer. On the other hand, when the playmate has been regarded as inferior, they quickly admonish their progeny to dissolve the relationship and send Jimmy home.

Fred Keller, who has long observed the effects of peer instruction, experimented with and later endorsed a system for teaching psychology to college students based on peer instruction. As a result of his research, he recommended that the course offerings should be first broken into identifiable modules. The students were then required to learn the behaviors in each module. When they had studied a module, they took a test. If they passed the test with a specific degree of accuracy, they then advanced to the next module. And so on. These tests were administered by peers of the current students: pupils who had just finished the course themselves.

If, in the Keller system, a pupil needed help with a particular unit, he was assisted by a peer instructor, not by an adult professor. The latter was responsible only for working with the tutors and for managing the administrative elements of the system. It is Keller's belief that when students have difficulty in understanding certain concepts or in solving certain problems, peers can be of greater assistance than adults. There are apparently three reasons supporting his belief. For one, Keller contends that since peers have themselves only recently mastered the concepts or exercises of a course, they can remember the steps they went through to arrive at solutions. A second supporting factor is that peers can easily communicate the steps required to solve a problem, since in many instances they use a language quite different from that of adults. They explain matters with their unique—and mutually understandable—vocabulary. Later in this chapter, a project is described which illustrates this point. A third reason for this peer effectiveness has to do with the previous experiences of the peers. Most pupils have all their school lives been well aware that adults administer tests, assign grades, recommend promotions, and give praise and punishment. Knowing these things, students quickly develop tactics for dealing with adults, tactics which will convince adults that they are learning and are eager to learn more. When peers run the show, however, and do not themselves give tests and grades, their students often relax; they rechannel the energies they formerly used to "snow" the instructor into the business of really learning the new behaviors. They ask questions about assignments, admit occasionally that they do not understand an explanation, and laugh at themselves when they make mistakes. Often, when pupils are taught by peers, they become more receptive, for they have removed their facades. Following are four illustrative examples of this phenomenon.

CURTIS HELPED JON ELIMINATE HIS NASTY COMMENTS

This project was conducted a few years ago by my wife when she was teaching a class for learning disabled children. She had ten youngsters in the group, their ages ranging from nine to twelve. Most of them had attended regular classes for a few years, but because of moderate learning or social problems they were placed in classes for the learning disabled (T. Lovitt, A. Lovitt, M. Eaton, & M. Kirkwood, 1973).

For the most part, these pupils were well behaved; they worked hard and were generally good citizens. One boy in the class, however, occasionally spewed forth some highly inappropriate verbalizations. Several times a day, Jon uttered phrases that psychiatrists customarily classify as being either a bathroom or a sexual topic.

Ordinarily, when Jon uttered one of these obscenities, my wife frowned at him and told him that the classroom was not the place for such language. She also wrote down each of Jon's outbursts in an effort to discern any pattern—the list came to be referred to as "Jon's notable quotes." When the verbalizations were studied, however, the analysis revealed no consistent pattern. Although related thematically, no two were exactly alike, save only that they shared the common characteristic of being definitely inappropriate in a classroom.

Since one of the purposes of this class for learning disabled youngsters was to rehabilitate their learning and social problems, then send them back to a regular class, my wife was convinced that Jon's verbalizations must be altered; one full-blown instance of this kind of language in a regular class, and he would be dead. She therefore decided to study the problem seriously.

For a number of days throughout a baseline phase, while my wife continued to write down Jon's remarks, she tried to determine whether any particular incident was triggering the outbursts. But after a few days of data keeping and studying the circumstances, it appeared there was no consistent event that prompted Jon's comments.

However, my wife noticed, during this baseline period, that Jon and Curtis, the boy who sat behind him, were very close friends. Jon, on occasion, would even turn around and ask Curtis if he liked him. Curtis candidly replied that either he did or he did not. Sometimes he said, "Yes, Jon, I like you," whereas on other occasions when Jon had done something Curtis was not pleased with, he responded to Jon's query with, "No, Jon, I don't like you when you do things like that." When Curtis admonished Jon in this way, my wife noticed that Jon would hang his head and mutter, "Curtis doesn't like me." She further observed that during such interactions Curtis never teased or made fun of Jon. It appeared that he was sincerely interested in Jon's welfare.

She decided, therefore, on the basis of these observations, to use Curtis as Jon's manager, in an effort to reduce his inappropriate verbalizations. Before beginning this stage of the project, she took Curtis aside and explained the situation to him, saying that she was not pleased with Jon's nasty words, that they must be stopped, and that Curtis could help. He agreed that Jon's words "were bad" and that he would help. My wife told Curtis that when Jon made one of his outbursts he was to go to Jon and say, "Jon, I don't like to sit by you when you say _____ _____ _____." Then Curtis was to slide his desk away from Jon's. After a period of time, generally following the completion of some activity, if Jon walked back to Curtis and talked about something appropriate, Curtis was to move his chair back to its original position.

So far so good. Curtis seemed to understand the plan, and when he was sure of these rehabilitation steps, he went to Jon and informed him about the whole arrangement.

On the day the plan went into effect, Jon let fall two outbursts. Subsequently, Curtis executed his part of the plan perfectly. He went to Jon, repeated what had been said, that he did not like it, and declared he was moving away. Later, when Jon came back to him in an effort to placate his manager with appropriate talk, Curtis responded at once by sliding his desk back toward Jon's. During the next few days, there were no incidents. After a week there was only one lapse; again Curtis reacted appropriately.

After this procedure had been in effect for about fifteen days and was running smoothly, a new boy, Jim, was assigned to the class. Since my wife did not anticipate any problems from Jim, he was seated alongside Jon. To her dismay, however, he began to taunt Jon from the moment he entered the class. Apparently Jon's reputation was widespread, for Jim did his best to elicit some of Jon's choice remarks. After a few taunts he was successful; Jon delivered, and Curtis reacted. Then Jim elicited another obscenity; Curtis reacted again. Curtis was beside himself, for on that day Jon delivered five of his remarks!

At the end of the day, my wife and a frustrated and ex-hausted Curtis convened. Curtis said, "Jim caused all the stuff." My wife agreed and decided to talk with Jim the first thing in the morning in order to arrange a contingency for *him*. This arrangement specified that for each attempt to elicit an outburst from Jon he would lose a recess.

The next day, after the contingency was explained, Jim behaved himself, Jon used only appropriate speech, and Curtis remained stationary. At the end of the day, my wife complimented all three boys. This arrangement ran for another ten weeks until the end of the school year. After the traumatic first day of Jim's entry into the class, there were no more outbursts from Jon.

Prior to Jon's placement in this class, he had received "aid" from several professionals. He had been from one clinic to another; from a psychiatrist to a clinical psychologist, from a guidance counselor to a social worker. The primary reason he had been sent to these professionals was because of his bizarre language. Upon reading the reports of Jon's visits to these agencies, we learned that the professionals were greatly concerned about Jon's obsession with "bathroom and sexual topics," as were all of his former teachers.

But a whole cadre of specialists and classroom teachers, despite their long and varied efforts, had been unable to clean up Jon's dirty talk. (This is not to say that had they used different techniques with Jon they would not have been successful.) The fact remains, however, that when a compassionate peer, Curtis, was given some straightforward procedures to use with his friend, he successfully altered the objectionable behavior. He was successful where all the learned adults had failed.

A conclusion to this story is that Jon continued to behave appropriately, as my wife learned from his next year's teacher. He had made no inappropriate announcements throughout the year, even though his new class was not based on contingency management.

PEERS RECORDED TALK-OUTS

This project took place with fourteen fourth graders in a remedial math class. Each day these pupils met for forty-five minutes. The purpose of the class was to assist the students to develop math skills equal to the abilities of their peers.

The teacher of the class was not pleased with the performance of the youngsters and believed that more improvement would be noted in these remedial sessions if there was less talking out of turn. Since she had pinpointed talk-outs as the behavior of concern, she began tallying each infraction during a baseline phase in order to determine the extent to which this behavior occurred. For a period of six days, she made a mark on a piece of paper each time a pupil talked out. When these data were analyzed, it was revealed that, on the average, there were about thirty-five talk-outs each period, slightly less than one per minute. (Throughout this project, the teacher did not obtain data in regard to arithmetic performance in order to learn [as was discussed in an earlier chapter, More on Direct Teaching] whether the talk-outs were, in fact, hampering the academic performances of the pupils.)

During the next condition of the project, students were randomly paired. They were then instructed to record the talk-outs of their partners. Throughout this condition, the data indicated that the pupils talked out of turn about twenty-two times each day—far less than they had during the preceding condition when the teacher herself recorded the talk-outs.

A third condition was then scheduled during which time the teacher once again recorded the talk-outs of the fourteen pupils. The infractions during this phase increased to about thirty-five times each session. In this class, insofar as talk-outs were concerned, it would seem that peers were better managers than the teacher. Whether or not similar findings would occur for children of different ages or for other "naughty behaviors" are other questions; more experimentation must provide those answers.

PEER POWER—HOW TO EXPLAIN

Another instance of the ability of a peer to educate a child was recently brought to my attention. Although no data are involved in this case, it amply supports Keller's contention that peers are sometimes better explainers than adults.

The setting was an elementary school class where a pupil had encountered in his reading the word *italics*. He went to his teacher and asked for an explanation of the word. In response, she began the explanation by citing situations in which italics should be used. She explained, for example, that a word was italicized when the author wanted to attach particular stress and emphasis to that word and that foreign words were sometimes italicized. The pupil seemed to understand these uses, but he then wanted to know what italics looked like. In response, the teacher said the italic letters differed from ordinary typography in that the letters slanted up and to the right and had other differentiating characteristics. But when she saw the pupil's uncomprehending, yet inquiring, expression greeting her efforts, she realized she had not been successful.

Meanwhile, throughout this explanation, another pupil had been standing by watching this "learning experience." It was obvious to him that his friend had not caught on, so he offered an explanation. "You know what they are, Mike," he said, "they're those bent letters!" Whereupon Mike looked at his peer with a relieved expression and said, "Oh, I see," and walked off. The teacher shrugged her shoulders, and she too walked off—to "instruct" another pupil.

LEARNING BY TEACHING: OLDER BOY TEACHES YOUNGER BOY

A few years ago a resource teacher in one of my classes at the University of Washington conducted a project where she obtained data from both participants in a teaching situation: the pupil and his manager. They had been referred to her by their classroom teachers because of their poor penmanship. Previous efforts to assist them in the classroom had failed to bring about improvement.

One boy was thirteen years old and a seventh grader. He had, for the past several years, received tutoring assistance in penmanship, as well as in other subjects. He had gone from one remedial instructor to another. When he entered seventh grade, however, he asked his parents to end the tutoring, and his request was granted. The second boy was an eight-year-old third grader. His teachers reported that he had problems with many visual-motor activities, including handwriting.

A favorite hypothesis of the resource teacher's in regard to learning was that the best way to learn is to teach. She therefore arranged a situation whereby the older boy instructed the younger boy. Another of her pet theories was that managers would be more effective if they were reinforced for pupil improvement rather than for simply putting in time. Therefore, she arranged a situation so that the older boy would receive payment dependent on the penmanship improvement of his pupil.

The project comprised three conditions: baseline, training, and maintenance. During the baseline period, both boys wrote a series of letters and words for five minutes. Following this period, the teacher checked each letter and scored it as either correct or incorrect. Since the penmanship of both boys was very poor, she was rather lenient in her evaluations; she was more concerned about basic legibility than about writing as an art form. If she could read the letters or words without too much effort, they were scored as correct.

Each day the number of correct and incorrect letters was graphed. Throughout the baseline phase, the data indicated that both boys formed most of their letters incorrectly.

Prior to the training condition, the adult manager and the older boy met for a planning session and agreed on the teaching method that would be arranged for the younger boy. It was decided that prior to the daily five-minute measurement period, the tutor would administer four teaching activities. The purpose of the first was to relax the pupil; for two or three minutes the tutor led him through a series of physical exercises which included jumping jacks, throwing darts, and playing catch with a softball. The second focused on visual discrimination and visual memory; the pupil worked on tracing and copying and was also shown objects, designs, and symbols and asked to recall what he had seen. The third involved modeling; the tutor wrote letters, one at a time, on the board, and the pupil, using these as models, was required to write the letters himself. The fourth period was devoted to writing phrases; here the tutor handed the pupil a paper on which were written a number of phrases, and he was then required to copy them.

As the reader will note, the tutor assigned his pupil a fair number of teaching techniques. Since the older boy had himself been tutored, he had a vast repertory of teaching techniques. He apparently believed, as do many adult teachers, that if pupils are to succeed rapidly, many approaches must be used simultaneously. (Some discussion regarding instructional overkill was included in an earlier chapter, Some Teaching Procedures Are Complex.)

Not only did this battery of instruction precede each five-minute writing session throughout the second condition of the project, but a reinforcement system was also in effect during this phase. At the end of each session, the pupil was given one point for each correctly formed letter. These points could be exchanged for money at the rate of one cent for every ten points. The tutor received a matching number of points each day, one for each point earned by the pupil.

The handwriting of both boys greatly improved throughout this phase. Each day they were credited with about 75 percent accuracy. During baseline, neither boy scored over 40 percent correct. Interestingly enough, the handwriting improvement for both boys was about the same.

Following this twelve-day instructional phase, a third condition was arranged, throughout which neither the instruction nor the reinforcement arrangement was in effect. The situation returned to what it had been in the baseline phase. The data from this third phase indicated that writing accuracy remained at the level it had attained during the teaching-reinforcement phase: about 75 percent.

Although, as I admitted at the outset, perfection was not reached by either boy, substantial progress had been noted in only a few days. The significant aspect of this project was that a peer was better able to teach a pupil than a number of adults had been previously. Some vital ingredient shared by the two boys, which was apparently missing when they were being "taught" by adults, resulted in their progress.

Many years ago, the use of peers as teachers was an integral part of the educational system. Back in the days of the country schoolhouses, when there were a dozen or so pupils in the entire school—first through eighth graders—the older children often taught the younger ones. The teacher maintained overall surveillance of the class, but much of the actual teaching was conducted by the youngsters. As the teacher worked with one group in reading, older youngsters assisted younger pupils in computing. As the teacher assisted some pupils in writing, the older ones helped their younger mates to memorize important historical dates.

Although schools at that time did not keep data which pertained to pupil growth, and certainly were not interested in educational research, there is no doubt that many pupils learned, and learned well, from their peers. Apparently, when the appropriate conditions for teaching are arranged, people other than "teachers" can teach very well. A later chapter in this book provides examples of parents as teachers.

Several interesting research projects could be arranged to determine the extent to which peers can teach peers. In the examples provided here, they were effective with a language behavior, penmanship, and talk-outs. It would be of additional interest to determine the general age at which children become more effective as teachers than adults. My premise is that, ordinarily, primary age children are much more reinforced by adults than by peers; but that in the third, fourth, or fifth grades the reinforcement systems of most youngsters change in such a way that they are more influenced by their peers.

As is suggested by the penmanship example, not only can peers be effective teachers, but they can also, in the process of teaching, learn certain skills themselves. There are possibly three reasons for the popular belief "the best way to learn is to teach." One relates to the initial presentation of a skill. If, for example, the basketball coach wishes to demonstrate dribbling to his pupils, he would be well advised to practice this skill beforehand. And, in doing so, he is quite likely to find his own performance improving.

A second reason derives from those instances in which the learner asks for information the teacher does not possess. When I was taking Spanish, for example, I occasionally asked questions about grammar that the teacher could not answer. She therefore had to look up the information prior to the next lesson and, conceivably, learned more about grammer herself in the process.

A third reason lies in a situation where the logic or reasoning of the teacher is challenged. For example, when I am expounding in one of my classes on what I consider to be a carefully thought-out progression of events leading to a logical conclusion, and an interested student challenges some step along the way, I invariably learn from the interchange, particularly if his challenge is new and has substance. If my thinking was, in fact, wrong, I am forced to reconstruct the steps. If I was right, but a new argument has been posed, I am forced to think some more and develop a suitable counterargument.

Whether or not people do in fact learn from teaching is still subject to research. Although many educators, I am sure, share my belief (and that of the resource-room teacher who arranged the penmanship study) that individuals do learn from teaching, only limited proof is available as yet to support the hunch.

Parents
as Teachers

EVEN parents can teach their children if they follow a few
simple rules.

"I can teach anyone but my own child." "Parents are the worst
teachers for their own children." "Don't let parents try to teach
their children how to read." "So you're a great piano player; if
you want your girl to learn, send her to another instructor."
Such comments made by and about parents have been around
for years on end.

When the topic of teaching and children comes up, parents
are full of stories about their attempts to teach their own children to do something, anything—read, play the piano, swim,
string beads, bowl, sew, you-name-it—which ended up with everyone screaming at everyone else. I have heard of fathers and
sons, mothers and daughters who have become lifelong enemies because the parent tried to teach his offspring how to drive
the family car.

Failures

On this touchy subject, I will have to admit to some failures of my own. Several years ago, for example, I tried to teach my daughter Kathy to play the trumpet. For a while it worked, but after a few more weeks I was screaming, and she was crying and threatening to run away from home. Nor did it work out much better when I tried to teach my oldest boy, Mark, to write more legibly. I did not allow our antagonism to reach the level that it had reached between my daughter and me, however, for I disengaged myself much sooner.

Along with these failures, I have had some small successes; occasionally, I have actually taught my children a skill or two. My biggest instructional coup came when I taught my second oldest boy "to read." Actually, I did not teach him to read from the beginning, but I was able to give him quite a boost in the right direction.

This instruction began when he was in the second grade. The teaching situation was precipitated by a teacher conference sometime before Christmas at which it was announced that Bryan was a poor reader. I was shocked; I couldn't believe it. I a college professor, an educator, one who deals with learning and development, with a boy who couldn't read!

That night I talked to Bryan about his reading, asked him whether he liked it, what his group did during reading, how he liked his teacher. Then I asked him to read from a second grade reader I had borrowed from his teacher. Sure enough, Bryan was a poor reader. Many thoughts ran through my mind. I blamed his teacher; I blamed him; I blamed his basal reader; I blamed myself.

Later, when I had settled down a bit, I realized that since Bryan could not read too well, and his teacher apparently assumed little responsibility for his condition, someone else would have to take over the job. Why not I? I had taught lots of other children to read. I had also taught lots of other people to teach reading to lots of other children. Surely I could teach my own son. But then I remembered my failures: my daughter and the trumpet, my son and his penmanship. I became increasingly apprehensive about beginning the lessons.

But, having no choice in the matter, I began. Each evening at about six-thirty we went into my office and Bryan read orally. I used the borrowed second grade book and required him to read four pages a night. As he read I gave him a reasonable amount of praise, and each time he made an error I told him what the word was and wrote it down on a sheet of paper. Following the session, I wrote out each word he had missed on a three-by-five inch card and plotted on a graph the number of errors he had made. Each day before Bryan began to read orally we rehearsed the words he had missed the previous day.

If he made fewer than four errors on the four pages he was advanced to new material. If he missed four or more words, he was required to read the same pages the next day. The total reading session, including oral reading and practice, required about five minutes.

Bryan and I had no problems; we didn't argue, I didn't scream, and he didn't cry. There were nights when he would have preferred to go directly to his television watching, but once he began reading, everything was all right. He knew that the reading session would be short. But even more important, he knew he was improving, for he made few errors and progressed through the book very rapidly. Not only did his oral reading speed improve, but he began talking more and asking more questions about the stories he had read.

By the end of the school year, Bryan's teacher said his reading was about on a par with that of the other children in the class. She was greatly relieved. I think she believed that I had simply had a man-to-man talk with Bryan and told him to quit goofing off during reading, and he had improved. She apparently did not know I had been working with Bryan at home, which was too bad because what I could have done, by teaching Bryan myself after she had told me of his problem and then sending him back to school an able reader, would have been to reinforce her role as a diagnostician. Some teachers are already heavily into this role. They tell the parents their child is bad or dumb, and it is up to the parents to fix him up and send him back to school for further diagnosis. Bryan's teacher was a shining example of a teacher who preferred diagnosis to teaching.

But back to parents as teachers. What was the difference? Why was I able to teach Bryan when I had failed with Kathy and Mark? Obviously I do not know all the reasons, but I have some inklings that may conceivably explain the differences. In fact, I see four differences in procedure that accounted for the success of the reading project.

First, I established a set time. I arranged a specific time of the day and stuck to it. In our project, the session was held each evening at about six-thirty. Almost anything can interfere with teaching if it is allowed to intrude. Since teaching and learning have so long been associated with punishing circumstances, very low strength activities compete with instruction. Such competition is more difficult, however, if a set time is scheduled.

Second, I scheduled short sessions. The time allotted for our sessions was about five minutes. The daily period required for teaching need not be long. I am more and more convinced that if the skills to be taught are clearly defined, the time required for instruction can be quite short. If the instructional period is brief—five or ten minutes—time for teaching can easily be found. Thirty-minute periods are too long; an entire TV show would be missed. Many behaviors can be learned over a reasonable period of time if a short session each day is devoted to practicing that skill.

Third, my responses were consistent. When Bryan missed a word, I simply wrote it down with little display of emotion. It is extremely important for the teacher-parent to determine what he will do when an error is made. Whatever response is chosen, it must be consistent. Some parents display a crescendo effect toward errors; they ignore the first few, then gradually respond to them with increasing concern. Finally, after a mounting number of errors have been made, panic sets in, and the parent explodes. He lashes out violently at his child, for now he realizes, or at least he fears, that he has spawned an idiot.

Fourth, I kept a record. In our project I kept a daily record of errors. By this time, a plug for daily record keeping should come as no surprise to the readers of this book, for that is one of the prime messages. Unless records are kept, the parent and child are never aware of the exact effects of the teaching. Furthermore, when a record is kept, it comes dispassionately between the teacher and the learner; the emotional distance between the pair is increased, and the emotional stress between them is correspondingly decreased.

Following are four projects where mothers taught their children. In the first example, a girl was taught to subtract; in the second, a girl learned to string beads; in the third, a boy learned to subtract; in the fourth, the mother worked with her entire family.

REINFORCEMENT CONTINGENCY, SELECTING DINNER MENU

The pupil was a seven-year-old girl in the second grade. The young lady was of normal intelligence, according to her teacher, but was having problems with her subtraction facts. The girl's mother conducted this project in the early afternoon in the home.

The pupil was required to work on subtraction problems for one minute each session. Daily she was given five sheets; each contained twenty problems of the type 3 −2 = [   ] and 11 − 1 = [   ]. Although the problems on each sheet were of the same class—the remainder was ten or less—no two were exactly alike. The pupil responded to them for one minute; more were presented than could be finished. I should point out that in those projects where the same measurement time is scheduled, for example, ten minutes, more materials should be provided than can be completed. (If the pupil's rate of response is desired, and the pupil finishes the material before the specified time is up, the rate calculation, computed by dividing the frequency by time, is invalid.)

During the baseline condition, the mother corrected the problems that had been answered and handed the sheets back to the girl. Each correct answer was marked with a C, while each error was underlined. No further instruction was provided.

Throughout the next condition, a menu contingency was arranged. During this phase, if the girl's correct rate equaled or exceeded fifty answers per minute, she was allowed to select the menu for that night's meal. She could determine everything that would be eaten that evening, from salad to dessert.

Throughout the third phase, the contingency was arranged for both correct and incorrect rates. Now, if her correct rate equaled or exceeded fifty, and her incorrect rate equaled or was less than three, she was allowed to schedule the dinner menu. In the final phase, the reinforcement contingency was removed. The conditions were as they had been during the baseline.

In the baseline phase, her correct and incorrect rate medians were fifteen and twelve answers per minute. During the second phase, when the contingency was based on correct answers, the correct rate increased to a median of forty-five, and her incorrect rate median fell to four.

During the third condition, when the contingency was arranged for both correct and incorrect rates, her correct rate median was sixty-four and her incorrect rate median was zero. In the final phase, when the contingency was removed, her correct and incorrect rate medians were sixty-one and five per minute. In summary, the menu contingency greatly influenced her rate and accuracy.

Although the mother did not report data regarding her daughter's subtraction performance at school, it would have been of interest and value to know whether the girl's proficiency in subtraction generalized from the home to the school. Ordinarily, a reverse generalization is expected.

One can only view with some suspicion, if not with alarm, the tactics of the teacher who sends a child home with a diagnosis of behaviors that need teaching and turns the job over to the parents and the home. Too many teachers are like the one in this project and my son's second grade teacher—long on diagnosing and short on treating.

A MOTHER SHAPED BEAD STRINGING

The pupil was the manager's two-year-old daughter, and the sessions were held each week-night at approximately eight o'clock. Baseline data were gathered and recorded for five days. The behavior measured was the number of beads the subject could string in one minute. Each bead that was appropriately threaded was credited as a correct response. An error was defined as any attempt that failed to put the bead on the string. Approximately one minute of warm-up time was allowed before the one-minute session began, so that the child could practice holding the string in her hand and placing the beads on the string. Thus, the measurement part of the sessions began without the child's knowing exactly when. No special feedback was given during this phase.

In the second phase, the manager held the leader portion of the string while the child placed the bead on the string. The manager then pulled the bead down to the bottom of the knotted string. This process was repeated until the minute was over. The child was quite capable, it developed, of performing this task. The difficulty throughout the baseline condition had been her inability to coordinate and alternate her hands properly. After she put the bead on the string with one hand, she could not pull the string through with the other hand and then pull the bead down to the bottom of the string with the first hand.

The purpose of this second phase was to give the child practice in one part of the behavior and some cues to model by watching the instructor follow through with the remaining two steps of the act. The data throughout this phase indicated that not only did the child attempt to respond more often, but also her correct rate accelerated, and her incorrect rate dropped to zero. The child, however, still did not perform the complete task by herself; therefore, another phase was scheduled.

Throughout the third phase, the second step of the shaping process was scheduled. During this time, the child held the leader portion of the string in one hand and placed the bead on the string with the other. The instructor then performed the third part of the procedure by pulling the bead down to the knotted end. As the data indicated, it was more difficult for the child to perform this additional step. Her correct rate was lower, and initially her incorrect rate increased. After a few days, however, her incorrect rate returned to zero.

The final phase was a return to baseline conditions; now, the girl performed the entire task. During the first part of this condition, her correct rate was rather low, but gradually, as her facility in manipulating the beads improved, her correct rate increased. During the final day of this condition, her correct rate was higher than it had been during the third phase. Her incorrect rate throughout this phase remained the same as it had been in the preceding two phases.

EXPLANATION AND PRACTICE WERE EFFECTIVE

The pupil was an eight-year-old boy in the second grade. The manager was the boy's mother. She was a former speech therapist and was, at the time of the project, working toward her master's degree in special education. The sessions were conducted each morning in the boy's room.

During each session the boy was required to respond to twenty-five subtraction problems of the type $48 - 29 = [\ \ ]$ and $33 - 24 = [\ \ ]$. Both the subtrahend and the minuend contained two numerals; borrowing was always required. Each day, different problems were assigned.

During the baseline phase, after the boy completed the problems, the manager checked them and handed the paper back to him. No further feedback was provided. Throughout this brief phase, the only problems he solved correctly were those of the type $80 - 23 = [\ \ ]$, those with a zero in the units column of the top numeral.

In the second condition, instruction was scheduled. First, he was told how to borrow; he was instructed to "take away" a numeral in the tens column of the subtrahend by crossing out that numeral and replacing it with one less and then to place a 1 in the subtrahend's units column. Next, he was directed to compute a sample problem. While doing this, he and the manager discussed each step. The second part of this process was scheduled every day of this condition. Instruction was offered only on the first day. On the first day of this phase, he missed fifteen problems; on the next, only seven. Thereafter, for a week, he never missed more than two problems a day.

Throughout the third condition, no instruction or practice was scheduled. The purpose of this phase was to determine whether the ability to borrow (which the pupil had developed during the second phase) would generalize from one type of subtraction problem to another. While the problems in the second phase contained two digit minuends and subtrahends, those in the third phase were three-digit subtrahends and two-digit minuends. Borrowing was required in only the units column of each class. As before, twenty-five different problems of the same class were assigned each day. On the first day of this phase, he missed eleven problems. Although he received no instruction, just feedback indicating which problems were correct and which were wrong, he never missed more than two problems throughout the remaining eight days of the phase.

During the final phase, the manager wanted to determine whether the lad's subtraction abilities would generalize to a second class of problems. These problems were of the type 818 - 39 = [ ]; they included three-digit subtrahends and two-digit minuends, and differed from those of the previous class in that borrowing was required in both the units and the tens columns.

The data from this phase indicated these problems were initially more difficult for the boy. On the first day he missed fourteen. On the next day, he missed four, then seven the next. On the seventh and eighth days of the phase, however, he missed only one problem.

This was obviously a rather sophisticated project for a parent to run. The matter began with a baseline which served to confirm that the boy could not borrow. Next, she taught him to borrow with simple problems; then, as proficiency was attained on that type of problem, she obtained data which confirmed that his ability to borrow had generalized to more difficult problems. It should also be mentioned that the teaching procedure she selected was effective and simple. During the phase when the most elementary problems were taught, the instruction was very simple; she told the child how to borrow, asked him to solve a problem, and discussed the steps as he worked the problem. Throughout the remainder of the project, when more difficult problems were scheduled, not even this technique was used. During these latter phases, the pupil received only feedback regarding which problems were correct and which were incorrect. In this case feedback was effective, unlike the project reported in an earlier chapter, Common Teaching Procedures.

This project ran for twenty-six days. On the average, each session lasted about 10 minutes. Thus, about 260 minutes were spent teaching an eight-year-old boy a rather complex skill, one that some school teachers would devote many more days to.

A MOTHER STRAIGHTENS OUT THE HOUSE

This project was managed by a mother of five children who was a graduate student in special education. She conducted this family project to fulfill a requirement in a class she was taking from me.

Her reason for arranging a measurement situation with her entire family, beyond the fact that she was required to do something for the course, was that she wanted to increase the household efficiency of a group of extremely busy people. She herself had a full schedule as a graduate student, and her husband, a physician, was away from home quite often. The five children, who served as the subjects for her study, ranged in age from twelve to nineteen; two boys were sixteen and nineteen, and three girls were twelve, fifteen, and eighteen. They were typically active teenagers.

Since this was a large and busy family, and particularly since the mother was away from the house a large part of each day, everyone had to shoulder a fair amount of responsibility. No one had time to do all the work.

As is the case with many busy families in their efforts to run their homes, various household chores were assigned to each member. These assignments included such chores as dusting, vacuuming, putting dishes into the dishwasher, putting dishes away, washing, drying, and folding clothes, scrubbing woodwork, feeding animals, doing yard work, preparing and serving meals, washing windows and floors, and ironing. As in many similar households, these chores were sometimes completed, but often they were not.

Prior to beginning her project, the mother listed all the chores. A family conference was then held, at which time the chores were distributed, all the members voicing their views on such matters as job preference, amount of time free for jobs, and other factors. After considerable deliberation, everyone accepted the duties assigned.

Throughout the project, the mother kept five graphs, one for each child. At the end of the day, she plotted the number of completed tasks for each child.

Throughout the baseline phase of the study, the mother did not inform the children that she was charting their performance. Neither did she nag them to finish their tasks. During this phase, there were about five chores completed each day, an average of one per subject.

In the next phase, the children were informed that their mother had been recording the number of tasks completed. Throughout this phase, graphs of their performances were posted. Apparently, as a consequence of the graphs, the average output throughout this phase rose to seven chores completed per day.

During the third condition, a point system was arranged, points being earned for completed chores. At a family conference, it was decided how many points each job was worth, and one point was redeemable for ten cents. Throughout this phase, the children had to earn their allowances, which formerly had been given whether they did their chores or not. The points were distributed across the jobs so that if the children performed all their tasks each day they could earn slightly more money than they had received when their allowances were noncontingently granted. Throughout this phase, the average output was eleven chores per day—slightly more than two chores per person.

Since the arrangement of earning money for jobs did not significantly alter the number of chores completed, another plan was then put into practice. Throughout this next phase, a dual contingency was arranged. Now, as before, the children received ten cents for each point but, in addition, ten cents was subtracted from their total for each job that was not completed. During this phase there were, on the average, seventeen tasks completed each day.

The mother then became venturesome and scientific and removed the double contingency. She informed the children that throughout this phase the payoff and penalty arrangements were being removed, but they were nevertheless expected to continue to complete their tasks. She also announced that allowances would be granted regardless of production rates. During this phase, the house was a mess. The average number of completed tasks fell to seven, the number it had been throughout the second phase, when only feedback was provided.

After a few days of disorder, a final phase was scheduled, during which the pay and penalty provisions were again put into effect. Once more, the effects of these arrangements were positive. On the average, the children completed eighteen tasks each day.

Many families have grappled with the problems of getting children to pitch in and help. Often elaborate schedules and assignments are worked out. Typically, in the wake of these "systems," the family unit functions satisfactorily for a while; then someone doesn't do her job and someone else does it for her, the shirker is reprimanded and the rescuer feels like a martyr—and very soon confusion is once again restored and chaos reigns supreme.

This woman's project was more successful than most home management efforts because she specified the tasks required of everyone (actually, they all agreed upon these), then put some teeth into the rules for completion of the tasks. During the conditions that were successful—payoff and penalty—if the children worked, they were paid; if they didn't, they were penalized. Little emotion was involved; once the contingencies were specified, *they* took care of the behavior, and the mother didn't resort to threats and reprimands.

Poor parents, they are a beleaguered lot. Although they are criticized if their progeny do not develop as good citizens, they are generally discouraged from teaching them to that end. Nonsense: parents *can* teach their children. It is only necessary that they be sane and systematic about their instruction. The four rules presented earlier were devised for that purpose, and I believe they are important enough to be repeated: (1) a set time should be established; (2) the instructional sessions should be brief; (3) the teacher's responses should be planned and consistent; and (4) daily record keeping should be maintained. The reader may observe that these rules for parent-teachers are not at all inconsistent with those suggested throughout this book for teacher-teachers.

Everyone
Measures

MEASUREMENT: if it's good enough for children, it's good
enough for big people.

One of the basic notions of this book, indeed, the underlying
message of its every page, is that measurement is indispensable.
Managers need measurement in order to determine (1) the effects of their teaching efforts, (2) whether their pupils are developing, and (3) where their pupils are. Certainly, measurement is
needed for the betterment of our profession—to lead us to even
newer concepts about learning and development that can be
added to those I have sought to advance here. This point cannot
be overstressed, for if managers of children do not learn from
children (and the use of measurement is fundamental to that
learning), they will never be able to improve their own teaching.
In fact, without some corrective system, something to dispel the
old, unfounded, developmental beliefs, some teachers will continue to plod their weary way, thwarting the progress and even
damaging the development of the children they are paid to
nurture.

Throughout this book, the ideas and recommendations expressed have been derived from *data*. They are not the product of dreamy conjecture. My reliance upon measurement, the reader will readily recall, is indeed a fact of my daily life. My book, then, makes use of lots and lots and *lots* of data obtained from children. Children's performances were meticulously measured in arithmetic, reading, creative writing, spelling, typing, penmanship, and many other school subjects.

I have consistently emphasized that if children's performances are measured it will be good for children. I have also stressed that if pupils measure their own performances it will be even better for them. The summation of these two hypotheses is that if teachers measure child behaviors and they do not share them with children, these data help teachers help children. Children are the *indirect* beneficiaries of the measurement. However, if the children keep their own data, if they look at it every day, if they plot their own scores, they will benefit even more from the data. For in these circumstances they also benefit *directly* from the data.

Thus, when children keep their own data they receive a double benefit. They are, of course, learning about their progress in a particular subject, but they are also learning about a data-keeping process that can be used to solve many of their future problems. This point was discussed in an earlier chapter, Contingent Free Time. At any rate, teachers should measure the important behaviors of children because measurement *is* good for them.

If children were trained or allowed to be independent and critical, and if they were told upon being measured that it was good for them, they should respond accordingly. "Look, if this measurement stuff is so good, how come you, the big person, are not measuring yourself?" They might also say, "Is this measurement another one of those things that's good for children, but not for grown-ups?" "Is this another one of those do-as-I-say-but-not-as-I-do, sort of things?"

Although more will be said about this later, children might very well ask this same question of their adult teacher about many educational matters. "If it's so good for us, how come you're not doing it?" Children could, in fact, ask of many of their adult supervisors, "How come you want me to change, to learn, to develop, when you're not?" "Why aren't you learning anything?" "From what I've heard, you tell the same dumb jokes every year, and you teach the course in exactly the same way every time." "Is it true that learning is only good for young people—then when they've had it, they need no more of it?" A pretty stupid idea to transmit to children, that only they need education and that they only need to learn until they are twenty-one or are finished with their formal schooling.

But once again I have digressed. The point I want to make in this chapter is that measurement is also good for big people. Measurement assists them to grow and develop in positive and discernible ways just as it does children.

In this section, I will discuss some projects where teachers measured certain behaviors of their own. I will also present some principal-kept data and, finally, some data I have logged.

TEACHERS CAN MEASURE THEIR BEHAVIORS

Sometimes in my college classes I have asked teachers to conduct self-projects; projects where they measured some aspect of their own performance. The primary reason for the request was to teach them certain charting and evaluating skills and to provide them with a rationale for measurement and change that would eventually enable them to individualize their programming and procedural strategies with children. Presumably, when teachers have successfully charted certain of their own behaviors and have perhaps altered some of them, they are better prepared to measure and change certain academic and social behaviors of children.

In many instances, teachers can benefit from these teacher-improvement projects in ways far beyond the fact that they have learned the rudiments of data keeping. Indeed, in certain instances, as teachers improve, so do their pupils. To assess this factor one might, during the first phase of a project, measure some pupil behavior and a teacher behavior. Then, during the next phase of the project, some element relevant to the teacher's environment, not the pupil's, could be altered. By comparing the data relative to the pupil's performance during the first phase with his activity throughout the second phase (teacher modification), one could readily ascertain if, and to what degree, teacher change was related to pupil change.

A third benefit derived from certain teacher-improvement projects is that the pupils can become involved in the management of the class. Perhaps if students were thus consulted and involved in class management, motivation for learning would increase, and, for the same reasons, the inclination for dissent would decrease. Following are three descriptions of instances where teachers measured their own behaviors. My first and third reasons for obtaining teacher data are illustrated.

In one project, a sixth grade teacher was concerned with a topic not particularly related to school. She wanted to measure the number of interactions she had with her pupils regarding nonschool topics—a discussion with a boy about last week's fishing trip or a talk with a girl about her plans for the coming weekend. This teacher wanted to know her pupils better.

During the first phase of this project, the teacher simply measured the extent to which she interacted with pupils; no attempt was made to alter the rate at which this behavior occurred. One interaction was tallied each time she talked with a different pupil; if she talked with a pupil, then talked with him again, only one tally was made. Throughout this phase, her median rate of interacting with pupils was about nine occasions per day.

Throughout the second phase, a contingency was arranged. It specified that if she contacted all twenty-seven pupils in the class, she would be allowed a full half-hour lunch period the following day. Otherwise she would have to eat in fifteen minutes, leave the lunchroom, and return to her classroom. The data from this second phase indicated that in sixteen days she was successful; she contacted all twenty-seven members of her class at least once.

A project such as this, where the teacher measured one of her behaviors and did not involve the pupils, can serve as an initial measurement effort. Some teachers, although convinced that pupil measurement should be an important part of their teaching, are reluctant to begin examining themselves. Some are uncertain about the various technical aspects of the data-keeping process: counting, calculating the rate, and charting. Many times, therefore, a teacher project can serve as the prelude for obtaining measurement relating to students. If a teacher can successfully conduct a self-project, she may be more inclined to measure some aspect of pupil performance. This was true in the present instance. After the teacher had successfully measured and changed one of her behaviors, she went on to obtain data from her students in several academic areas.

Another project of this type was conducted by a first grade teacher. The behavior she counted was the number of times she asked her class questions which required only a yes or no reply. Believing that one of the primary objectives of the first grade should be the development of language and general communication skills, she wanted to stimulate responses, at the proper times of the day, that required more than a simple yes or no answer. This called for more open-ended questions, which would require children to construct whole-sentence responses.

During the first phase of this project, the teacher kept a record of each question that required only a yes or no answer; she tallied these questions for thirty minutes during the language development time. The median rate throughout this phase was about eleven such questions per period. During the second phase of this project, she asked the children to remind her whenever they heard her ask a question requiring only a yes or no. They were only too willing to comply throughout this phase. When they heard her commit an "infraction," they often, in chorus, reminded her that she had "done it again." The data throughout this phase indicated that the behavior of asking simple questions had slowed down considerably. The median in the seond phase was about three infractions per thirty-minute period.

In order to determine whether the children's reminders were needed in order to maintain a low rate of asking simple questions, the teacher then withdrew the contingency; she asked the children throughout the final phase to stop reminding her. The data from this phase indicated that her rate of asking questions requiring yes or no answers remained about the same as during the preceding phase.

By involving the children in this project, the teacher not only had many helpers to monitor the reliability of her measurements, but, in the process, many of the pupils learned to discriminate between open-ended questions and those which required only single-word responses. This is an important behavior to learn, because such a discrimination is basic to the development of an effective communication system. We may possess a vast repertory of words and phrases, but unless we know how and when to use them, they are of little use to us. The inability of many people to communicate may stem as much from the fact that they are uncertain as to the type of question that has been asked as from a limited verbal repertory.

In this project, since the teacher recorded only the frequency of her asking simple questions, she, in effect, counted only her errors. It is possible, therefore, that although her errors decreased from the first phase to the second, her correct rate, that of asking open-ended questions, also decreased. She should have kept two tallies: one which depicted correct responses (asking open-ended questions), and another which revealed incorrect responses (asking simple questions).

SO CAN PRINCIPALS

A few years ago, I was associated with a demonstration project, the purpose of which was to train teacher consultants. It was our belief that if we trained a group of consultants who, in turn, assisted classroom teachers to manage children who "behaved inappropriately," more children would be adequately educated in their regular classrooms and would not be reassigned to special education situations.

These consultants were to serve in an advisory capacity and were to be assigned to elementary schools. It was our task throughout this two-year project to provide the consultants with the skills necessary to function in such a system.

Throughout the first year, we instructed the consultants (all former classroom teachers) in ways to pinpoint academic and social behaviors, to chart the frequency of those behaviors, and to analyze data. We also taught them to arrange various reinforcement contingencies, and to use modeling, shaping, and other instructional procedures. They were provided with a large repertory of potential teaching techniques.

After the consultants demonstrated that they could work successfully with children, our next task was to teach them to be as effective with teachers, who were, in turn, working with the children. This was not as simple, for not only did the consultants have to teach the teachers certain new skills, but also they had to work through certain archaic and ineffective techniques the teachers had acquired. In order to work effectively with the teachers, they had to keep in mind many of the truths they had learned when they themselves were working with children. They had to take into account that teachers, like children, are individuals; they are unique and must be so treated. They had to remember that teachers must be shaped, not raped; that is, if teachers are to be taught a skill, they must be allowed to develop "at their own rate." If they are to be taught to measure certain behaviors and to use reinforcement contingencies to alter those behaviors, they must be allowed to develop these competencies at their own pace, not that of others.

Once the consultants were trained to work effectively with teachers and had expressed confidence they could do so, the next step of training began. Now our task was to teach the consultants to work effectively with their building principals. By "working effectively," we had in mind that the consultants would explain to the principals, in minute and inspiring detail, the operation of the project, and, thus indoctrinated, the principals would in turn support our endeavors by encouraging their teachers to participate. It was also our hope that his contagion would spill over into a zeal, on the principal's part, to evangelize parents, leading citizens, and other interested parties as to the worthiness and adaptability of our cause.

The four principals involved in the project varied widely as to their interest in what was going on, in their general support of the program, and in their ability to articulate to others what their own contributions were to be.

One principal in particular, we soon discovered, was not at all committed to the enterprise and remained shaky as to the project's real purposes. This in spite of the fact that we had taken meticulous precautions prior to launching the undertaking to select principals who wanted the measurement program in their schools. His ignorance of the plan was particularly vexing—and perplexing—in that orientation periods had been conducted with the four men prior to the opening date expressly to acquaint them with our purposes and aims, in precise and thrilling detail. But in spite of our best efforts to select motivated and knowledgeable men and brief them expertly, we had picked a real dud.

About the best that could be said for this principal was that his relationship with the project, particularly with the consultant assigned to his school, was one of benign neutrality. He did not actively attempt to sabotage the project, but he certainly made no attempt to support it, either.

And support the consultant needed. When the announcement went out to teachers in the building to request assistance from the consultant for their pupils' academic and social problems, few cries for help came. This in spite of the fact that in the days and months before the project was initiated, teachers in the lounge were amply vocal about their terrible situations and their need for help. They complained about the kids who couldn't read, the ones who couldn't add, the ones who were late for school, the ones who were chronically absent, and the ones who misbehaved.

These teachers, like many others, were perhaps suspicious of anyone who proposed to tell them how to interact with their pupils. Or there could have been other good reasons for their reluctance. Perhaps in the past they had asked for needed help that was never received. Or perhaps they had been offered "help," and it had proved useless (our diagnostic centers have done a great deal to encourage such skepticism and resistance). There are the teachers who never ask for help because they are "above it all"—they are sure no one can possibly help them. And there are those who believe that it shows weakness to ask for advice and, wishing to appear strong, they stoically go it alone.

At any rate, when the call for clients went out in this school, only a few friends of the consultant sought her assistance. It may have been that even some of these gestures were purely of the token variety; the appearance of need was purely cosmetic.

Many of the teachers went to the principal and asked him to level with them—Did they *have* to request help? He replied, "No, not if you don't want to." And that was that. A number left his office knowing that, for them, the project was finished before it began. Many believed it was unnecessary for them to request help in measuring the progress of their pupils, for they "knew" exactly how they were getting along.

But teachers who have never measured a pupil behavior do *not* really know how their pupils are getting along. They are like drivers who "know" they have enough oil but never bother to look at the dipstick. Some succumb to another fallacy: they do not want to be troubled with measurement because it takes time from their instruction. What they do not know (because they do no believe in measurement) is that what they call instruction can be, for some children, a sheer waste of time and, for others, even damaging. They do not realize that without the sharp focus of day-by-day measurement, they are only guessing at their pupils' progress—or lack of it. What is perhaps even worse, they themselves will never grow, never change. They will continue to plug along, fooling themselves, deluding parents and principals, and, in some tragic cases, demoralizing rather than developing some of their pupils.

But all this was far, far over our uncooperative principal's head. He could not, or would not, see that the primary mission of our project was to obtain measurement, so that teachers would *know* what they and their pupils were doing, would grow and improve as teachers, and, along the way, would find, develop, and refine new ways of teaching each successive group of children more efficiently than they had taught the last.

He could not see that as a principal he should have been our project's staunchest advocate. When the reluctant teachers came to him with their complaints of how measurement interfered with their teaching, he should have explained—gently but firmly—that unless they measured, they would never know just how effective their "teaching" was.

For several days, we were angry and disappointed that our nonparticipating principal should be jeopardizing the success of our project with his indifference. And when even these reactions on our part failed to alter his behavior, we knew something had to be done.

So we set to work on those behaviors. We reminded him of our goals. We flattered him that only through his high office would we best carry to his teachers the gospel of daily measurement and of adroit contingency management. We gave him the most instructive readings to read, scheduled discussions and then discussions of these discussions, invited his questions for our answers. He read, discussed, and questioned brightly enough and made many encouraging sounds—even gave some of the signs of becoming a true believer. But his behavior back at his school was the same unenlightened routine of being superpermissive with the reluctant teachers (who saw no point in measurement) and stolidly nonreinforcing to the fearless few who *were* measuring. We had gotten precisely nowhere.

Then we remembered the Delphic oracle's "Know Thyself" dictum and had a clue. We scheduled a new program for our friend, dedicated to the proposition that even principals must have *something* to measure—and persuaded him to help the consultant make the list. What *were* his daily jobs during a typical week? He talked, and thought, and talked some more. The consultant jotted it all down.

Finally, the following behaviors—all of them measurable—were drawn up into a fairly respectable total: contacts with teachers, contacts with specialists (speech therapists, music teachers, the librarian), contacts with students, contacts with the central office. It was also agreed that the data would specify the initiator of the contact; for example, the principal-teacher contact data were differentiated as to whether the principal or the teacher made the first move.

A contact was defined as any interaction. It could be a face-to-face conversation, a written note, or a telephone call. Although all were classified as to initiator, no attempt was made to separate them on the basis of topic, quality, or length; the consultant believed it was better, initially, to obtain a general measure of performance. Later, if the principal desired more sophisticated measures, he could easily obtain more refined data as to these other dimensions.

For the first few weeks, the consultant assisted the principal to plot these data. On a ruled form he tallied each activity: nine teachers contacted that day, nine checks in that column. At the end of each day, the consultant helped with the graphing, but on the seventh day the principal was doing it for himself—and that was good, too.

And so our problem principal learned for the first time what he was really doing—or, on some days, what he was not doing. His chart was not exactly an ego builder, though it could probably have been worse. It ran something as follows:

As to teachers, he was both pained and piqued to discover that on most days they got along very nicely without him, though he sought them out at the rate of about five (of the twenty in the building) a day. As to students, he found them also notably principal-shy, and he did not fare much better with them, except for the disciplinary cases that he handled. As to parent contacts, he had about three a day, most of them initiated by him. As to the specialists, he averaged six per day, all of his own seeking. And with the central office, it was a chummy seven per day, evenly divided as to the initiator.

Our near-convert was amazed at these revelations of the way he actually spent his time. He was especially shocked at how much time was taken up by central-office people and how little time went to the teachers and pupils of his own school.

But, sadly enough, he was not shaken up sufficiently to make really wise use of the data he had obtained. Although manifestly displeased at his track record, he did nothing about it; he simply continued keeping his books and scratching his head over their revelations. The central office got just as much of his time as before; the teachers and students just as little.

We consoled ourselves, however, with the thought that in a sense our major purpose in working with this man had been realized. In spite of himself, he had learned to measure; its mysteries had been dispelled and its values at least glimpsed. He had learned that one does not have to be in serious trouble before data can be useful—a sound therapeutic discovery. But the larger truth, that measurement can be used to prevent failure, to maintain a desired level of behavior, and to foster further development, he never fully grasped. The change occurred in only his most frequent, most natural behavior. His verbal.

Because of his own data experience, there were real changes in his attitude toward measurement as a working principle applicable to principals. He also became more supportive of our project, even to the extent of encouraging those of his teachers who had been in favor of it to involve themselves even more actively in the cause and of making an honest effort to evangelize the heathens. No more could they tell him they had no need to measure their classroom results, or that it would take valuable time away from their invaluable teaching to do so, or that they had no personal inclination, anyhow, toward juggling with figures, charts, and graphs. They were officially and emphatically enjoined to get with it.

He had, indeed, learned much from his brief bout with self-analysis. We like to think that his school will never be quite the same again. And once more we were agreeably fortified in our belief, as educators committed to progress in the schoolroom and out, that one is never too old to learn (as discussed in an earlier chapter, Teaching Youngsters and Oldsters) or too dull to be quickened.

This case happened to center upon a school principal. But we know of many other school personnel who have profited by measuring some of their behaviors. Speech therapists have kept data on the number of clients served, the types of speech problems they have worked on, and the tools, materials, and remedial devices they have worked with. School psychologists have tallied the number of children seen, the reasons for their referral, and the type of intervention they recommended. In this age of accountability, many of our auxiliary personnel are experiencing new pressures to communicate more effectively with the public regarding the ways they spend their time. They would do well to incorporate the data system described here.

EVEN PROFESSORS CAN MEASURE

For more than a decade, I have kept data on several professorial behaviors in my own life. Not always on the same ones—my concept (and that of my respected colleagues) about what constitutes the job of "professoring" has changed from time to time. But my constancy to a few basic disciplines has remained, and five or six of these I have charted quite religiously.

My core curriculum has run about as follows: contacts with students, preparation time for classes, planning completed, planning not completed, hours spent writing, and writing rate.

Through the years, I have also kept private-eye data regarding my research associates. I have counted the times we have discussed research, the number of graphs we have made and studied, the number of questions I have asked about the progress of various projects. And in my classes I have asked my students such intriguing trivia as how many ambiguous statements I have made, how many of their first names I have used correctly, how many questions I have asked—and answered myself, how many vocalized pauses (uh's) I have been guilty of, and how many laughs I have intentionally elicited. Not too academic, but we profs do need to keep a check on these things.

Generally, there are two reasons for obtaining personal data: a desire to modify the measured behavior and/or to improve communication and accountability. The data obtained in regard to classes taught, workshops presented, and the measures of my research endeavors were used to modify and improve my performance. For example, I discovered some years back that when I discussed several research studies during a single class session, the tally of ambiguous statements went up. But when I limited my presentations to fewer studies the score went appreciably down.

Some of the data kept have served both purposes: they provided me with personal information and were also useful in communication. This is particularly true of data regarding my contacts with students. At one period, I discovered that I had about fifty contacts each week. (I defined a contact as any interaction—phone call, letter, visit—not, however, a greeting as we passed in the hall.) I learned further that I saw the most students at the beginning of the quarter, at the end of the quarter (when they enrolled for a new term and began to worry about exams), and after tests. I also saw the most students on Monday and the fewest on Friday—they were more TGIF-minded, apparently, than I. I was faithfully available on Friday, as on every other day of the school week. These data were doubly useful to me. I was able to anticipate and prepare for busy periods by scheduling fewer committee meetings and appointments with my dentist;

and, for purposes of communication, I had something useful to include, among oceans of other data, in my reports to the ever-increasing number of officials ever solicitous about my account-ability and that of my colleagues.

One might be more specific than I have been to date as to the various topics discussed in these student contacts. Some are about assignments, quizzes, or exams; some are about enroll-ment procedures or future plans; some students simply want to talk to someone about something, anything—though these aimlessly amiable visits are all too rare. It would also be of inter-est to discriminate as to the type of contact: whether a face-to-face interview or a phone conversation. Informative, too, would be data as to the length and quality of the interactions; for some last five minutes and others two hours; some are productive, and others are an unconscionable waste of time. A few really valu-able pieces of information should be obtainable from such data. One that comes immediately to mind would be the con-firmation of a consummation devoutly to be wished—that 88.9 percent of the student conferences could be handled using the time-saving method of a telephone call.

And speaking of what we may loosely and charitably refer to as my writing, I have learned through the years, thanks to my data keeping, a few random facts about My Yellow Pad and Me. For whatever it may be worth, I know something about the aver-age number of minutes per day spent in writing in a given month, the average number of words written per minute, and the average number of pages of a first draft that I can revise in an hour. I am talking here chiefly about writing articles for journals. It is of some use to me to know that on the average I write, in longhand, about ten words per minute and can generally revise one page of my own stuff in twenty minutes. I also know that my writing and revising rates for technical descriptions are about twice my rates for reflective and synthesizing material.

Travel and writing, for me, coexist in an inverse ratio; the more I travel, the less I write. I am not an airport writer. But I am, the data reveal, a fairly productive pretrip writer, prompted, no doubt, by feelings of guilt over the approaching escape from my desk. Professional travel, too, encourages a search for fresh top-ics: trips mean workshops, workshops means speeches, and speeches mean finding something to say that is not already as "old hat" as new math. I figure that I should make about one short trip a month for these regenerative purposes. When I follow such a regime, the trips provide a wholesome stimulus, as well as practical motivation, for gathering, organizing, and writing fresh material. The presentations themselves provide me with feedback and broad hints as to sorely needed revisions. Too much traveling, however, can lead rapidly to a point of diminishing returns; the same speech used too many times can become an exercise in futility for all concerned. A new trip, it has always seemed to me, should, in all fairness, include a brief-case well stocked with truths to be heralded abroad.

Fortunately, or unfortunately, I do not have to turn down many traveling engagements because of my data. Geography tends to keep my wonderlust in check and my market unsaturated. Organizers of symposiums in Philadelphia, Boston, or New York can usually find able consultants nearer at hand than the West Coast and can thus avoid paying the hefty airline fee from Seattle and back. They like me in Idaho and Montana.

What have I tried to say in this chapter? Simply that teachers, principals, professors—all those concerned with development in our educational programs and practices—should measure, measure, measure. As I remarked at the outset, if it's good enough for children, it's good enough for big people. It would, as a matter of fact, be a beneficial and eminently fair procedure for teachers to perform most of the things they expect children to do. In our classroom, we made it a practice to read through all the material, work all the math sheets, and do all the writing assignments that our children were required to study. It was amazing how many times, after a teacher had worked through one of the pupil assignments, we found it advisable to modify the materials before the children were subjected to them. Some assignments were too long, some too short, some painfully dull, some just plain stupid. It is a far cry from handing out any old work sheets to children and expecting them to do them and be happy in the doing, to making an intelligent—yes, even a measured, data-processed—effort to provide them with really stimulating and meaningful material. Let the big people try things out first.

Let the teachers read all the books and do all the exercises they assign to the children. Let them occasionally run through a typical child's day. They should—if they are teaching elementary age children—come to school in the morning and hang their coats on a rack. They should quietly take their seats, answer roll call, read in a group, answer comprehension questions, take a spelling test, work on math problems, line up to go to the bathroom, eat in the cafeteria.

They should, by all means, sit at a desk for long hours at a stretch without getting up to roam about, and never, never talk to anyone. Have you ever seen a group of teachers, or any group of adults for that matter, in the throes of sitting for longer than sixty minutes in the same place? They fidget and squirm, light and stub out cigarettes, talk to their neighbors, mutter to themselves, scribble notes on the programs, scratch their arms, twirl their hair, trim their nails, look at the clock, adjust their coats, take off their shoes, slip back into their shoes, and fold and refold the notebooks in which they are supposed to be writing down the speaker's golden words.

And yet we expect children to sit for hours, listen to all the teacher says, make nothing but intelligent responses (*only* when asked), keep their feet on the floor and their shoes on their feet, and be happy, young, and gay throughout the whole process.

Incredible! Yes, and inexcusable.

By all means, big people, measure your own behaviors, just as you measure the behaviors of others.

Enjoy
Your Children

TEACH those kids, but along the way get some laughs.

No one would deny that teaching is a difficult job. Difficult not only in that a lot of skill is required to show or tell people how to do something they cannot yet do; but difficult because teaching, at least school teaching, is just plain hard work.

There are, I am certain, jobs that are harder than teaching. But not too many. The third grade teacher, for example, goes to work every day at 7:30 A.M. or thereabouts, and returns home around 4:30 P.M. He goes through his routine day after day. He has to see to it that all his pupils learn how to read, write, do arithmetic, and many other things; he must keep them happy throughout the year. He must contend with all types of administrators and educational experts, like myself, who are quick to criticize him and tell him how his job should be done. He must also contend with parents, many of whom are also experts in all matters of educational practice. Furthermore, teachers must contend with a herd of children each day, many of whom are undeniably a pain in the neck.

Strong evidence that teaching in the public schools is a difficult job is that many people, including myself, have spent lots of time and money trying to escape doing it. Many of us have worked hard to obtain additional degrees in order to become college teachers or public school administrators. We realized that it takes a lot out of you if you work with youngsters for a long time.

The approach to teaching I have advocated throughout this book would not make the teacher's job any more restful. Although I believe the notions advocated here—underscored by the suggestion that pupil performance can and should be measured—will be helpful to teachers, I am aware that, if the ideas advanced here are followed, teachers will be more and more committed to the ideas that children can be taught and they are worth teaching. If teachers subscribe totally to those ideas, the business of teaching is not an easy one.

If the teacher is dedicated to children's development, his workday will be filled with worry and concern. He will constantly be looking at data and revising programs. He will always be thinking about the best ways to solve the thousands of classroom problems—problems that are never going to be totally solved; for if the teacher wholeheartedly believes in the idea that people can change and that the potential for change is limitless, there are always dozens of new behaviors to teach after certain behaviors have been taught.

Not only will the good teacher be concerned about his pupils throughout the day, he will take these concerns home with him, even on vacations. When we were living in Mexico, two elementary teachers, friends of my wife, visited us. Although they were vacationing, they were constantly searching for new behaviors to teach and show to their children. Many a harassed husband or wife has spent one thrilling night after another listening to their teacher spouse talk about the pupils. I am certain that many marriages and other relationships have been dissolved because of this single interest of the teacher.

In addition to the fact that teaching school is hard work, teachers are dealt many frustrations and disappointments. Although they are very significant persons in the lives of children, they cannot control all the circumstances of a child's life. (Most of us would agree this is as it should be.) Many things can go wrong with the teacher's plans, for there are many other forces that influence children—some in directions contrary to the thrusts of the teacher. Many teachers have had to cope with matters such as the following: a pupil who has been making significant progress is sent to a bad foster home situation, a boy who is already messed up just lost his dad, a girl who was taught to read last year is not reading in her new situation, a child who is beginning to bloom is being sent to special education.

By mentioning the fact that teaching is hard and that there are counter-forces and uncontrolled circumstances, I am not encouraging teachers to be fatalistic or discouraged about the whole business of teaching. But since teaching *is* a very hard job (it makes people tired), and there *are* lots of accompanying frustrations, I would advise teachers to get some laughs along the way. I hasten to add that I am certainly not advocating that teachers laugh *at* their children, for that isn't nice. I am suggesting that teachers laugh *along* with their children because they are amusing and because they can be very educational. As I have indicated throughout the book, even I have learned from children. Often their insights and proclamations can help straighten out *las personas mayores* ("adults"). When those times occur, when children express their thoughts differently or creatively, and teachers are entertained, if not educated, those moments and, better yet, those memories should be cherished.

Being in a position to receive these vignettes is one of the big advantages of being with kids. Being able to be with young people who have fresh insights is the major fringe benefit of teaching. Whether they like it or not, teachers are apprised of the new dress styles, the new expressions, the new music. If teachers have been in the business for many years, they have seen many changes, and, to some extent, they have had to adjust to these changes.

I would like to advance, rather cautiously, another notion about being with children. I believe that because teachers are with youngsters and can witness their insights and revelations, teachers are relatively sane, nonviolent, and honest. Certainly, we have all known some teachers who were crappy people, but, by and large, they are not a bad lot. I don't know too many teachers who have done really bad things to others. Most of the people I know who work day after day with children do not rape, pillage, plunder, or get involved in extortion plots. Perhaps the reason they don't engage in such high-powered, societal wrongdoings is that they are too tired from teaching and don't have the energies. But I would contend that the primary reason that teachers are adequately socialized is that their children have helped them. Their pupils have kept them honest by challenging some of their values and by providing them with fresh strategies for viewing the environment.

Youngsters are, by definition, fresh. They have not been around as long as old people; therefore, they see life differently. They have not learned the cliches, the established ways to act and describe articles and events. They often develop their own approaches and language systems for dealing with and talking about their lives. In the process, they use new words and phrases. They use different analogies; they even use different descriptive strategies.

Thus, children entertain teachers; they keep them sane, pure in spirit, and incorruptible. With such gains, it would appear to be "worth the pain" of being tired throughout the week and bringing home a few school-related problems.

I have been fortunate to have had hundreds of memorable experiences with children during my life; every teacher has. I certainly don't want to present all of them, but I would like to share some experiences I have had throughout the years and tell why these experiences were important. My only regret in regard to these incidents is that I have not kept as careful track of them as I have of children's progress in reading and arithmetic. Please don't accuse me, however, of not being able to see the forest for the trees—it is vitally important to know about them, too. What I have done for the past year or so has been to keep a rather loose diary of the funny, interesting, witty, and inspirational things that children say and do. I heartily recommend, too, that others consider keeping such additional records, for along with the graphs of academic performance, they provide a valuable narrative account of the "whole child."

One instructive incident served to point out vividly a glaring inconsistency in one of our great educational controversies. My oldest son and I were talking one day about the great "reading" debate—phonics *versus* nonphonics. I explained that some teachers of reading believed pupils should be taught phonics—sound-symbol relationships—before they were taught to read in context and that other teachers believed pupils should be taught isolated sight words instead of the part words. I explained that the first group believed phonic rules or generalizations should be taught, but the others insisted that, since the English language has so many inconsistencies and exceptions, teaching rules is futile.

I then pointed out some of the phonic elements that teachers stressed, mentioning that most of the time the c sound is made with a c, but this sound is also made with other letters. I also explained that usually the f sound is made with f, but occasionally this sound is represented by ff and ph. "Wouldn't you know," Mark then said, "the name of the movement itself, phonics, isn't even a regularly spelled word." He suggested that the least phonics proponents could do would be to relabel their method and call it p-hon-ics or change the spelling to fonics. When I thought about his amazement that even the name of the cause is inconsistent with the message it professes, I began to consider other educational inconsistencies, some on a much grander scale. For example, when teachers tell children to behave in a certain way, yet they themselves behave differently; when administrators tell teachers to upgrade their skills, yet they do nothing to alter their own behaviors; and when parents blame teachers for not teaching something they previously warned teachers *not* to instruct.

Another story that comes to mind serves to illustrate how children look upon adults, particularly teachers. It came from my daughter Kathy when she was doing her student teaching. For this experience, she was assigned to a beautiful first grade class; the children were multicolored and came from all kinds of homes and environments. One day in her class, she was seated with a group of three or four youngsters, working on some school activity. While she was busy with the group, another boy came up to her and stood waiting. Although obviously eager to ask the teacher something, he patiently waited to be recognized. But Kathy kept on with her group. In a few minutes, another boy came up to the group, and she overheard him ask the first boy what he wanted. The first boy whispered something that she was unable to hear. Whereupon the second boy said, "You might as well sit down. She won't talk to you about that; it doesn't have to do with school," and both boys took their seats. Kathy was crushed. Although she would have been glad to talk to the young man about any topic of interest to him, she realized that she had somehow failed to make her availability known to her pupils and now this boy, like his companion, believed teachers were interested only in school matters, and not really in them. I'm afraid too many of us are responsible for developing just such opinions of us and attitudes toward us, without really intending to do this at all. And as Kathy learned so early in her career, you can't fool the kids. In the preceding chapter, however, there is an example of a teacher who *was* concerned about the lives of children outside the school. It's worth rereading.

I recall another story worth telling, not because of its message but just because I was greatly amused by the event. The incident took place a few years ago in my Curriculum Research Classroom, where we had another interesting color mixture among the kids. There were seven children in the group, among which were two black boys and one white girl.

In spite of, or because of, this racial mixture, the children got along very well; there were only a few fights and not too many quarrels. One day, however, Jenni, our token girl, and Fredi, one of our black boys, got into an argument. I can't remember how it started or what it was about, but they called each other all the bad names they could think of. Finally, Fredi administered what he thought was the coup de grace. He called Jenni a white honkie. When Jenni heard this, she quickly retaliated and called Fredi a black honkie. Fredi was stunned; for once in his life he was speechless. Then, after a few moments, he put his hands on his hips, stuck out his chin, and looked firmly at Jenni. He said, in his most deliberate way, "Man, there ain't no such thing as a black honkie!" Of course, there are some social, racial, and perhaps linguistic overtones to the incident, and hence a message of some sort, but mostly I simply found it amusing.

We all need to be reminded at times that the notions of big and little people sometimes differ widely when it comes to providing assistance. Some times adults—parents and teachers—"help" children who do not want to be helped; and sometimes they help them in one area only to make the situation worse in another.

The principal person in this account was the son of a good friend of mine. When Billy was born, he had many physical problems. His little head was misshapen, his pulmonary system was inadequate for the job, his ears did not line up properly, and several other facial features were somewwhat abnormal. In spite of these problems, he was, and still is, a bright, engaging little chap.

When he was about two years old, he was taken to a large medical center for extensive plastic surgery. The doctors intended to repair his ears and restructure and patch up other parts of his face. He would look normal again. Needless to say, his parents and grandparents were thrilled at the prospect of the normalizing procedure. All concerned knew they were doing something for Billy's own good; he would now look just like other two-year-old boys.

Following the operation, when the scars had healed and the bandages were removed, Billy was taken to a mirror to see himself. He looked for a long moment at his reflection, then ran away from the mirror and began to sob uncontrollably. When asked why, he sobbed, "It doesn't look like me." Apparently Billy had not been so displeased with his original face as his folks had thought, and he was certainly not so turned on by his new one.

Again, I reflected. How often do we, as teachers and parents, make attempts to change behaviors without ever actually telling the children why. The obvious moral to this story is to tell the poor kids what we are up to. Of course, another moral is that beauty is in the eyes of the beholder. We adults say this, but perhaps children—Billy, at least—really mean it. The great thing about kids is that beauty, for them, does not exist only within certain, narrow, adult-defined limits—it is boundless. Children are not afraid to love and to accept differences. Adults would do well to recapture this ability, to again be able to see and feel a wide diversity of experiences and to express the fact, at least to themselves, that they have encountered a moment of beauty. There are many other skills, too, that we can relearn from children.

Epilogue

In the course of the book I have described fifty-two diverse projects. Most of them dealt with a single student. In some instances, a few individuals participated; in a very few, an entire class was involved. The ages of the pupils ranged from the two year old in the bead-stringing project to one of the teachers in the "teacher measurement" study who was about fifty years old. Most of the individuals, however, were from eight to twelve.

Many different behaviors were dealt with in these projects. Certainly, the basic academic skills—reading, writing, arithmetic, spelling—were amply represented. Other projects were concerned with verbal behaviors, cooperative play, inappropriate speech, and chores around the house. Most of the studies were conducted by classroom teachers.

Likewise in these pages, twenty-one notions were presented in as many chapters. These dealt with various aspects of teaching and learning. Certain topics related to diagnosis, the establishment of goals, and the selection of appropriate teaching procedures. Others focused on various processes of learning, such as maturation, generalization, and discrimination. Some notions pertained to managers other than school teachers: peers, parents, principals, and professors.

Several of the positions taken in my book were stimulated by the false implications of many, often heard educational bromides. For example, the Motivation, Reinforcement Contingencies, A Hierarchy of Reinforcers, and Contingent Free Time chapters reappraised some of the false meanings of the ever-popular saying, "You can lead a horse to water but you can't make him drink." The old cliché, "Practice makes perfect," inspired the Benefits of Practice chapter, and the truism, "You can't teach an old dog new tricks," was challenged in the chapter, Teaching Youngsters and Oldsters. In all those chapters, I have presented arguments based on data that should cause educators to proceed with caution when it comes to being influenced by such pearls of wisdom.

A significant amount of data has been given in order to substantiate most of the contentions in this book. Certainly, more data have been considered in support of them and their implications than has been submitted by many educators in generating their procedures, postulates, and laws.

In special education, for example, several persuasive special-treatment plans have been advocated in the past that were based on severely limited data. It has been recommended, for instance, that if hyperactive children are placed in cubicles they can be instructed more easily, that children who reverse letters should be instructed by a multi-sensory regime, that children who reverse letters should be provided laterality training, encouraged to crawl, and shown how to make angels in the snow.

Indeed, an entire instructional method which began in Europe several years ago is based on little, if any, data. Yet this method has enjoyed considerable popularity among many middle- and upper-class parents who want only the best for their offspring. It advocates self-instructional techniques and procedures and also leans heavily on the concept of multi-sensory stimulation.

Although this approach, which has swept America, is ostensibly based on logic and the observation of children, there is little evidence that demonstrable data were regarded in its conception. In fact, the advocates of this method appear to be actually anti-empirical. That is, they are so opposed to data gathering and evaluation that should one of their number find any part of their approach faulty or nonfunctional, and should then attempt to modify that procedure and make it workable, he would be discredited and be banished from the cult. The proponents would believe their system had been damaged. Even if the method becomes outmoded and stagnant, it is, according to them, better to remain pure than to change—particularly because of empiricism.

Other educators and psychologists have advanced theories of development which were derived from a meager data source. Some have proclaimed that children pass through certain developmental epochs at rather precise ages; others have stated that a definite heirarchy or taxonomy of learning exists. Although many of these theories are based on a fair amount of observation and deduction, rarely have they been the product of abundant data.

As I have already noted, there are twenty-one speculations on teaching and learning problems in this book. But it has certainly not been my intention that all of my recommendations should be used by teachers in their efforts to instruct every child. And nothing is to be taken necessarily in the order prescribed; that is, I don't intend that the first chapter should be used first, then the second, third, and fourth chapters. I would hope, rather, that the notions would be used as appropriate teaching situations arise.

There appears to me to be a certain logic, however, in the order of my earlier chapters. The Diagnosis chapter, for example, should be used when instruction begins. It seems reasonable to me that if the teacher knows exactly what a pupil can do, what he cannot do, and why he cannot do it, her job of teaching him that skill should be relatively simple. In many instances, teaching will be simple if enough time is taken to identify the precise point at which instruction is to begin.

Once a pupil's starting point is identified, the Behavioral Objectives chapter should come into consideration. I cannot imagine teaching—good teaching, that is—commencing until some careful attention has been given to the identification of the extent to which the behavior of concern should be developed. As I have tried to point out in that chapter, objectives or desired rates can be calculated in many different ways; but without some clear identification of intended outcome, the teaching process may all too readily—and dangerously—become misleading or irrelevant. The greatest hazards here invited are that in the absence of specified objectives, the pupil may be either undertaught or overtaught—with regrettable consequences to all concerned in either case. But when teaching objectives *have* been determined, teachers are able to shift their teaching efforts from one skill to another as a consequence of performance level, rather than because of mere factors of time or a specified number of pages read.

After a point for the inception of instruction has been identified and the objectives for the teaching effort are defined, instruction should begin. At this point, we face several possible choices. Basically, however, the teacher should use the simplest, most direct approach possible. Quite possibly the simplest is that described in the chapter about Clarifying Expectations; the pupil should be plainly told what is expected of him.

As to the form of instruction itself, the teacher should give careful consideration to the suggestions made in the Reinforcement Contingencies chapter that pertain to capabilities and stages of development. If such a survey determines that a specific instructional technique should be employed, perhaps the notion that is basic to a preceding chapter, Common Teaching Procedures, should be given a fair chance; that is, arrange a good, old-fashioned way that might even have been good enough for your grandmother. It may be good enough for you. In any event, you won't know until you try. If, on the other hand, it appears that some motivational technique should be arranged, go to the chapter titled A Hierarchy of Reinforcers and restudy the steps that lead to a successful selection of reinforcers. But remember also, in the doing, that too much of a good thing may be only bad. There is further enlightenment, I hope, on this all-important matter of selecting and arranging the proper kinds of reinforcement in the Motivation, Reinforcement Contingencies, A Hierarchy of Reinforcers, and Contingent Free Time chapters.

Another highly significant factor in the handling of every teaching situation is elaborated in the Pupil Management chapter. Regardless of the age or the capabilities of the pupil, some kind and degree of pupil management skills can and should be taught. I emphatically believe this to be one of the most important features of any curriculum.

But surely there is no need for me to lobby for each one of my remaining "notions" and chapters. They should speak for themselves. And if they don't, perhaps my down-to-earth, off-the-cuff, adage-epigraphs will speak for them. The suggestions, at any rate, are there, and the concerned, compassionate teacher can look at them in the light of her own specific circumstances as they arise and choose her own appropriate sequence. But I am hopeful that no one will get any cart-before-the-horse ideas and suspect me of offering any solutions in search of problems. We can't any of us, in our baffling business, always know and do the right thing the first time. But we can all try to be a quick study. And to that end, I know of nothing that can speed up our search for certainties as surely as does the technique that is the theme song of this book—direct and daily measurement.

WHAT'S AHEAD, THEN?

My crystal ball is not infallible. But I see in it several reflections that raise some interesting questions—and some high hopes, too—for the future of educational research as the "teacher's best friend."

One of these, undeclared up to the present moment and as yet untried in any laboratory, is an iconoclastic pronouncement that goes something like this: "Children will listen to almost anything but silence." This hypothesis burst upon me several years ago, when I was doing some basic research in another direction. I was intrigued by the notion and even collected a moderate amount of data in support of the lunacy.

What else is one to conclude, however, when in several studies the data revealed that many children preferred listening to stories read backward, speech replayed at about any speed, and many types of music and nonmusic . . . to *silence!* If data from applied situations, homes and schools, reveal similar findings, we may indeed be compelled to rearrange our priorities as to curricular offerings and reformulate some of our ideas about noisy classrooms and their relationship to distractibility. We may have to research the teacher's reactions to this fearsome eventuality, too, before we get very far with the idea.

Another wave of the future might be deeper inquiry into the ramifications of this surmise: "If you want children to appear to be working, reinforce that; if you want them actually to work, reinforce that. But don't confuse appearing to work with actually working." This is a concept related, to be sure, to those discussed in earlier chapters, Direct Teaching and More on Direct Teaching. But the two ideas are not identical.

In the past few years, a number of studies have reported that attending (appearing to work) can be perceptibly changed by contingent reinforcement. The implication here conveyed is that if a pupil increases the amount of time he appears to be working, his actual work output will also—and commensurately—increase. My response to this is maybe so, maybe not. Recently, a few studies have focused on this issue, and while their data are not conclusive (certainly the proclamation stage has not yet been reached), at least a corollary seems likely: "If attending is reinforced, *it* will increase, but production won't; and when production is reinforced, it will increase and so will attending." However (Is this the Catch 22?), attending does not increase as much when production is reinforced as when attending is reinforced. These preliminary findings do appear, at least at first blush, to support those of the Direct Teaching chapter, which deals with direct and indirect instruction.

A third pronouncement of the future may relate to pupils as their own diagnosticians. It would conceivably run as follows: "If a child isn't doing what he is supposed to do, you can often find out why if you ask him why he isn't doing it." I have only a few uncodified anecdotes to support such a contention, but a systematic research project that dealt with self-awareness and anticipated need should yield some extremely interesting results. Sometimes children do not do things (refuse to do them) for reasons that, *when discovered,* prove to be entirely logical. Why not be as logical ourselves and simply ask them how come they have been "uncooperative" and have displayed an "inability to learn." We will be surprised at what good sense their answers often make, and we will be inclined to ask ourselves—so wise we always are in our hindsight—why we didn't think of that solution before.

Another inquiry of high potential might focus on this theme: "If we give children the time to do the things we want them to learn, they will learn these things more quickly than if they do not have the time in which to learn them." And that is not at all as enigmatical a dictum as it may sound at first hearing. In advancing this notion, I am not in the least advocating a free, permissive, "do I have to do the things I want to do?" environment in which children are completely at liberty to do whatever impulse directs, wherever and whenever. I simply mean that pupils, like anybody else in the world, need time of their own in which to *use* the skills they are being instructed in and urged to learn. Put them into practical, empirical operation.

Take reading and creative writing as two examples. I have observed many and many a class where teachers—conscientious and dedicated and even experienced teachers—professed to teach these skills and allocated an impressive amount of time for *their* comments, instructions, and exhortations. But the children were allotted no time whatever of their own to read and write! What is the logic of supposing that they did not need free time of their own in which to assimilate the newly taught skills into their own systems? I am sure that such a provision would dramatically increase the speed of the learning process. Jim Herndon, in *How to Survive in Your Native Land,* strongly advocates such a practice. He points out, with great cogency, that, particularly in the area of reading, children are often given all manner of workbook exercises, phonics, drills, and word-defining assignments, yet they are never allowed to go off by themselves and enjoy some reading. Here is another point to chalk up for my advocacy of some of the old-fashioned, folksy wisdom of a bygone day, as effective instructional methods.

Now take a deep breath. And don't shout until I finish. My next to the last glance into the future is really a blockbuster. For It states: "Escape from school is the biggest reinforcer of all, and we may come to something like that." Let me explain the thrust of this decree—as best I can.

No one in his right mind, of course, is going to permit himself to be accused of trying to set up any paradoxical antithesis between school and learning—"the less schooling, the more educating." Such a self-canceling statement sounds as phony as a tour that lists eight days and only four nights.

In an earlier chapter, Contingent Free Time, I wrote about leisure time and its reinforcing effect for many pupils. I also mentioned that it was difficult to determine whether leisure time was reinforcing because the pupils earned the privilege of playing with a toy or game or whether they were reinforced by the boon of no longer being required to work. I wouldn't be at all surprised to learn that the latter is true for many children; in fact, I am veering more and more toward this belief, and I would be quite surprised to learn that it is untrue. And if children are motivated by being able to cease work temporarily, imagine the atomic impact of a motivation that would permit them to escape from school for an entire afternoon!

Such a contingency, of course, could never be arranged in most schools because of bus and kitchen schedules, if nothing else. But imagine, if only for a moment, a school situation in which each pupil was given his total daily assignment the first thing in the morning and told that as soon as everything was satisfactorily completed he could leave. I would predict that most children would be gone by noon—many of them of the type that theretofore had been called lazy and motivationless, or worse, because they never finished their work.

It's too bad, if only for experimental verification, that schools cannot operate in this way, for I can see all sorts of advantages, to the quick as well as to the slow. And to the teacher! With so many of her brood gone, what wonders could she not perform in the way of giving precious extra time to those left behind because of their slowness. What a spur to the initiative of all the pupils when they realized that it was strictly up to them whether they stayed or left. And—a consequence even more appealing to the teacher eager for maximum effectiveness in her relationships with her students—there would be nothing to keep the ambitious student from staying, despite his earned freedom, for an added boost along the educational road. There would be more individualized instruction—and more of it—in any event. Pupils would be learning, perhaps even arriving, at different times all through the day.

It is, indeed, a fascinating development to contemplate. I have said nothing, it may have been noticed, about just how the parents would fit into this new order. That is another problem and, admittedly, a big one. And I don't care to tackle it just now.

Perhaps, though, my favorite among these potential developments—because, unlike the no-school proposal just discussed, its feasibility is distinctly high—is the last one. It can be capsuled in some such statement as this: "Children will do no better than you expect them to do; so be sure to expect them to do what you think they should do." Recently there has been a great deal of talk about this panacea, and it has an identifying label, the doctrine of "self-fulfilling prophecies." Translated, this simply means behaving in the way you are expected to behave—which the proponents of this view would have us believe is exactly what people will do, given the proper stimulus. These theorists have a point, I am willing to concede. But it is pretty heady stuff, I warn. Let me explain.

The view was given impetus, if not actually instigated, by the authors of *Pygmalion in the Classroom*. They contended, to be a bit simplistic about it, that if teachers believe their pupils are dull, those pupils will be dull and will perform in a dull manner. By the same token, if teachers believe their pupils are bright, they will be bright and will perform intelligently.

A year or so ago, a young woman in one of my classes conducted a simple little project with a couple of her students, dealing with this matter of teacher expectations. Initially, during the baseline phase, she obtained data pertaining to their correct and incorrect rates in arithmetic. Throughout the next condition, she agreed to give them a few minutes of free time if their correct and incorrect rates were above and below preset figures. On many days, she found, they earned their bonus minutes, but their rates barely exceeded the agreed-upon limits.

In the next condition, she extended the correct and incorrect requirements. When this was done, the pupils stretched accordingly. On most days, they earned their points, but again their rates barely surpassed the minimum requirements. She altered the goals a third time—and again the rates of the pupils improved.

Although a performance peak would ultimately, of course, have been reached, it was an interesting development, in this experiment, that apparently the pupils did successively what was expected of them, but no more. As the teacher's expectations rose, so did the performances of the participants. It is also a little frightening to consider the implications and possible extensions of this phenomenon. And it can be nothing short of appalling to weigh the ultimate potentiality for mischief in the procedure.

There is, indeed, an alarming aspect to the self-fulfilling concept. If it is possible to influence behavior beneficially by this manipulation of objective standards and goals, it is also a force that can work in the opposite direction—a two-edged sword that cuts both ways. And if the exercise of such influences and controls should take a turn toward the enormity of brainwashing and the like, the consequences are unthinkable.

Children have too often been given labels indicative of inferior performance, to their lasting damage. And it is quite possible that in our efforts to overclassify our exceptional cases, with the desire to be either more precise or more humane, we are in danger of increasing the number of pathological labels. And all we will be doing, in this misguided effort, will be to increase the number of pathologies—a self-defeating technique, surely.

Reasonable care, however, and a decent sense of responsibility, should hold such abuses in check. On balance, the potentiality for good seems far to outweigh that for mischief. If data continue to support this labeling, or self-fulfilling, prophecy, the phenomenon may well be used to everyone's advantage. For one thing, children could be given labels that are precisely in accord with their strengths. Such titles as "rapid runner,"

"careful calculator," or "perfect penperson" would be reinforcing in a highly beneficial and desirable way. For that matter,
children might well have several such labels at any one time,
and these names could be readily changed from time to time.

Another provocative wrinkle in the game would be that
children might be allowed to name themselves, or contingent
naming could be arranged. (Readers of these pages know what
my ideas on pupil participation in the learning process are. If
you've forgotten, reread the Motivation and Children as Managers chapters.) If the latter strategy were adopted, a child
would be required to run off a specified rate before being permitted to select his name.

And so we come to the last of our crystal ball fore-
shadowings. It has to do with errors, and its distillation might
run: "Although making too many errors is a waste of time, a few
have to be made if learning is to occur." Some mention of this
notion regarding errors was made in an earlier chapter, Relationship Between Errors and Learning, but the matter is admittedly still debatable. The summary I have just made might well
be a misunderstood, and misused, idea, but it seems increasingly apparent to me that a pupil *must* make a few errors so that
his teacher can know where to start working. The pupil's error
shows the teacher precisely where remedial attention is needed.
And, by the same reckoning, if the pupil performs some task er-
rorlessly, the teacher knows that there would be little point in
going over the material or the activity again. A study of a pupil's
few errors, moreover, would enable the teacher to analyze the
pupil's type of responding and give him immediate feedback.
Conceivably, then, a teaching technique could be designed to
focus on his unique pattern of response.

There has been a tendency among educators, in recent
years, to refer to errors as "learning experiences," and I heartily
applaud the attitude this label expresses. It seems to me a far
more productive description to employ, particularly if the phenomenon of the self-fulfilling prophecy I have just been dis-
cussing proves to be valid.

Certainly labeling a child an "error maker" could prove
damaging. This, in fact, is exactly what has happened to many
problem children who have moved from one diagnostic clinic
to another. Errors have become traumatic experiences for them.
They have learned from bitter, cumulative experience that
when they make errors, negative consequences generally fol-

low: they are sent to another clinic, reprimanded, given poor marks, or perhaps given a newer, even more distasteful, label. Many of these unfortunates have learned simply to cease responding, for this is the only way they can avoid being punished for the errors they are certain to commit. And what about the label becoming only a placebo, devoid of any remedial virtue and serving only as a convenient handle for the clinicians to grasp in disposing of the case as handily and expeditiously as possible?

As I have admitted earlier, the idea of euphemistically calling errors something else and running the risk of encouraging children to make mistakes is not a good practice. Neither I nor anyone else would want pupils for any reason to increase their incorrect rates. But somewhere along the line, human nature being what it is, people must learn that errors are bound to be made by everyone, error responses *can* be changed, and, most important of all, it's much easier to shape an error response into a correct response than it is to shape no response at all. It gives you something to work on.

DAILY MEASUREMENT CAN MAKE YOUR DAY

I have said so much in praise of direct and daily measurement already in these pages that any reiteration may be at the risk of overkill. My readers must be on a first-name basis by now with all the catchwords as well as the prerequisites of our cause. But I am nearing the end of my campaign, and endings call for summaries. So let me try once more to sum up the advantages, to the teacher, of full and participating membership in the club.

First of all, the teacher who measures pupil progress will learn about the effects, and hence the effectiveness, of her teaching. She will know whether that new "reading technique" that looked so promising really works or not—and with whom, and to what extent, and when the effects, if any, took place. And if they didn't take place, she will have the invaluable, negative evidence that she must abandon that tactic and look for another.

In the second place, the teacher who measures will be able to communicate accurately and acutely. With data, she knows exactly what happened; she doesn't have to guess about progress, she doesn't have to make anything up. And since data are not transient, she has a history of a part of a child's development that can be stored and retrieved at any time. She can inform principals and other administrators as to her teaching effectiveness; she can even tell them off and set them right, very discreetly of course, if they presume to question her teaching effectiveness. Bolstered by her bedrock of facts and figures, she can communicate objectively with parents concerning their child's progress or problems—and how beautiful the substitution of hard evidence for free-wheeling emotionalism can sometimes be for all concerned! And, finally, her communication with her pupils can be on this same controlled and mutually agreeable level—kindly, clear, and convincing.

A third advantage to the teacher who measures, and one of the central by-products of this book, is that the teacher who obtains data and reflects upon all the information, implicit and explicit, that she has gained by the effort is in a position to assess and develop herself, as never before. She will be able to test her classroom techniques and procedures, to provide an instant replay, if she so desires, of new devices at work, to check and recheck her results and know, not merely guess, when they should be used again, or modified, refined, or abandoned for fresh ideas and materials. No more false equating of mere busy work with valid instruction, or of wheel spinning with progress. No more substitution of idle hopes for hard-nosed experiences. The data are not to be denied. Nor will she become obsessed with any one type of method, system, or technique. Since the one reinforcer that works for *her* is the progress of her pupils, she will cheerfully cast about for another approach when one has failed, because her data have told her she must.

And that vital little matter of refinement of method. Our data-conscious teacher is in a position to discover the sometimes unwelcome fact that a technique that works for a certain child in a certain subject works not at all for another pupil in the same area. She learns that a motivational event for one pupil may be wholly nonreinforcing for another, and so faces the back-to-work truth that such events can be sadly temporary. Just when a reinforcer has been found for a certain child in a specific area, the effect wears off, and it's all to do over again.

Then, too, the teacher who measures has a great opportunity to learn the true meaning of individual differences. No two of her pupils will perform exactly alike in the basic skill area, and her data will show her just how, and to what degree, they differ. Some children will read advanced materials at rapid rates but be poor spellers and even poorer cipherers. Kim loves arithmetic but loathes spelling and barely tolerates her reading assignments. Martha is good at both reading and math, but regards the "rules" of spelling as just so much nonsense. The combinations of abilities are as diverse as is always the distribution of talents to mortals here below.

And as though these variables were not enough, there is the added fact that pupils develop at different *rates* in different areas. One might advance rapidly in math but at a snail's pace in reading; another might achieve a fast rate in spelling but develop slowly in penmanship. All of which means that our perceptive teacher is likely to be deeply unimpressed by such labels as "first" or "third" graders, just as she is by such special education labels as "emotionally disturbed," "learning disabled," "educably mentally retarded," or "neurologically impaired." She is much more challenged by the fact that she can, by the employment of direct, daily measurement over a period of time, be armed with the tangible means of describing her pupils' performance records in a number of academic and social areas.

THE WORTHY OPPOSITION

A preacher has been said to enjoy the protection of speaking always six feet above contradiction, and a writer operates (for a time, at least) within the safety of his book's two covers. But this is not to imply that we true believers in direct and daily measurement are immune from criticism; and it is the practicing teacher herself, of course, who is most exposed to the wrath of her nonmeasuring colleagues. They may often seem to regard her, indeed, as the bringer of some form of a voodoo cult into the schools and warn that as a fanatical mystic she must be watched very carefully—even destroyed.

There are, I suppose, several reasons why she should encounter such scorn and opposition. Some teachers do not believe in measurement for the simple, self-preserving reason that they do not want the product of their efforts to be measured. They fear that someone will learn they cannot teach. Others avoid measurement because they do not want to work hard enough to learn how to do it. They expect their children to learn and change, but they do not believe in change for themselves, such being one of the high privileges of being an adult. I have commented on all this in the Teaching Youngsters and Oldsters chapter. And of course there is always the plight of the teacher who always wanted to teach so badly—and did. She just hadn't yet heard of measurement! Others decry measurement because they believe that time thus spent is time taken away from their teaching—you will remember, I trust, the reluctant teacher and the dunderhead principal in the Everyone Measures chapter.

Those who use this last argument are right, but for the wrong reasons. There is no denying that measurement, because it takes up time and entails effort, will encroach upon the time a teacher has for "teaching." But we must take pains to discriminate between teaching and learning. Teaching is the attempt to instruct someone in the doing or knowing of something by telling or showing him how to do or know it. Thus, teaching can be measured by the clock. The teacher began her program at 9:00 A.M. and continued until 4:30 P.M. She had taught for 6 1/2 hours.

In contrast, learning is indicated when a person has acquired some new behavior. Therefore, learning must be evaluated in terms of some response unit: words, numbers, whatever. In addition, these units are often expressed in relation to time: minutes, days, weeks. It is possible to obtain information about these units of performance only if data are obtained. If, therefore, we accept these definitions of teaching and learning, measurement is bound to infringe upon teaching time. *But only with measurement will an instructor know if learning has taken place.* And isn't this the name of the game, to coin a phrase?

But let's proceed with the charges. Over the years I have heard dozens of critical comments, and although I have not spent much time categorizing them, they appear to fall into four main groups. To wit:

One. "I see you are trying to measure _____. Don't you know that _____ can't be measured?" If the teacher under attack is trying to measure reading, writing, or arithmetic, the critic will tell her, with a smirk of superior insight, that the *real* ability to perform these tasks simply doesn't lend itself to measurement, and if data on the issue are being gathered, they will pertain only to relatively unimportant surface skills. The critic is fairly certain to go on to say that *she* is teaching by such sophisticated and complex processes that it would be impossible for performance at this rarefied level to be measured. In other words, we have here the glorious *non sequitur* that if it *can* be measured it's not worth teaching. I have made a few well-chosen remarks on this form of criticism earlier in the Epilogue.

Two. "Okay, I realize you can measure _____, but you shouldn't." These are the critics who, while they are willing to grant that certain behaviors can indeed be measured, fear that applying such measures will do some sort of damage to the measuree. In my own mind I classify them as the "Don't rub the bloom off the rose" school of philanthropy. They are usually extending their protectiveness to the victims of a teacher's efforts to measure the performance of her pupils in the so-called creative subjects, particularly creative writing, about which there tends to be a sort of hushed mystique.

Recently, we set out to measure several elements of children's writing. total words, new words, sentences, punctuation, and capitalization. We also used a scale that allowed us to obtain data on several literary aspects of their writing.

Invariably, when we explained this project to any interested group of visitors, there were those who felt we were doing something we shouldn't be doing. They believed that, because we were measuring creativity, the creative capacities of the youngsters would somehow be impaired if not destroyed. According to our data, however, and many subjective reports about the writing capabilities of the youngsters (which for the nondata oriented were the best endorsement of success), the pupils improved in every respect following several weeks of teaching, in spite of the fact that they had been subjected to measurement right along.

Three. "I see you are measuring _____. That's commendable, but I believe you're measuring the wrong behavior; you should be measuring something else." This third type of criticism comes from those who are willing to concede that many behaviors can be measured, and that perhaps if behaviors are monitored very judiciously, no harm will be done. But they have another concern, as the quotation indicates. They don't approve of our taste in testing. Reading, especially, was a target for their objections. If we explained that we were measuring the naming of letters, we were told, "You should have measured the ability to say sounds." If we measured oral reading, we should have measured silent reading. If our concern was for factual comprehension questions, we were told that it should have been for data on the ability to answer sequencing questions.

Four. "I'm pleased that you are measuring _____, but I believe you're measuring _____ in the wrong way." These critics acknowledge that many behaviors can and should be measured and that occasionally the measurer is tapping the right skill. But they attack the *form* of the measurement. They don't like our style.

And this brings us to the perennial argument over the relative merits of reporting pupils' progress in terms of rate or in terms of percentage. (The reader is undoubtedly aware that both forms of measurement have been used in describing the results of several projects in this book.)

Without going into great detail, I may quickly point out that the basic difference between reporting data as *rate* or as *percent* is that rate encompasses the element of time, whereas percentage does not. Perhaps a simple example will suffice. Suppose that a pupil has answered eight problems correctly and missed two when he has worked for five minutes. His percentage score would then be 80 percent ($8 \div 10 \times 100$); his correct and incorrect rates would be 1.6 and 0.4 ($8 \div 5$ and $2 \div 5$).

Thus, percentage reveals a measure of accuracy, and rate (correct and incorrect) reveals a measure of speed. As with other issues of this type, measurers must consider what results they are seeking and choose those measures which will best yield the desired information. These factors are always relative, and it's all in the pupose and point of view.

Although data keepers argue among themselves with some lack of amiability over the various ways of measuring and charting performance, most of the violent disputes over what kind of measurement to use are provoked by the nonmeasurers. It often appears that they are interested not so much in evaluating measurement techniques as they are in finding yet another way to discredit its proponents. Divide and conquer.

I am certain there will be more sophisticated arguments posed by the devotees of nonmeasurement in the future; but it has been very interesting to follow the evolution of their type of reasoning. They have swung all the way from the early philosophical arguments to the pragmatism of current technological criticism.

But where would we be without the critics, bless 'em! Just as a free press watches a government's actions and reports any wrongdoings, critics of educational measurement provide feedback and serve to keep us honest. As a result, the government, and we measurers, have been forced to correct, or at least to give very serious thought to correcting, the flaws in our respective systems.

This is not to imply that the believers in measurement have sought to take over the educational world by any devious or deceitful means, and so have merited the rebukes and the cleansing action of critical surveillance. It simply means that critics have assisted us to become more aware of our own misjudgments and to work more strenuously for their amendment. Because of our critics, we are assessing more significant behaviors than we once addressed ourselves to, are evaluating the effects of a wider range of variables, and have generally improved our methodology for obtaining more valid and reliable data.

It would be a dangerous and a sad state of affairs, indeed, if there were no critics, for without their feedback there would be less motivation—and far less opportunity—for change and growth on our part. Pity the poor educators who do *not* measure, and thereby have fewer critics to fear. They have no compulsion to amend their beliefs or their teaching methods. They trudge along, teaching the same courses in the same way they have taught them for decades. Their lesson plans are yellowed and moldy. Their students, all to often, go away uninspired and unfed.

Even if they do alter their techniques and procedures, however, they are prone to do so for questionable reasons. As I pointed out in my introduction, their innovations will usually be based on a quest for novelty or mere caprice or on pressures from parents or edicts from the central office. Rarely are they derived from data.

AND FINALLY THERE'S "TECHNIQUE"

Throughout this book, I have made every effort not to endorse any particular teaching method or technique—not team teaching or solo teaching, television instruction, or multi-media instruction. I have certainly not wished to give my stamp of approval to any instructional kit or package; neither have I sought to condemn, out of hand, any teaching plan or technique. At times in my career I have been critical of multi-component instructional packages; but I have had what I consider good reasons for this stand—two of them, to be specific. One is that I am opposed to recommending such packages simply because I am certain not all those elements are required for every learner—and I hate waste. I have examined this issue at some length in the Some Teaching Procedures Are Complex chapter. My second objection is made not because of the approach itself, but because of the overzealousness of its advocates. All too many of them believe there is but one way to teach language, one way to teach math concepts, one way to teach reading. I need no more information than I now possess, thank you, to be convinced that every pupil is unique. He learns in unique ways and, therefore, a single approach simply isn't going to work for all individuals.

The fundamental article in my professional credo is that it is the responsibility of educational researchers to seek out educational truths, if necessary, to shatter some old illusions, and to rearrange the picked-up pieces into a newer, truer pattern. Researchers must unearth the basic, the ultimate, fundamentals of education. Then, they must explain those basics to teachers and learners, explain them in such terms that they all can understand and implement them. It is not enough for researchers to say, "The findings of this study should have immediate applicability in all classes," or "Teachers should include the findings of this study as part of their basic technology." Teachers must be given an epitome, a maxim, a rule, a "notion" that is the central core of the researcher's conclusions, along with specific case studies or projects in support of that central point. If this is done, the chances of a teacher's adopting research evidence and pronouncements would, it seems to me, be greatly enhanced, for she would be able to generalize from both the specific instance and the broader, final truth. I felt the answer to this need did not really exist anywhere else. Ergo, my book. And it is in this spirit of humble hope that the informal, chatty epigraphs have been composed.

The obvious danger this procedure encourages is that researchers will be tempted to speak beyond their data—to arrive at too neat a package too glibly. This has happened in the case of so many of the "popular" educational maxims I tried to discredit or, at least, sternly reappraise in the Common Teaching Procedures chapter. Eager for the portable proverb, researchers might be tempted to generate principles and postulates on the basis of too limited information. It must be insisted that all such maxims must have their basis in rock-ribbed data.

Once these notions are disseminated to teachers in clear, concise language, they must implement the new ideas and report back to researchers—so that they may know what to investigate next. It is my belief (as I have stressed in my introduction) that if research results are carefully distilled and labeled so that generalizations from one situation to another are encouraged, teachers will welcome these ideas about the basics of teaching as much as they now hunger for educational materials.

This reconciliation between educational researchers and public school teachers is not a pipe dream. We have been actively striving for such a rapprochement in our little research setting for some time and recently have become greatly encouraged. A couple of summers ago, we started our "skip" project in reading. Our basic premise was that it would be reinforcing for pupils to skip through books which were below their grade level, in order that they might be advanced more rapidly to materials of higher challenge and interest.

In order to verify our hunch, we first divided the material of the readers into four parts, and the students ranked the stories of each part in descending order, from most to least favored. The skipping provisions were then explained. In order to skip, a pupil's correct rate, incorrect rate, and comprehension score on the material read had to be at least 25 percent better than those scores had been during a baseline. If all the scores on the same day exceeded the requirements, the students were allowed to skip to the next part of the book and on toward the next grade level. If one or more of their scores were not up to criterion, they could not skip; they had to read the next story, without making the jump, the following day. Our data indicated that, for most of the children in our class, skipping was a very motivating arrangement. Presumably, because the pupils were not reading at grade level and knew it, it was reinforcing for them to be able to go through their readers rather quickly (Lovitt & Hansen, in press).

After our project had been in operation for several weeks, the director and I were invited to a nearby school district to discuss some of our programs. Naturally, we mentioned our project "skip." Many of the teachers present were impressed by the idea of allowing students to make more rapid progress in their reading, contingent on a high level of performance, and we explained our program in every detail. They decided to try it themselves.

Some time later, I heard from one of these teachers, and I was pleased to learn that she and ten others in the same building were using the skip program with great success; they were enthusiastic about it. I told her that we were still engaged in the project and had made several improvements in the system, a point that still further engaged her interest. In short, our collaboration led to several other meetings together, at which the researchers and the teachers "shared and told" to their great mutual benefit. This proved a very reinforcing experience for all concerned.

This rapid implementation of research was in large measure possible because their school system and our research organization used the same measurement system—direct and daily mea-

surement. We spoke the same language. Since the basic ingredients of this technique—designing behaviors, designing
research patterns, gathering, charting, and analyzing data—can
be used equally well by both teachers and researchers, it should
intensify the desired rapport between the two camps. Use of the
same system should do much to unify and coordinate the efforts
of both groups. Individuals from one group can easily move to
the other. If teachers have been gathering data from their pupils
using daily and direct procedures, they will have little trouble
transferring those techniques to a research setting. Conversely,
researchers would be able to conduct their work in a classroom
setting.

I hope the message of this book may help close the teacher-
researcher gap. I hope that my plan of distilling the data from
several projects and attaching a label to characterize those data
will enable teachers to use the findings of research more readily.

There are, however, at least two modifications in current
practices that must be made. For one, the image of research
must be enhanced; currently, it is viewed by too many as irrelevant. Capable researchers must convince teachers, students,
funding agencies, and the general public that research is indispensable if the best educational practices are to be determined.
People must be convinced that research will save them money
and serve them better.

This image will not be altered by testimonials and plati-
tudes. Data must be gathered to substantiate claims, and those
claims must be disseminated to all citizens in appropriate ways.
Researchers must boldly and clearly present their findings; they
are fighting for their lives and for the betterment of their clien-
tele.

The second needed alteration, if researchers and teachers
are to develop harmoniously, is the enhancing of the reinforcement system for both groups. Teachers should be reinforced in
tangible ways for effectively implementing valid research
projects. Likewise, researchers should be reinforced for investigating school problems and presenting their data persuasively
to teachers. Perhaps in time the two will communicate fully and
will progress together. When this happens, there is a great
chance that education, too, will progress efficiently, and that the
patrons of our profession, as a consequence, will be more effectively served.

What other system offers the sweeping benefits of direct and daily measurement? To my knowledge, there is no other methodology that so inclusively encompasses the needs of both teachers and researchers. I do not believe an alternative system exists that can do this vital job.

But let me hasten to say, with all the conviction and earnestness at my command, that education *is* a serious business and that the members of my profession, with a unanimity and dedication few professional groups can equal, know this. They are challenged by the knowledge. And they are one in their determination to rise to their great opportunity and responsibility.

The children of today, who will become the citizens of tomorrow, are the ones who will determine our future. And we are their privileged teachers.

Let us measure, monitor, and manage their progress toward maturity wisely and well, using every analytical, instructive, and remedial device our wits can devise—and so move them more surely toward the fulfillment of our hopes and their dreams.

For their potential, we all know, is *im*measurable.

REFERENCES

Featherstone, J. Notes on educational practice. *Harvard Graduate Bulletin,* Spring-Summer 1975, pp. 2-5.

Harris, F. *The new populism.* New York: Saturday Review Press, 1973.

Herndon, J. *How to survive in your native land.* New York: Bantam Books, 1972.

Illich, I. *Deschooling society.* New York: Harper & Row, 1970.

Keller, F. S., & Ribes, E. *Behavior Modification: Applications to Education.* New York: Academic Press, 1974.

Lovitt, T. C. Self-management projects with children with behavioral disabilities. *Journal of Learning Disabilities,* 1973, *6,* 138-150.

Lovitt, T. C., & Curtiss, K. A. Effects of manipulating an antecedent event on mathematics response rate. *Journal of Applied Behavior Analysis,* 1968, *1,* 329-333.

Lovitt, T. C., & Curtiss, K. A. Academic response rate as a function of teacher- and self-imposed contingencies. *Journal of Applied Behavior Analysis,* 1969, *2,* 49-53.

Lovitt, T., Eaton, M., Kirkwood, M., & Pelander, J. Effects of various reinforcement contingencies on oral reading rate. In Ramp & Hopkins (Eds.), *A new direction for education: Behavior analysis.* Lawrence: University of Kansas Press, 1971.

Lovitt, T. C., & Esveldt, K. A. The relative effects on math performance of single versus multiple ratio schedules: A case study. *Journal of Applied Behavior Analysis,* 1970, *3,* 261-270.

Lovitt, T. C., Guppy, T. E., & Blattner, J. E. The use of a free time contingency with fourth graders to increase spelling accuracy. *Behaviour Research and Therapy,* 1969, *1,* 151-156.

Lovitt, T. C., & Hansen, C. L. Round one—placing the child in the right reader. *Journal of Learning Disabilities,* 1976, *9,* 347-353.

Lovitt, T. C., & Hansen, C. L. The use of contingent skipping and drilling to improve oral reading and comprehension. *Journal of Learning Disabilities,* in press.

Lovitt, T. C., & Hurlbut, M. Using behavior analysis techniques to assess the relationship between phonics instruction and oral reading. *Journal of Special Education,* 1974, *8,* 57-72.

Lovitt, T. C., Lovitt, A. O., Eaton, M., & Kirkwood, M. The deceleration of inappropriate comments by a natural consequence. *Journal of School Psychology,* 1973, *11,* 149-154.

Lovitt, T. C., Schaaf, M. E., & Sayre, E. The use of direct and continuous measurement to evaluate reading materials and procedures. *Focus on Exceptional Children,* 1970, *2,* 1-11.

Lovitt, T. C., & Smith, D. D. Using withdrawal of positive reinforcement to alter subtraction performance. *Exceptional Children,* 1974, *40,* 357-358.

Lovitt, T. C., & Smith, J. O. Effects of instruction on an individual's verbal behavior. *Exceptional Children,* 1972, *38,* 685-693.

Mager, R. *Preparing instructional objectives.* Palo Alto, Calif.: Fearon Publications, 1962.

Rosenthal, R., & Jacobson, L. *Pygmalion in the classroom.* New York: Holt, Rinehart & Winston, 1968.

Smith, D. D., & Lovitt, T. C. The educational diagnosis and remediation of *b* and *d* written reversal problems: A case study. *Journal of Learning Disabilities,* 1973, *6,* 356-363.

Smith, D. D., & Lovitt, T. C. The use of modeling techniques to influence the acquisition of computational arithmetic skills in learning disabled children. In E. Ramp & G. Semb (Eds.), *Behavior analysis: Areas of research and application.* Englewood Cliffs, N. J.: Prentice-Hall, 1975.

Smith, D. D., Lovitt, T. C., & Kidder, J. D. Using reinforcement contingencies and teaching aids to alter subtraction performance of children with learning disabilities. In G. Semb (Ed.), *Behavior analysis and education—1972.* Lawrence: University of Kansas Press, 1972.

Smith, J. O., & Lovitt, T. C. Pinpointing a learning problem leads to remediation. *Teaching Exceptional Children,* 1973, *5,* 181-182.